G000150759

UPPER INTERMEDIATE
OUTCOMES

HEINLE
CENGAGE Learning

Australia • Brazil • Japan • Korea • Mexico • Singapore • Spain • United Kingdom • United States

HEINLE
CENGAGE Learning

Outcomes *Upper Intermediate Workbook*
Amanda Maris

Publisher: Jason Mann

Commissioning Editor: John Waterman

Project Manager: Karen Jamieson

Development Editor: Karen Jamieson

Product Manager: Ruth McAleavey

Content Project Editor: Amy Smith

Production Controller: Richard Gogarty

Cover and text designer: Studio April

Compositor: eMC Design

ISBN: 978-1-1110-5413-7

Heinle, Cengage Learning EMEA
Cheriton House, North Way, Andover, Hampshire
SP10 5BE United Kingdom

Cengage Learning is a leading provider of customised learning solutions with office locations around the globe, including Singapore, the United Kingdom, Australia, Mexico, Brazil and Japan. Locate our local office at **international.cengage.com/region**

Cengage Learning products are represented in Canada by Nelson Education Ltd.

Visit Heinle online at **elt.heinle.com**
Visit our corporate website at **cengage.com**

CREDITS

Although every effort has been made to contact copyright holders before publication, this has not always been possible. If notified, the publisher will undertake to rectify any errors or omissions at the earliest opportunity.

Text

The publisher would like to thank the following source for permission to use their copyright protected text:

Page 29: From http://www.citizenshipfoundation.org.uk/main/page.php?286 © The Citizenship Foundation, www.citizenshipfoundation.org.uk

Photos

The publisher would like to thank the following sources for permission to use their copyright protected images:

Alamy – pp25tr (vario images GmbH & Co.KG), 27bl (Powered by Light/Alan Spencer), 32br (Stan Gamester), 67tr (Nick Haslam), 84br (Tim Jones), 87ml (Randy Green), 97 (OnTheRoad), 97tr (Niall McDiarmid), 98b (Ian Dagnall); Corbis – pp44bl (Beau Lark), 90d (Ulet Ifansast/Stringer); Getty – pp38tr (Shafiq Alam/Stringer, AFP), 55br (AFP/Getty Images), 61tr (Lisa Peardon/Taxi), 76mr (Baoba Images), 80mr (Image Source), Ulet Ifansast/Stringer; iStockphoto – pp4b (Kemter), 4c (Jodi Matthews), 4d/73tr (Justin Horrocks), 4e (Jani Bryson), 4f (Francisco Romero), 5t (Robert Kohlhuber), 11t (Klaas Lingbeek van Kranen), 13b (Neustockimages), 14/15b (Oleksiy Mark), 23t (Juan Collado), 28a (Adrian Assalve), 29t (morganl), 35t (Brian Jackson), 37br (Brasil2), 41t (fotoVoyager), 43bl (Don Bayley), 44tl (YinYang), 47t (arturbo), 53t (LajosRepasi), 53bl (Lev Olkha), 55t (Mark Evans), 59t (Sean Locke), 62bl (Alija), 65t (Loic Bernard), 71t (Alexander Raths), 72tr (DamirK), 77t (Tatiana Morozova), 78bl (Chris Schmidt), 81bl (Jennifer Trenchard), 83t (ilbusca), 86tr (Anthony Brown), 89t (Baloncici), 90c (anzeletti), 95t (Jacob Wackerhausen), 96bl (H-Gall), 99br (Susan H. Smith); The Press Association – pp51bl (Peter Byrne/Press Association Images); Photolibrary – pp31br (Anthony Weller), 56br (Christian Arnal Photononstop); Shutterstock – pp4a (AZPworldwide), 7bl (Corepics), 17t (26kot), 19tr (Baevskiy Dmitry), 28b (Dmitry Yashkin), 28c (iofoto), 34a (Marek Slusarczyk), 34b (olly), 42br (worldswildlifewonders), 43tr (Kim Seidl), 49b (Izabela Zaremba), 73tl (Howard Sandler), 79m (niderlander), 89br (Kheng Guan Toh), 90b (graph), 90e (efka), 94tr (Monkey Business Images); Topfoto – pp50mr (Shaun Greenhalgh).

Illustrations by Mark Draisey

Printed in China by RR Donnelley
2 3 4 5 6 7 8 9 10 – 14 13 12 11

CONTENTS

GRAMMAR Habits

A Read the answers to the question *Do you ... much?* What are the people talking about? Match the answers (1–6) to the questions (a–f).

1 Hardly ever nowadays. We used to get away about twice a year but it's just too expensive now. We've got a tent so we go camping along the local coast whenever we can.

2 Not as much as I used to. To be honest, I got really overdrawn at one point and so I had to stop. Now I'll pick up a bargain in the sales but only if I really need it.

3 Not if I can avoid it! The local service is never on time and it's always packed. I tend to cycle everywhere but I'll take the tube if it's pouring down.

4 All the time. I think they're a brilliant local resource. Most of them are free and you can learn such a lot. Even my kids enjoy the interactive exhibitions.

5 Whenever I get the chance. My sister lives abroad so we use the net a lot for email and stuff. But I also like to chat, so I end up with a huge phone bill!

6 Not as much as I'd like to. I really enjoy having a day off from cooking but it works out quite pricey. As a rule, it's usually to celebrate someone's birthday.

Do you ... much?

a use public transport
b visit museums and galleries
c go out to dinner
d keep in touch with family and friends
e travel abroad
f go shopping

B There is one missing word in each sentence. Add the word in the correct place.

1 As rule, I go out once a week, usually on Saturday evenings.
2 I don't read for pleasure as much as I like to.
3 I tend see my family just on birthdays and at Christmas.
4 We used go to the cinema about once a week before they put the prices up.
5 Why you always sitting in front of that computer? Go outside and get some fresh air.
6 She must be really busy. She ever comes to the badminton club anymore.
7 I enjoy going to the theatre but we only go once a while.
8 We used to go walking every weekend. We get up early and be out on the hills to see the sunrise.

Language note *used to* and past simple

You can use the past simple or *used to* to talk about habits in the past. For single actions in the past, use the past simple.
I used to go / went for a run every day when I was in my 20s.
I went for a run yesterday.

VOCABULARY
Describing films, music and books

A Choose the correct words.

1 I could listen to it all day. The music is so inspiring, just so *uplifting / weird*.
2 I saw it twice. The plot was really exciting, just really *gripping / disturbing*.
3 Why is this play so popular? I thought it was terrible, absolutely *catchy / awful*.
4 I can't stand her acting. She's just too much, always so *dull / over-the-top*.
5 It all sounds the same to me. It's only produced to make money, just very *hilarious / commercial*.

B Complete these sentences using the adjectives that weren't the answers in exercise A.

1 I couldn't stop laughing. The show was so funny, absolutely ....
2 The second half was so boring, just very ....
3 I wouldn't take your kids to see it. The special effects are quite upsetting, really quite ....
4 I didn't get it at all. The dialogue was really strange, just really ....
5 I can't stop singing it. It's so easy to remember, really quite ....

DEVELOPING CONVERSATIONS Disagreeing politely

Add the words in brackets in the correct place.

1 A: I'm really into heavy metal.
   B: Oh, right. I find it loud and scary, to be honest. It's the kind of thing my teenage son listens to. (a bit)
   Oh, right. I find it a bit loud and scary, to be honest.

2 A: Wasn't that a brilliant film?
   B: Did you think so? It didn't do anything for me, I'm afraid. (really)

3 A: Do you listen to jazz much?
   B: Er, I'm not keen on jazz. I prefer something lighter, a bit more commercial. (that)

4 A: Do you fancy coming to see a musical at the theatre tonight?
   B: Thanks, but I'm not very keen on musicals. I prefer something more serious, more realistic. (a bit)

5 A: Have you read the latest Philip Roth novel?
   B: To be honest, I'm not interested in fiction. I tend to read about politics and current affairs. (really)

6 A: I've seen all the Bond movies at least twice.
   B: Really? I'm not fond of action movies. I'm more into romantic comedies, to be honest. (that)

LISTENING

🔊 **1.1 You are going to hear people talking in six different situations. Choose the correct answer, a, b, or c.**

1 What did the woman think about the film?
   a The main character was too complicated.
   b They changed a lot of the original story from the book.
   c It wasn't very exciting.

2 What does the man think about modern forms of entertainment?
   a There's too much choice.
   b You need too much technology to enjoy them.
   c It's made people less sociable.

3 Why doesn't the man go to the theatre very much anymore?
   a He doesn't have much time.
   b The shows are too dull.
   c It's too expensive.

4 What does the woman say about the facilities in her town?
   a She prefers to go out in the bigger cities nearby.
   b She doesn't approve of the number of pubs.
   c There needs to be more provided for young people.

5 Why does the woman criticise her son?
   a He watches TV in his bedroom.
   b He doesn't have a range of hobbies.
   c He's always asking for money.

6 What was the problem with the exhibition?
   a Not many artists contributed their work.
   b It wasn't very well attended.
   c The standard of the art was disappointing.

PRONUNCIATION
Strong and weak forms

> **Language note** strong and weak forms
> --
> Many function words (such as prepositions, determiners, conjunctions, pronouns and auxiliaries) can have two pronunciations:
> • the weak form, which is unstressed and contains a schwa /ə/. This is the most common pronunciation.
> • the strong form, which is stressed.
>   /ə/
>   He's <u>from</u> the north of Italy.
>   /ɒ/
>   Where are they <u>from</u>?

A 🔊 **1.2 Listen to the sentences. Choose the correct symbol for each <u>underlined</u> sound.**

1 /ə/   /æ/
   I wish they wouldn't do th<u>a</u>t. ....
   I just think th<u>a</u>t they should be true to the original story. ....

2 /uː/   /ə/
   People used t<u>o</u> go out to have fun. ....
   People don't socialise like they used t<u>o</u>. ....

3 /ə/   /uː/
   You used t<u>o</u> be a really keen theatre-goer. ....
   Not as much as I'd like t<u>o</u>. ....

4 /ɔː/   /ə/
   It's the teenagers I feel sorry f<u>or</u>. ....
   I mean, there really isn't much f<u>or</u> them to do. ....

5 /ə/   /uː/
   I'm not asking <u>you</u>, I'm telling <u>you</u>. ....
   I don't want <u>you</u> to watch any more TV. ....

B **Choose the correct words. Then practise saying the sentences.**
   When the function word is at the *beginning / end* of a sentence, the pronunciation is usually *weak / strong*.

VOCABULARY Talking about pictures

A **Complete the paragraph with the correct form of the words in brackets.**

There are nearly as many opinions on art as there are paintings themselves. Describing a painting is always open to ¹ .... (interpret). What appears ² .... (atmosphere) or ³ .... (drama) to one person may seem dull or ⁴ .... (date) to another. Abstract art is perhaps the style that is most difficult to appreciate because its meaning is often ⁵ .... (ambiguity).

B **Complete the conversation with the words in the box.**

life-like   intimate   pretty   abstract   sombre

A: Can we skip the modern art section? It's all a bit too ¹ _abstract_ for me. I like things to be a bit more realistic.

B: Yeah, sure. ... Look, this one is very ² _life-like_. You feel you could almost pick up the fruit and eat it.

A: You're right. It must be difficult to get in all that detail. And what do you think of this one?

B: Oh, it's a bit depressing, isn't it? The whole mood is very ³ _sombre_. They all look so sad.

A: I know what you mean. I find it a bit disturbing to look at a private moment like this. It's too ⁴ _intimate_ to share really.

B: Yeah ... but this one is completely different. Maybe a bit old-fashioned but very nice, just a very ⁵ _pretty_ scene of the countryside.

C **Match the sentence halves.**

1 This one is so realistic. It looks as ...... d
2 Come and look at this. The man in the picture .... g h/c
3 I don't see the attraction. To me all his paintings c
4 She looks furious so they've .... f
5 The artist was born in Belgium and that could ...... b
6 It all seems very weird. I think it must .... h
7 It's a celebration and they appear .... a
8 Looking at this one, I get .... e

a to have just got married.
b well be his hometown.
c look really dull.
d if it's been photographed with a camera.
e the impression the artist was rather depressed.
f obviously just had a row.
g looks a bit like your brother.
h show some sort of nightmare.

> **Language note** uses of *look*
> ---
> They **look** *really dull.* (look + adjective)
> It **looks as if** *it's been photographed.* (look as if + clause)
> He **looks like** *your brother.* (look like + noun)

GRAMMAR Adjectives and adverbs

A **Find and correct the six sentences that contain mistakes with adjectives or adverbs.**

1 You look tired. Have you been working hard recently?
2 She said it was an absolute dreadful film.
3 If you arrive lately for work again, you'll be in real trouble.
4 Don't forget to check your work really careful.
5 She looks very sadly. Do you think she's been crying?
6 Funny enough, I was thinking exactly the same thing.
7 We hardly ever go to the cinema nowadays.
8 It's important to read carefully the instructions.

B **Complete the sentences with one word from box A and one from box B.**

A	unusually wrongly terribly absolutely completely badly

B	rebuilt amazing injured chilly sad arrested

1 Both the driver and passenger were .... in the accident.
2 The gallery was .... after the fire.
3 It was .... to hear the news of his death.
4 The gig was .... – the best I've ever been to.
5 The man was .... but then was released after new evidence came to light.
6 This month has been .... We haven't had such low temperatures for years.

DEVELOPING WRITING A review – making recommendations

A **Read the possible headings for a gig review. According to the information in the *Learner tip*, which two would make you want to read the whole article?**

QUEST
– THE NEXT BIG THING?

Triumphant Quest
return of

A good gig

Quest

There are lots of reasons to go and see Quest at the City Hall this month

Full review

B **Read the review quickly and choose the correct heading from exercise A.**

How often do you go along to a gig and see something new? Well, Quest's Friday night gig at the City Hall certainly caught my attention. Having heard one or two tracks online, I was expecting a group of about six musicians. Imagine my surprise when just three young men walked on stage.

It was clear that the band already have a small but loyal following. A group of fans in front of the small stage were singing along to at least half of the songs. And it was easy to see why. Quest have a clever combination of catchy lyrics, an irresistible beat, and very much their own sound. All three of the band members play with great energy and expertise despite their age.

The only downside was when it came to the encores. They ended up repeating some of their material and giving us cover versions of early rock classics. A bit disappointing, but give them time and I'm sure they'll be writing a lot more.

I'm sure we'll be hearing a lot more from Quest. Check them out every Friday at the City Hall until the end of the month. It's well worth it.

C **Complete the sentences with the words in the box. There are two words that you don't need.**

downside	encores	irresistible
singing along	following	expertise
disappointing	worth	

1 One of the best things about the concert was the .... of the conductor.
2 It was amazing to hear the crowd .... to all the bands hits.
3 It's well .... the price of the concert ticket.
4 The biggest .... was the acoustics in the hall. It was very difficult to hear the singers.
5 I can't see why this pianist has such a large .... To me, she's very dull.
6 After playing three ...., the band finally went off stage leaving the crowd still wanting more.

D **Match the collocations.**
1 give
2 play
3 develop
4 compose
5 give
6 put on

a an individual style
b a memorable performance
c an exciting light show
d an old cover version
e a two-minute standing ovation
f an inspiring piece of music

E **Write a review (150–190 words) of a gig / concert you have been to. Use the language in this section and the following plan to help you:**
Include:
- an interesting heading and first sentence. Where and when the concert was, and your expectations.
- positive aspects of the concert.
- negative aspects of the concert.
- your overall view and recommendation.

FANCY A MASTERPIECE FOR JUST £40?

The market for contemporary art shows no sign of falling and the opportunity to snap up an original at a bargain price just can't be missed. Every year London's Royal College of Art (RCA) organises its Secret exhibition and sale. [1] ... The College invites both established, well-known artists and young art students to create an original piece of art based on just two rules – the work must be done on a postcard and must be signed on the back [2] ... . All the cards are exhibited for a week and then sold in a one-day sale at a price of just £40 each.

Since the first exhibition, Secret has really captured the public's imagination. [3] ... The list of famous contributors includes: artists Damien Hirst, David Hockney and Tracey Emin, designers Manolo Blahnik, Paul Smith and Stella MacCartney, and musicians David Bowie and Paul Simonon from The Clash. [4] ... Part of the fun is deciding which of them is by a famous artist or designer, and which is by a hard-up art student. Buyers could end up with a great investment or just a pretty picture by a student the public has never heard of.

At one recent exhibition, a lucky visitor bought a sketch of a human skull with an eye in the middle of its forehead, only to discover that it was by fashionable British artist Damien Hirst. It was later auctioned at Sotheby's for over £15,000. Another good investment was the painting of a bearded man in a canoe by British artist, Peter Doig. It sold for £42,000 at the same Sotheby's auction as the Hirst postcard.

Secret was set up in 1994 and was the brainchild of an RCA student who wanted to help raise funds for fine art students at the college. Since its beginnings, over one million pounds has been raised for the Royal College of Art Fine Art Student Award Fund. [5] ... Professor Glynn Williams, Head of Fine Art at the RCA said: "RCA Secret is about securing the future of the next generation of artists and when the public buy postcards at the event they are helping to make this possible. [6] ... – everyone has an equal chance of getting a big name."

As well as raising much-needed funds for the students at the College, RCA Secret has attracted loyal support from a group of art lovers who have been visiting the show since it started. It is not only one of the most popular events at the RCA, [7] ...

> **Glossary**
>
> **hard-up:** short of money
> **skull:** the bone structure of the head
> **auction:** to sell something at a public event at which things are sold to the person who offers the most money

READING

A **Read the article on page 8 quickly. Who do you think wrote it?**
a   an art student
b   the director of an art college
c   the arts correspondent of a newspaper / magazine

Learner tip

As well as looking for logical connections between the main text and missing sentences, remember to look for words that link parts of the text together. These include pronouns like *it*, them, etc. and connectors like *because*, *in order to*, *also*, etc.

B **Seven parts of the article have been removed. Write the correct letter (a–g) in the gaps in the article. There is one extra sentence that you do not need to use.**
a   The postcards can be viewed in person at the RCA or online.
b   in order to keep the artists' identity a secret
c   It's one of the most democratic art sales in the world
d   Most examples are much too expensive for the average buyer.
e   The idea behind it is simple.
f   but it has also developed into an important date in the British art calendar.
g   The money has helped hundreds of students in the early stages of their career.
h   Now over 1,000 artists take part in the event each year.

C **Number the paragraph summaries in the same order as the article.**
☐ who benefits from Secret
☐ the overall role of Secret
☐ how Secret works
☐ who made a good investment from Secret
☐ who has taken part

D **Choose the correct words. Look back at the article if you need to.**
I'd never [1] *heard* / *known* of Secret until I went along with a friend last year. I wasn't really hoping to [2] *find* / *snap* up a bargain, more just interested to see the art. We spent ages [3] *viewing* / *looking* the postcards and the hall was packed. The exhibition has obviously [4] *taken* / *captured* the public's imagination. In the end, I bought just two cards and neither of them will make anything at [5] *auction* / *investment*. I don't really mind. I think it's a great way to [6] *rise* / *raise* funds for young artists.

Vocabulary Builder Quiz 1 (*OVB* pp2–4)

Try the *OVB* quiz for Unit 1. Write your answers in your notebook. Then check them and record your score.

A **Replace the underlined words with an adjective from Unit 1.**
1   That film was so underlined{boring}, I almost fell asleep.
2   She seemed really serious and sad. She hardly spoke.
3   I didn't like the ending. What happened to the main character was unclear.
4   I couldn't watch it. It was just too upsetting.
5   The story is so exciting. You won't be able to put it down.
6   His jokes were extremely funny. I've never laughed so much.
7   His first reaction was positive but then he changed his mind.

B **Which words that are both verbs and nouns can complete these sentences?**
1   The bigger screen is a new .... of the computer.
    The series of films .... the same group of actors.
2   Why did he .... himself as a clown?
    He managed to escape because he was in ....
3   He burned down the factory in an act of ....
    He's spent years trying to .... himself on his attackers.
4   Don't .... Everything will be OK.
    Being declared bankrupt drove him to ....

C **Complete the sentences with adjectives ending in -al.**
1   It wasn't my fault. The damage was ....
2   The .... decision to increase taxes led to protests in the streets.
3   All countries must unite and make a .... effort.
4   Having lower costs and faster production gives us a .... advantage.
5   He was excluded from school due to .... problems.
6   We give large bonuses only in .... circumstances.
7   Her writing style is very different. She never uses .... ideas.

D **Write the missing word in the correct place.**
1   I can't bothered to cook tonight.
2   The message in the poem is open interpretation.
3   He corrupted by mixing with older gang members.
4   The roles of hero and villain been reversed.
5   The police accused of burglary but he denied it.
6   Do you think they will get away the robbery?
7   His reasons for leaving struck me odd.

Score ____/25

Wait a couple of weeks and try the quiz again.
Compare your scores.

VOCABULARY Buildings and areas

A Complete the descriptions with the pairs of adjectives in the box.

deprived / residential	rough / run-down
high-rise / hideous	affluent / stunning
up-and-coming / trendy	historic / grand

1 People say it's an .... area. They're starting to open a lot more shops, bars and stuff like that. I hope it doesn't get too .... , though, as the house prices will go up.

2 The architecture is amazing. It's full of .... buildings like the first synagogue in the area but there are also .... palaces and squares.

3 It's always been a bit .... with lots of litter and graffiti everywhere, but now it's starting to look really .... All the houses are in a terrible state.

4 It's always been the most .... district in the city and I could never afford to live there. The houses are .... with up to seven bedrooms and enormous gardens.

5 About 20 years ago this part of town was quite .... There were lots of empty houses and shops, and very few facilities. Now it's been transformed into a quiet, ... area. Loads of young families live there.

6 They're planning to build some .... blocks of about 25 floors on the edge of the old town. I think mixing old and new like that is going to look ....

B Complete the conversations with the correct form of the verbs in brackets.

1 A: Wow! Look at that castle. It totally .... (dominate) the whole area. What does it say about it in the guidebook?
 B: Apparently, it .... (date back) to the sixteenth century and it .... (renovate) several times since then.

2 A: Why have they bought a flat down by the station? It used to be really rough down there. I always told visitors .... (steer clear) of it.
 B: It's all changed now. They .... (knock down) the run-down old buildings about a year ago and built some trendy new flats. Needless to say, prices over there .... (soar) now.

3 A: Do you remember where I used to live?
 B: Yeah, it was quite trendy. Lots of small shops and businesses .... (base) there.
 A: You wouldn't recognise it now. They .... (open up) a huge shopping mall and all the individual shops have gone.

GRAMMAR
Non-defining relative clauses

A Add commas where necessary.

1 We'd walked round the same streets five times at which point I decided it was time to buy a map.

2 The local people who had at first appeared rather unfriendly couldn't do enough for us.

3 Our hotel turned out to be in a pretty run-down part of town which really spoilt the trip.

4 Most of the old town where my parents lived for many years had been knocked down and completely rebuilt.

5 We booked several day trips to the surrounding areas all of which were really good value for money.

6 The first day of the festival when everyone dresses up in amazing costumes is the one not to miss.

B Match the information (A–F) in the box to sentences 1–6, rewriting it each time as a relative clause.

| A It was completely amazing. |
| B We had missed dinner by then. |
| C She had done a course in Mandarin Chinese. |
| D His family is from South Africa. |
| E My brother-in-law has a boat there. |
| F None of them were open when we actually got there. |

1 It was very relaxing to spend a few days in Cannes, *where my brother in law has a boat.* .... E

2 The tour didn't finish until 10 p.m.
 ....
 ....

3 We spent a week exploring the coastline.
 ....
 ....

4 We couldn't have managed in Beijing without Nicola.
 ....
 ....

5 My old boss gave us a lot of travel tips about Cape Town.
 ....
 ....

6 We spent ages planning to visit different vineyards.
 ....
 ....

DEVELOPING CONVERSATIONS
Agreeing, using synonyms

A Match the opinions and responses.

1 I've never seen such a run-down area.
2 The architecture in the old town is amazing.
3 The height of that tower is unbelievable.
4 What wonderful old buildings!
5 The people round here must be quite wealthy.
6 They've turned this into quite a trendy area.
7 Aren't those high-rise flats awful?
8 The design of the roof is a bit strange.

a You're right. It's absolutely stunning.
b I know. They're beautiful, aren't they?
c Yes, it does look quite an affluent area.
d I agree. It does look a bit weird.
e Yes, it does look pretty rough, doesn't it?
f Yes, I heard it was quite fashionable now.
g I know. It's incredible, isn't it?
h I agree. They look hideous.

B Agree with these opinions, using a suitable synonym.

1 A: The view across the bay is lovely.
   B: *Yes, it is beautiful, isn't it?* ....

2 A: This looks quite a fashionable area.
   B: ....

3 A: I think the new architecture round here is really hideous.
   B: ....

4 A: I'd hate to live here. It looks really rough.
   B: ....

5 A: The design of the new gallery is a bit weird.
   B: ....

6 A: Just look at the design of that cathedral. Isn't it stunning?
   B: ....

7 A: The condition of the buildings in the old town is incredible.
   B: ....

8 A: I think this must be the most affluent part of the whole city.
   B: ....

LISTENING

A ◎ 2.1 You are going to hear two people planning a day's sightseeing. Listen and tick the places / events they decide to visit.

the annual parade   ☐ ☐
the City Museum   ☐ ☐
a tour of the temple ruins   ☐ ☐
the street market   ☐ ☐
the old town   ☐ ☐
old Merchant's House   ☐ ☐

B Number the places in the order they are going to visit them. Listen again if you need to.

PRONUNCIATION Connected speech

A Underline the main stresses and mark the linking (final consonant + vowel sound).

1 It starts in the town square and then goes all the way through the main streets.
2 The city museum has one of the best collections of modern and abstract art in the country.
3 It's not the kind of place you can see in just a short time.
4 Take a trip into the past and soak up the atmosphere at the street market.
5 So, we spend the morning at the market and we end up at the parade.
6 We need to be up there for the parade anyway.

B ◎ 2.2 Listen and check. Practise saying the sentences.

VOCABULARY Festivals and carnivals

A **What are the people talking about? Match the statements (1–5) with the items in the list (a–j).**

a fireworks display
b costumes
c parade
d confetti
e sound system
f bonfire
g steel drum band
h masks
i floats
j silly string

1 'Wow! Look at how many people there are. It stretches all the way back to the main square. And the music is brilliant. I love all those Caribbean rhythms.' ..g...

2 'Look at that one with all the flowers. That must have taken ages to build. And the one in the shape of the boat is beautiful. But I can't hear the commentary very well. It isn't loud enough.' ....

3 'I'm freezing. Let's get a bit closer to the flames. ... Oh, it's started! Aren't they amazing? Like little coloured stars hanging in the sky.' ....

4 'There were people dressed as Romans, characters from Disney, birds all sorts. I didn't even recognise my own sister. Her face was completely covered with feathers.' ....

5 'Look at me! I'm covered in bits of paper. And you got caught by that kid with the spray can. It's all in your hair.' ....

B **Cross out the verb in each set that doesn't collocate exactly.**

1 *set light* / *make* / *sit round* / *throw wood on* a bonfire
2 *watch* / *light* / *cancel* / *miss* a fireworks display
3 *listen to* / *form* / *play* / *book* a steel drum band
4 *set up* / *test* / *record* / *hire* a sound system
5 *watch* / *hold* / *look* / *take part in* a parade
6 *carry local* / *dress up in a* / *design a* / *wear national* costume
7 *forbid* / *have fun with* / *spray* / *get covered in* silly string
8 *decorate* / *build* / *ride on* / *sit* a float
9 *get dressed* / *make* / *wear* / *hide behind* a mask
10 *throw* / *spray* / *ban* / *be showered with* confetti

READING

A **Read the blog opposite quickly. Match the headings (a–f) to the correct sections (1–6).**

a Learn something new
b Declare your home a work-free zone
c Keep a record
d Indulge yourself a little
e Plan ahead
f Set start and finish dates

B **Read the blog again. Which of these statements are true, according to the writer.**

1 The only reason for doing a staycation is lack of money. ☐
2 At first, the writer's children weren't keen on the idea of a staycation. ☐
3 It's important to decide a fixed period for your staycation. ☐
4 A staycation is a good time to catch up on household jobs. ☐
5 Only one person should plan the family activities. ☐
6 It's a good idea to explore your local area on foot. ☐
7 You should be prepared to spend a bit on money on something special. ☐
8 People don't often bother to look back on their staycation experiences. ☐

C **Add one missing word to each sentence. Look back at the blog if you need to.**

1 Our kid aren't very demanding. They usually .... along with what we suggest.
2 You can't trust to luck if you want a successful party. It's .... in the planning.
3 If you want to improve your language skills, staying with a host family is just the .... for you.
4 I don't drink much – just the .... glass of wine with dinner.
5 There's a lot to choose from but have what .... your fancy.
6 You've been very kind. I'd like to .... you to a nice dinner.

HOLIDAYS FOR THE HARD-UP

Short of money, time or just energy? Fed up of being ripped-off at hotels, restaurants and theme parks? Tired of getting stuck in endless traffic jams and airport queues? Then a staycation may just be the thing for you. Adapted from the word vacation, a 'staycation' is becoming the trend for families who opt to stay at home during their summer break. And it can be more fun than you might think.

My family and I have been 'staycationing' for the last couple of years. At first my kids went wild at the thought of not going abroad. What on earth would they tell their friends or put on their Facebook profile at the end of the summer? But then they realised they wouldn't have to put up with an exhausting journey, sharing a room with siblings, communication problems and endless arguments over the plans for each day. Suddenly, exploring the area near their own home and being able to hang out with their friends seemed like heaven.

Basically, as with any family activity, it's all in the planning. Don't expect to have a successful break by just staying at home and hoping that something interesting will happen. Here are a few pointers to get you started:

1 ......

Schedule a beginning and ending to make your staycation seem like a 'real' holiday. Otherwise, it might end up feeling like a series of days just hanging around at home.

2 ......

That means no housework, no paperwork and no homework. You are on holiday, after all.

3 ......

Have a daily activity in mind and a back-up in case the weather changes. Let each member of the family choose what they would like to do for at least one afternoon ... and make sure the others go along with it.

Check out what's free

Everything from bike rides in the countryside to family fun days in the local park. Pack your own picnic and set a budget for treats like ice creams, boat trips and the odd glass of wine for mum and dad.

4 ......

Most colleges and sports centres run summer schools that offer a wide range of courses. Have a go at something the whole family can enjoy – pottery, cookery, local wildlife – whatever takes your fancy.

Explore your own backyard

Take the time to explore the area near where you live. Walking or cycling is a great way to enjoy the scenery without adding to your carbon footprint.

5 ......

Add up all the money you're saving on travel and accommodation and treat the family to something really nice. It could be a banquet-style takeaway, a fancy dress party, or an evening out.

6 ......

Take photos or videos, just as you would if you went away from home for your holiday. Remember your kids will want something to show their friends, and you will want to keep those staycation memories too.

Have a happy staycation!

Glossary

back-up: a second plan in case a situation changes
your own backyard: the area near where you live
carbon footprint: a measure of the amount of carbon dioxide produced by a person / organisation

GRAMMAR The future

> **Language note** referring to the future
>
> Remember that there is no single future tense in English. We use a range of different forms and sometimes more than one form can be used with little difference in meaning.

A Cross out the one future form that is not possible.

1 It's pouring down. *Shall I give you a lift? / I'll give you a lift. / I'm planning to give you a lift.*
2 What *will you do / are you going to do / do you do* when you finish your contract?
3 When *are they hoping to / going to / bound to* move house?
4 *We check out / We've got to check out / We'll have to check out* by midday tomorrow.
5 Where *shall we meet / are we going to meet / do we meet* later?
6 The strike *plans to start / is due to start / starts* on Wednesday.
7 Look at all this traffic. We're *going to / bound to / hoping to* miss our train.
8 *I'm taking / I'm going to take / I take* next week off.

B Rewrite the sentences using the word in brackets. Make any necessary changes.

1 It's inevitable that you will get the job. (bound)
....
....
2 When should your train arrive? (due)
....
....
3 It's possible I'll see you at the party. (might)
....
....
4 It's our intention to take on more staff next year. (plan)
....
....
5 I feel very worried about my next exam. (dread)
....
....
6 They think house prices will fall in the next six months. (expect)
....
....

DEVELOPING WRITING
An email – making a request

A Read Martin's email to Kati. Choose the main reason for writing.

a to ask for help with money
b to ask for some travel tips
c to give and ask for news

B Read the email again and underline examples of these aspects of informal writing.

- contracted forms
- short sentences
- direct questions
- phrasal verbs
- two abbreviations
- a more informal way of saying:
  1 *thank you*
  2 *fine*
  3 *send you a message*
  4 *you don't have to hurry*

C Complete the sentences with the verb phrases in the box.

get around	drop off	book up	put on	hang out
picking me up	eat out	put us up		

1 We'd like to stay with a family. Do you know anyone who could .... ?
2 I'm arriving in the early hours of the morning. Would you mind .... ?
3 We like to get away from the tourist areas. How easy will it be to .... on public transport?
4 We'll be travelling out of the peak season, but do we still need to .... in advance?
5 We're hoping to try some local specialities, so where would you recommend to .... ?
6 We'll be in town for just 24 hours. Is there a safe place where we can .... our bags?
7 Annie is desperate to see some flamenco, so where do they .... the best shows?
8 I'd like to sample the nightlife, so where are the best areas to .... in the evening?

D You are going to spend time in a place that an English-speaking friend knows well. Write an email (150–190 words) to ask for some help in planning your trip. Remember to use a fairly informal style and include some of the language from this section.

○○○

To _____

Subject _____

Hi Kati,

How are things? I hope all the family are doing OK.

I wanted to drop you a quick line to ask you a favour. As you know, I'm finishing uni at the end of this term and I'm going to do some travelling with a friend over the summer. We're planning to visit Hungary and I was wondering if I could ask you for some local info. We won't have a huge amount of spending money so can you recommend any bargain hotels and places to eat in Budapest? Also, when would be the best time to visit in terms of the weather and things to do? Apart from the capital, where would you recommend we go? A friend of mine suggested Lake Balaton. Do you think it's worth a visit? Any advice you can give us on transport, sightseeing and local customs would be very welcome.

I'm really looking forward to the trip but I've got to get through my finals first! There's no rush for a reply as I know you're really busy, too. Just get back to me when you can.

Cheers

Martin

Learner tip

Before you write an email or a letter, think about how well you know your reader and the level of formality to use. A very formal style to someone you know well can sound silly or even pompous; an informal style in a work or business context may cause offence.

Vocabulary Builder Quiz 2 (*OVB* pp6–8)

Try the *OVB* quiz for Unit 2. Write your answers in your notebook. Then check them and record your score.

A Complete the sentences with *up* or *down*.
1 They've moved to an ....-and-coming area of the city.
2 I can't seem to .... load these images to the website.
3 They knocked .... the wall to make the room bigger.
4 The days leading .... to the exams are always frantic.
5 That painting looks odd. I think it's upside ....
6 I was surprised to see the old high street looking so run-
....

B Replace the <u>underlined</u> words and phrases with more expressive language from *OVB* Unit 2.
1 I <u>briefly saw</u> the sea between the mountains.
2 The new design for the town hall is <u>very ugly</u>.
3 She was <u>given lots of</u> presents when the baby was born.
4 Rollercoasters make my heart <u>go fast</u>.
5 I'm <u>not looking forward to</u> going to the dentist today.
6 Wages have fallen <u>by a large amount</u> during the recession.

C Which five of these sentences describe decreases?
a There's been a crash in the value of sterling.
b There's been a surge in house prices.
c Book sales plummeted after the scandal about the author.
d Why have prices plunged so dramatically?
e Soaring inflation is the biggest challenge we face.
f Interest in the project has been sliding for months.
g Orders have risen dramatically since last month.
h What accounted for the drop in bookings?

D Correct one letter in the <u>underlined</u> words.
1 It took us ages to <u>elect</u> the tent.
2 The house was very <u>grant</u>, with ornate decoration.
3 The <u>bombs</u> of the Egyptian pharaohs attract millions of tourists.
4 There was a sudden <u>burnt</u> of activity and then everything went quiet.
5 There's a <u>brought</u> so we can't water the garden.
6 Don't <u>spit</u> me around, I get really dizzy.
7 Make sure the children are <u>stripped</u> into their chairs before we set off.
8 Don't bother with that ride. It's rubbish, just really <u>same</u>.

Score ___/25

**Wait a couple of weeks and try the quiz again.
Compare your scores.**

02 SIGHTSEEING 15

03 THINGS YOU NEED

VOCABULARY Useful things

A **What do these people need?**

1 'I've made a mistake in my homework.'
   a rubber   correction fluid
2 'The button's come off my shirt.'
   ....
3 'Dad's cut his finger on the bread knife.'
   ....
4 'You've dropped rice all over the floor.'
   ....
5 'I'm too short to reach the lightbulb.'
   ....
6 'My mobile is completely dead.'
   ....
7 'I need to stick down this envelope.'
   ....
8 'You've spilt water all over the floor.'
   ....

B **Choose the correct words.**

A: Mum, I've found the clothes [1] *pegs / clips*, but where's the [2] *washing-up liquid / washing powder*? I need to wash my favourite top for tonight.
B: What? You can't do that now. You'll just have to wear something else.
A: But the rest of my stuff is still in suitcases.
B: Well, unpack it. The [3] *drill / iron* is in that box over there. And here are the [4] *scissors / staples* so you can cut the [5] *string / rope*.
C: Mum, I'm setting up my computer and stuff, but my bedroom has only got one socket. Have you got [6] *an adapter / a stapler*?
A: Dad packed all the electrical stuff, so ask him.
C: He's putting up some pictures. I just saw him with the [7] *hammer / saw* and some [8] *pins / nails*.
A: Why on earth is he doing that now? He should be looking for the [9] *tin opener / corkscrew* so we can have some lunch.
D: Any sign of the [10] *lighter / torch*? I want to go up the loft but there's no light in there.
A: Do you have to do that now? I'm just warming up some soup so can you find some [11] *buckets / bowls*?
D: I was just about to go to the DIY store down the road. I need some [12] *screws / pads* to repair the garden gate.
A: Don't bother doing that now. The previous owners have left a huge [13] *file / wire* of paperwork that we need to go through first.

GRAMMAR
so, if and to for describing purpose

A **Write new sentences with the information from box A and box B.**

A	I popped round to my neighbour's house.
	~~I'm just going to get the hammer.~~
	I need a plaster.
	I went to the DIY store.
	I bought some files.
	I'm looking for the dustpan and brush.

B	I want to sweep up this broken glass.
	I want to cover this cut.
	I needed to organise all the papers from my course.
	I wanted to borrow her stepladder.
	I needed to get some paint.
	~~I want to knock in this nail.~~

1 *I'm just going to get the hammer to knock in this nail.*
2 ....
3 ....
4 ....
5 ....
6 ....

B **There is one word missing in each sentence. Add the word in the correct place.**

1 This cream is great you need to treat a bite or sunburn.
2 I found some really nice paint decorate the bedroom with.
3 Wipe up that wine quickly it doesn't stain the table.
4 Here's the corkscrew open the wine with.
5 The plasters are in the cupboard your finger's bleeding.
6 Please turn off all appliances when leaving order to conserve energy.
7 Keep the iron on low so that you burn your silk scarf.
8 Here's a needle and thread so you repair the hole in your top.

DEVELOPING CONVERSATIONS
Explaining and checking

A Complete the conversations with the words in the box. There is one extra word each time.

thing	sort	mean	what	how	made

1 A: .... do you call that thing you use for DIY?
  B: Can you be a bit more specific?
  A: Yeah, sorry, it's .... of plastic and metal and it has a .... of pointed .... at the end. You use it to put screws into pieces of wood.
  B: What? You .... a screwdriver?

mean	like	use	what	stuff	as

2 A: What's the name of that .... you use to hold pieces of material together? It's a bit .... a zip or something.
  B: ....? You mean the stuff they .... to fasten trainers and bags?
  A: Yeah, it has two layers that kind of lock together.
  B: Yeah, yeah. I know exactly what you .... but I don't know what it's called. Sorry.

Language note questions with *what / how*

Remember we say **What** *is ... called?* and **What** *does ... look like?*
How can be used like this:
How *are you?*   **How** *are things?*   **How** *come?*

B Choose the correct words.
  A: Ow! I've just cut my finger. Are there any plasters in the first aid kit?
  B: No, sorry. We need to buy some. [1] *Don't / Can't* you use a bandage?
  A: I don't think so. Not on my finger.
  B: You just need a piece of cloth or [2] *somewhere / something* to keep the dirt out. Would a tissue [3] *do / make*?
  A: It wouldn't be strong [4] *enough / too*.
  B: What about a cotton pad? You could [5] *use / to use* some sticky tape to hold it in place.
  A: Yeah, that [6] *ought / should* do.
  B: Let me help you.
  A: Ow!
  B: Oh, sorry. Have I made it worse? ... And you've got blood on your top now.
  A: Don't worry. These things [7] *result / happen*.
  B: You might want to soak your top in water or [8] *it'll / it shall* leave a stain.

LISTENING

🎵 **3.1 You are going to hear five people talking about shopping, and the difference between *wants* and *needs*. Match the speakers (1–5) to the letters (a–f). There is one letter that you don't need.**

Speaker 1   ....
Speaker 2   ....
Speaker 3   ....
Speaker 4   ....
Speaker 5   ....

a I've given up buying luxury brands.
b I got into debt by having what I wanted.
c I think it's good for people to have what they want.
d I've stopped impulse buying.
e I try to buy only what I really need.
f I can never resist a bargain.

PRONUNCIATION
Intonation and lists

A Mark the intonation arrows on the sentences.
1 They think they really must have that bigger house, the latest mobile phone, a designer top, or some luxury food.

2 We all only really need somewhere to live, food and water, basic health and hygiene products, and clothes for different situations.

3 I remember in one weekend I bought six pairs of trousers, eight shirts, around 20 CDs and a new mobile phone.

4 In fact, just yesterday I bought a bag, a pair of sandals, a pair of jeans and two white shirts.

5 It didn't matter if it was in a shop window, in a magazine or catalogue, on a website, or even in an auction.

6 Our economy would suffer, workers in the developing world would lose their jobs, and life would be very dull.

B 🎵 **3.2 Listen and check. Then practise saying the sentences.**

VOCABULARY Word families

A Complete the questions with the correct form of the words in brackets. Then give true answers.

A question of personality

1 What things make you feel full of .... (optimistic)?
....

2 In what ways in life do you think you are .... (caution)?
....

3 When in your life have you felt most .... (pessimism)?
....

4 What childhood .... (afraid) have you overcome?
....

5 How do you react if people .... (critic) you?
....

6 Do you tend to shop in an .... (economic) way?
....

7 Which two .... (able) are you most proud of?
....

8 What's your idea of perfect .... (happy)?
....

B Complete the words in the text with the missing endings.

When I was about seven, I started a collection of football programmes. This started as a [1] harm.......... hobby but over time it became an [2] obsess.......... – I had to have every programme from every Liverpool match, even some from before I was born. By the time I was 20, I had literally thousands of programmes in different locations in my parents' house. I saw this as one of my greatest [3] achieve.........., but they couldn't stand the lack of space. I was always full of good [4] intent.......... about sorting them out but never did. In the end, my parents threatened me with [5] evict.......... if I didn't do something with the collection. Not wanting to be [6] home.........., I finally agreed that I would [7] advert.......... them for sale on *eBay*. The whole collection was bought by a local man as a gift for someone, but I never found out who. So, on one [8] rain.......... afternoon in February, my programmes were sent by courier to their [9] myster.......... new home.

READING

A Read the title and the introduction of the article opposite. Choose the correct reason for writing the article.
a to talk about the history of shopping
b to complain about shops on the high street
c to highlight the amount of consumer choice

B Read all of the article. Are these statements true or false?
1 The range of items available in shops stops people buying things.
2 The Internet has made choosing products easier.
3 No part of life has escaped from having too much choice.
4 Professor Schwartz thinks the prices we pay for products are too high.
5 Having a lot of choice raises people's expectations of products.
6 Scientists have shown that people feel less stressed when given less choice.
7 The article advises buying fewer products.
8 Professor Schwartz recommends researching but only for a short time.

C What do these numbers in the article refer to?
1 50 (line 4)
2 154 (line 10)
3 thousands (line 11)
4 10,500,000 (line 35)
5 six (line 47)
6 30 seconds (line 55)

D Complete the text with the words in the box. They were all taken from the article.

choice	missed out on
got round to	dissatisfied
range	choose between
overwhelming	popped

Last time I [1] .... into my local coffee shop, I couldn't believe the [2] .... on offer – full-fat, low-fat, americano, cappuccino, decaffeinated, even something called an iced mocha latte. It took me ages to [3] .... the drinks in the list. It was completely [4] .... When I [5] .... making a decision, I went for a white coffee, which is what I always drink at home. As I left the shop, I felt a bit [6] .... with my [7] ...., as if I'd [8] .... something much better.

Spoilt for choice?

Do you remember the old days? The time when buying a pair of jeans or a mobile phone involved choosing between two or three options. Now, pop into a shop on the high street and you'll find about 50 different styles
5 of jeans and literally hundreds of mobile phones. But is more necessarily better?

We've never had so much choice. Take supermarkets, for example. A local store could offer you 38 types of milk, 107 varieties of pasta, over 170 types of salad dressing,
10 and 154 flavours of jam. The average supermarket offers more than 30,000 products, with thousands more being added each year. In the words of one shopper, 'It's so overwhelming that it just makes you feel awful. If you carefully considered every aspect – ethics, food miles,
15 price, flavour and ingredients – you'd never get round to buying anything, ever.'

But it isn't just about food. For every aspect of life, there's an incredible range of products and services on offer – from clothes and gadgets to educational
20 and financial services, not forgetting holidays and entertainment.

Access to the Internet has of course widened this choice. It not only offers the products themselves, but detailed reviews of product ranges with comparisons of style,
25 price and reliability. These are intended to make our lives easier but in reality just lead to information overload.

It now seems that all this choice isn't good for us. Professor Barry Schwartz, a psychologist from Swarthmore College in Pennsylvania and the author of *The Paradox*
30 *of Choice* says, 'There is vastly too much choice in the modern world and we are paying an enormous price for it. It makes us feel helpless, mentally paralysed and profoundly dissatisfied.' But shouldn't we be happy to have all this information and choice? Why is it a problem
35 to have 275 types of breakfast cereal or 10,500,000 hits to an Internet search for 'holidays in Spain'?

The bigger the range of products available, the less satisfied we are with our choice. We imagine that the perfect mobile or pair of jeans must exist in such a big
40 number of products and that we might have chosen the wrong thing. Or that by choosing a particular service or form of entertainment, we might have missed out on something better.

Experiments seem to indicate that less choice is better.
45 A team of researchers at Stanford University in the USA ran a test on consumers choosing jam. Those who tested just six jams felt happier and bought more products than consumers who had 24 jams to taste. Another experiment showed that students who were given a smaller range of
50 essay topics produced better work.

So what can we do? One technique is simply to choose smaller shops with fewer products. And Professor Schwartz advises, "Choose when to choose. ... Don't worry about what type of mobile-phone package to opt for. Pick a sofa
55 from IKEA in 30 seconds and you'll feel better than if you spend hours researching sofas – because you won't know what else you're missing out on."

GRAMMAR
Indirect questions and statements

A Make indirect questions, using the words in brackets. Where are the people in each situation?

1 Can I take some time off next week? (I was wondering)
2 Could I speak to the chef? (Do you think)
3 Does this train stop at Middleton? (Would you happen to know)
4 Will you get any more of these jeans in? (Do you know)
5 Can I ask the pharmacist for some advice. (I was wondering)
6 Do all the planes from Paris land at this terminal? (Do you have any idea)
7 How long does the film last? (Do you happen to know)
8 Which aisle are the nails and screws in? (Do you know)

B Correct the sentences.

1 I can't remember does the shop open on Sundays.
2 I don't understand what are you saying.
3 I don't know how long does the guarantee last.
4 I wonder what he was so upset.
5 I can't remember where are we supposed to meet.
6 I wonder where are they living now.

VOCABULARY Problems with things

A Choose the correct words. Then match the sentences (1–10) to the objects (a–j).

1 It makes a *strangely / funny* noise every time I press 'play'.
2 I wouldn't use that brand again. I had a nasty *allergic / allergy* reaction as soon as I put it on my skin.
3 I can't finish building the cupboard. There's a *string / part* missing from the kit.
4 The *format / screen* keeps freezing when I try to tap in the address.
5 One of the back pockets was all *ripped / broken* when they arrived. I'll have to send them back.
6 I bought it as part of an *accessories / outfit* for a wedding but I think the sleeves are too long.
7 The lens was all *scratched / sprained*. I couldn't see a thing when I put them on.
8 I can't use it indoors or at night because the *flash / file* doesn't work properly.
9 Don't buy that one. The frame is *cracked / packed* up in the corner.
10 The *label / strap* is very thin. You won't be able to carry much in that.

a   a sat nav
b   a pair of jeans
c   some face cream
d   a pair of glasses
e   a camera
f   a CD player
g   a jacket
h   a bag
i   a cupboard
j   a picture

DEVELOPING WRITING
An anecdote – complaining

A Read the anecdote. What is the main reason for writing it?

a   to warn people about a specific company
b   to request a refund from customer services
c   to tell a story about something that went wrong

I'd been saving up for my girlfriend's birthday and I wanted to treat her to something really special. Then a friend recommended a balloon flight. He'd organised one just a month before, which had been a real success. It sounded ideal so I went for the 'celebration package' with a flexible booking date, an hour in the balloon, champagne and a DVD of the flight. Perfect, or so I thought.

Milly was delighted and she wanted to do the flight on her actual birthday. This is where the problems started. It turned out that they were already fully booked. When I insisted, they just said, 'There's nothing we can do. We appreciate your booking.' No explanation, no apology, nothing. We finally got a flight three days later but things didn't improve. We were up in the air for only 35 minutes, the champagne glasses were cracked and the DVD arrived scratched.

I promised Milly I would get a refund and we would go away for the weekend. Three months later I'm still waiting. The company won't reply to my emails and I can't get through to customer services. Without wanting to sound over-the-top, it's been the most stressful thing I've ever tried to organise.

B Read the anecdote again. What's the main purpose of each paragraph?

1 a to explain who the people in the anecdote are
 b to give background to what was bought/ordered
2 a to explain what went wrong
 b to criticise the company
3 a to say what action the writer intends to take
 b to describe the end result

C Are these statements about the anecdote true or false?

The anecdote:
 contains direct speech.
 is addressed to a specific person.
 includes short sentences to keep the reader interested.
 uses a fairly formal style.
 describes how different people felt.
 uses full forms, rather than contractions.

D Complete the collocations with the words in the box.

| keep | insist on | fall | customer |
| refund | wrong | sort out | waste of |

1 .... services / helpdesk / care
2 .... going wrong / breaking down / calling the company
3 .... my money / the payment / €750
4 a .... money / time / effort
5 .... the booking / the problem / the mistake
6 the .... colour / size / model
7 .... speaking to the manager / getting a refund / getting a new one
8 .... apart / to pieces / off

E Write an anecdote (150–190 words) about a situation when you had to complain. Use one of these ideas or an idea of your own.

A product
- a laptop that arrived damaged
- a pair of trainers that fell apart

A service
- an awful meal
- a special treat that went wrong

Learner tip

When you write an anecdote, try reading it aloud to check that it flows and sounds natural. If possible, read it to another person to see if you have kept their attention to the end!

Vocabulary Builder Quiz 3 (OVB pp10–12)

Try the OVB quiz for Unit 3. Write your answers in your notebook. Then check them and record your score.

A Complete the names of the household objects.

1 Hang your coat up. There's a h _ _ _ behind the door.
2 Do you need a c _ _ _ to hold your papers together?
3 What lovely flowers. I'll just get a v _ _ _ .
4 Be careful! That electrical w _ _ _ isn't safe.
5 Don't leave your rubbish there. Put it in the b _ _ .
6 Have you got a n _ _ _ _ _ and thread? I need to sew on a button.

B Choose the correct words.

1 When I got back to the car, it was all *squashed / scratched* on the side.
2 What's the best way to get a coffee *stain / leak* out of a carpet?
3 Can you pass me a drawing *pin / peg*?
4 Don't *rip / rub* your eyes, you'll make them sore.
5 She gave me a free *purchase / sample* of make-up.
6 He always thinks the worst will happen but I'm much more *optimistic / pessimistic*.
7 We're pretty *obliged / resigned* to selling our house.
8 She's full of *well / good* intentions but she never follows through.

C Which word do you need to complete the sentences in each set?

1 Please .... the documents away. / I've kept a copy in my .... / I need a box .... for all these papers.
2 Keep the .... for the new laptop. / The TV is still under .... / It comes with a one-year ....
3 Long hours are an occupational .... / The old wiring was a fire .... / Smoking can be a health ....
4 What's that .... smell? / The TV is making a .... noise. / It's .... we haven't seen him for days.

D What form of the words in brackets do you need to complete the text?

The number of [1] (evict) is rising and it's clear that people should have been more [2] (caution) about the property market. Many of my own friends became [3] (obsession) with owning bigger houses without giving any [4] (consider) as to how they would pay the mortgage. They had unrealistic [5] (expect) that the value of houses would continue to rise. And they would often ask, rather [6] (sarcastic), when I was going to get on the property ladder. [7] (Funny) enough, they are now asking about vacant flats in the block where I live.

Score ___/25

Wait a couple of weeks and try the quiz again. Compare your scores.

04 SOCIETY

VOCABULARY
The government, economics and society

A Replace the <u>underlined</u> words in the conversation with the words in the box.

booming	recession
too soft on	make ends meet
have gone bankrupt	made a difference

A: So what do you reckon to this new government? Are they any good?

B: I think they've done quite a lot. They've certainly [1] <u>had an effect</u> since they came to power three months ago. Things have improved since last year's [2] <u>economic decline</u>.

A: But the economy is hardly [3] <u>a great success</u>, is it? A lot of businesses [4] <u>are unable to pay their debts</u>, you know.

B: Sure, but it's getting easier for most families to [5] <u>have enough money to live on</u> because taxes are lower.

A: That's true. I just wish they would do something about youth crime. They're [6] <u>not strict enough with</u> young offenders.

B: You're right there.

B Choose the correct words. Then match the sentences (1–5) to the topics (a–e).

1 It's almost *non-existent / non-existing* nowadays. You need a really good salary even for a tiny flat in a decent area.

2 The rate has *shoot / shot* up over the last six months. It's getting harder and harder to get a job.

3 I think it will *undermine / underline* people's confidence. They are already worried about the threat of rising inflation.

4 This *shortage / shortness* is really hitting hard. Nearly all international flights have been cancelled.

5 It's bound to *rise / boost* our standing in the world. An important sporting event always does.

a lack of fuel
b the Olympic Games
c the economy
d unemployment
e affordable housing

GRAMMAR *so* and *such*

A Write new sentences with *so* or *such* and the information from box A and box B.

A	
	There were a lot of demonstrators.
	This area has become run-down.
	The economy is doing badly.
	Some students are in serious debt.
	The government have wasted a lot of money.
	~~Petrol is expensive.~~

B	
	No-one will vote for them again.
	~~We hardly use our car.~~
	It will take years to pay it off.
	No-one wants to move there.
	People are struggling to make ends meet.
	The police had to close the road.

1 *Petrol is so expensive that we hardly use our car.*

2 ....

3 ....

4 ....

5 ....

6 ....

B Find and correct five mistakes in the sentences.

1 The factory closing caused so lasting damage to the local economy.

2 Such few young people vote nowadays, they are thinking of making it compulsory.

3 The demonstration passed off so peacefully, there were no arrests.

4 There are so little green spaces, it's hard to find somewhere to sit and relax.

5 The parade was such great success that the city decided to hold one every year.

6 So many high-rise blocks have been built in the city, it's now unrecognisable.

7 Air pollution has risen so high that people are finding it hard to breath.

8 There are so a lot of positive things that he's done for the city.

DEVELOPING CONVERSATIONS
Responding to complaints

A Choose the correct response from the box for sentences 1–6. There are two sentences you don't need.

a I know what you mean, but they're not all bad. They just need somewhere to go after school.
b Well, maybe, but at least unemployment is falling.
c I know! Her voice drives me mad. I wish they would bring the older guy back.
d I know what you mean, but it isn't all bad. Some of the new offices are quite elegant.
e Tell me about it! I can't remember the last time I saw a good film.
f I know! It just keeps getting noisier and noisier.
g Well, maybe, but some are better than others. You just have to find out what they stand for.
h Tell me about it! If I'd tried that, my mum would have marched me into class herself.

1 It's rubbish on TV. I don't know why I bother with the satellite channels. ....
2 I don't think I'll bother to vote this time. All the candidates seem the same. ....
3 Young people are so rude nowadays. I don't like walking past them. ....
4 Some parents are too soft on their kids when they skip school. ....
5 That woman who reads the news is so annoying. ....
6 Modern architecture is a nightmare. All concrete high-rises and no green spaces. ....

B Write responses for these complaints. Use your own ideas.

1 They're not doing anything about the lack of affordable housing.
....
2 They never invest in public transport in my region.
....
3 The news is always so depressing.
....
4 Voting in local elections never changes anything.
....
5 There's a real shortage of jobs for young professionals.
....
6 All new rock bands sound the same.
....

LISTENING

Don't watch the news on your birthday. It'll only depress you!

A 🔊 4.1 You are going to hear two friends, Natalie and Adam. Listen and choose the main topic they talk about.
a the best way to catch up on the news
b problems in modern society
c a different type of news coverage

B Listen again. Are these statements true or false?
1 Adam doesn't read newspapers any more.
2 Talking about the news with a colleague made Adam feel depressed.
3 The Good News Network is a TV channel.
4 Adam assumes the Network covers just silly stories.
5 The Network aims to deal with serious issues in a positive way.
6 The stories reported on the Network are all American.
7 Natalie thinks that the stories that get the most coverage give bad news.
8 In the end Adam agrees to read the news on the Network.

PRONUNCIATION Same sound or different?

A Are the letters in bold the same sound (S) or different (D)?
1 I've given up on buying a p**a**per. / It just gave a bit of b**a**lance. ....
2 They deal with serious issues like the ec**o**nomy. / I just can't be b**o**thered reading it. ....
3 The only thing you hear about is the r**e**cession. / You should check out that w**e**bsite. ....
4 They had headlines on signs of economic gr**ow**th. / How do you find out what's g**o**ing on? ....
5 I listen to the h**ea**dlines on the radio. / My coll**ea**gue replied, 'What's good about it?' ....
6 They cover international n**e**ws. / They must have quite a lot of c**u**te stories. ....

B 🔊 4.2 Listen and check. Practise saying the sentences.

VOCABULARY Social issues

A Complete the newspaper headlines with the phrases in the box.

family size	school dropout rates
racism	family breakdown
drug and alcohol abuse	

1 IMPROVED TEACHING LEADS TO REDUCED ....

2 DIVORCE RATES FALL THANKS TO NEW POLICY ON ....

3 Average .... **falls leading to reduced risk of overpopulation**

4 MULTI-ETHNIC POLICIES AIM TO DEAL WITH ....

5 NEW CLINIC OPENS TO TREAT ....

B What are the people in these sentences talking about? Match (1–5) to the social issues (a–e).

1 They're opening a whole network of shelters so the number of people on the streets should fall.
2 They have a very good track record on this. Seven of the top directors are women.
3 The head has a zero tolerance policy on this, so the number of complaints from parents has dropped.
4 Several new species have been returned to the wild thanks to the preservation of the birds' habitat.
5 An innovative anger management programme has led to a fall in the number of attacks in the home.

a bullying in schools
b the destruction of the environment
c homelessness
d domestic violence
e gender discrimination

READING

A Read the introduction to the webpage opposite and just headings 1–4. In which paragraph would you expect to find this information?
what society gets from learning about citizenship ....
what you might do in a citizenship class ....
a definition of citizenship ....
reasons for teaching citizenship ....

B Read the webpage quickly and check your answer to exercise A.

C Read the webpage again. Choose the best answer to the questions.
1 Citizenship programmes aim to help people
  a become more established in the UK.
  b get a better education.
  c participate more fully in public life.
2 Citizenship doesn't include
  a being offered tuition.
  b the right to become a legal member of any country.
  c having the right to vote.
3 Modern citizens need to know
  a what they can and have to do.
  b how to win arguments.
  c about the geography of the world.
4 Citizenship education improves
  a the organisation in schools.
  b younger students' grades.
  c motivation and participation.
5 Citizenship students are likely to
  a practise what they have already learnt.
  b talk about what's in the news in a fairly informal way.
  c teach other people in their community.

D Complete the text with the correct form of the words in brackets.
I started a citizenship course with a group of rather difficult teenagers last term. They seemed to enjoy the [1] .... (topic) content of the course and slowly their [2] .... (behave) started to improve. They liked having more [3] .... (involve) in their learning through debates and [4] .... (discuss), and improving their [5] .... (know) of law and the economy. Perhaps the most surprising change was their interest in [6] .... (political). One of them is even thinking of becoming an MP!

Language note *it's* or *its*

Remember that *it's* means *it is* or *it has*.
It's a difficult issue. = It is ...
Its is a possessive form and doesn't need an apostrophe.
*... the behaviour that society expects of **its** citizens.*

Understanding citizenship

Home **About** Resources Contact

Many countries around the world have been looking at ways to encourage people to take a more active part in democratic society and in their local community. One of the ways of doing this is through citizenship programmes and education in schools. In 1989, an organisation called the Citizenship Foundation was established in the UK and in 2002 citizenship education became compulsory in UK secondary schools.

After a decade of interest in this subject, here are the answers to some FAQs on citizenship.

1 What exactly is citizenship?

The word citizenship can have different meanings:

- **legal and political status** Put simply, being a legal member of a particular country or state. This brings with it certain rights and responsibilities under the law, such as the right to vote and the responsibility to pay tax.
- **involvement in public life** Sometimes called 'active citizenship', this refers to the behaviour that society expects of its citizens. It can include a variety of activities including voting in elections and taking an interest in current affairs.
- **an educational activity** In other words, ways of helping people become active, informed and responsible citizens. This can be achieved in a number of ways – formal types of education in schools, colleges, universities, training organisations and the workplace, and more informal education in the home or community groups.

2 Why teach citizenship?

The main reason is to support modern society and the democratic process. A democracy needs citizens who are able to take responsibility for themselves and their communities, and to contribute to the political process. This requires a number of skills and characteristics, including:

- knowledge of rights and responsibilities
- awareness of other societies in the world
- concern for other people
- ability to express opinions and arguments
- willingness to act in the local community
These skills cannot develop without an education programme that includes everyone, whatever their background and whatever their age.

3 How does it benefit people?

People in general benefit by being able to make a positive contribution on a local and national level. Schools and other organisations develop motivated and responsible learners, who relate positively to each other and to the surrounding community. Younger people in particular find that citizenship education helps them develop self-confidence and find a voice.

4 What is involved in citizenship education?

It is typically different from other education programmes in these ways:

- **content** Including topics not usually covered in other subjects, such as law, government and politics, taxation and the economy, and the role of organisations such as the United Nations.
- **focus** Highlighting topical everyday issues that are not usually discussed in an educational setting, especially with younger learners. These may include health care, public transport, policing, and the environment.
- **approach to learning** Encouraging active involvement through discussions and debates, and active participation in the life of the wider community. Students are given opportunities to develop as learners and to put their learning into practice.

Glossary

current affairs: events that are happening now and are discussed in the news
United Nations: an international organisation that encourages countries to work together to solve world problems

GRAMMAR *the..., the...* + comparatives

A Choose the correct words in brackets to complete the sentences. There is one extra word in each set.

1 The .... you practise, the .... playing the piano becomes. (easier / less / more)

2 As a rule, the .... the plan, the more .... the project. (more / successful / simpler)

3 In my experience, the more .... a person is, the less .... they really are. (aggressive / less / confident)

4 If you ask me, the .... you are, the .... you learn. (younger / faster / fewer)

5 It's human nature – the .... people earn, the .... generous they become. (less / richer / more)

6 In general, the .... people work, the .... mistakes they make. (serious / faster / more)

7 The .... I thought about his suggestion, the .... I liked it. (worse / more / less)

8 You have to admit, the .... the economy does, the more .... the government becomes. (popular / better / good)

B Choose the correct responses from the box.

> the more, the merrier
> the bigger, the better
> the faster, the better
> the sooner, the better
> the simpler, the better
> the smaller, the better

1 A: They've brought forward the date for mum's operation. It's in June now.
   B: Good. ....

2 A: I've added twenty more people to the guest list. I hope that's OK.
   B: Sure. ....

3 A: I've booked tickets on the express train to Paris. It takes only 90 minutes.
   B: Great, thanks. ....

4 A: I've shortened the presentation to just 10 minutes and taken out a lot of the details.
   B: That was a good move. ....

5 A: We've managed to reduce the budget by about a third. I'll see if I can make any other cuts.
   B: Brilliant! ....

6 A: I'm upgrading my laptop to a 40cm screen. That should be easier on my eyes.
   B: Good for you. ....

DEVELOPING WRITING
An essay – giving your opinion

A Read the essay title and the first paragraph of the model text. What does the writer think about the statement?

> 'Interest in elections has been dropping for years. It's now time for compulsory voting.' How far do you agree with this statement?

B Choose the correct words in the rest of the model text.

It is clear that turnout in general elections has been declining in most democracies since the Second World War. In Britain, for example, over 72% of voters took part in the general election in 1945 compared with just 59% in 2001. Given this trend, it is worth asking if voting should be made compulsory. Personally, I think it should.

There are several reasons for [1] *these / this*. Compulsory voting makes politicians consider the views of the whole population, [2] *no / not* just of the regular voters. It brings young people, [3] *that / who* are traditionally less likely to vote, into the political process. It also makes the public take an interest in government and share the responsibility of checking their actions. [4] *Finally / Last*, it can encourage a sense of community, [5] *that / as* everyone takes part in it together.

[6] *Furthermore / Addition*, the system of compulsory voting has been successfully introduced in a number of other countries. In Australia and Belgium, [7] *by / for instance*, the system has been in place for many years and more than nine out of ten voters regularly take part in elections.

[8] *In / For* conclusion, I believe that compulsory voting is a way of reuniting people with the political world and so with democracy.

C Match the verbs in the box to the nouns and phrases they go with.

take part in	introduce	take	share	bring
consider				

1 .... an interest in / seriously / responsibility for
2 .... the possibility of / doing / people's views
3 .... a campaign / a discussion / elections
4 .... a law / a system / a change
5 .... the same opinions / enthusiasm for / responsibility for
6 .... people into a process / people together / up an issue

Learner tip

Remember to plan before you write! In an essay question:
- think about your own opinion / experience first.
- make notes of your ideas and the vocabulary you need.
- plan each paragraph and the topic sentences you are going to use.
- use connecting words and phrases to link sentences and paragraphs.
- check your essay carefully when you have finished.

D Write an essay (150–190 words) based on the title below.

'Young people are the least likely to vote. It's now time to lower the voting age to 16.' How far do you agree with this statement?

Vocabulary Builder Quiz 4 (*OVB* pp14–16)

Try the *OVB* quiz for Unit 4. Write your answers in your notebook. Then check them and record your score.

A Match 1–5 and a–e to form compound nouns.

1 tuition   a permit
2 gender   b tribunal
3 residency   c group
4 employment   d measures
5 pressure   e fees
6 safety   f discrimination

B Complete the expressions that start with *non-*.

1 I'm not really into stories, so I read a lot of non-..............
2 Omelettes can burn quite easily so use a non-..............
3 We don't land until 6 a.m. but at least we're on a non-..............
4 I asked for more money but they said it was non-..............
5 I like to support charities and other non-..............

C Write the missing words in the correct place.

1 They're planning to cut on investment in roads.
2 Why do you think their marriage broke?
3 How long have the police been carrying the investigation?
4 Even cooking meat goes my vegetarian principles.
5 The price of oil shot to $65 a barrel.

D Which words that are both verbs and nouns can complete these sentences?

1 How can we .... interest in the campaign?
   Promotion has given a .... to my confidence.
2 The school won't tolerate any form of racial ....
   Research shows that many criminals .... drugs.
3 Why did he .... he was innocent?
   No-one believed the .... that the cream could make you lose weight.
4 Newer varieties of wheat might give a higher ....
   How much will this year's crop ....

E Replace the underlined words with an adjective from *OVB* Unit 4. Make any necessary changes.

1 He isn't strict enough when the children misbehave.
2 According to experts the economy isn't likely to change suddenly.
3 The decision to fire him seemed very unfair.
4 People already know about the issue of recycling.
5 The report gives a very bad picture of the future.

Score ____/25

Wait a couple of weeks and try the quiz again.
Compare your scores.

05 SPORTS AND INTERESTS

VOCABULARY Health and fitness

Complete the conversations using the pairs of words in the box.

stamina / hand-eye coordination	breath / speed
junk / healthy lifestyle	demanding / sweat
shape / uncoordinated	flexibility / strength

1 A: Wow! You look amazing. What have you been up to?
  B: I've lost 10 kilos. I decided it was time to give up the ....
  food and go for a ....

2 A: I get such a stiff back after sitting at the computer all day.
  B: You should come to my yoga class. It's great for ....
  And it's good for .... too. I can lift much heavier
  weights than before.

3 A: How's your squash course going?
  B: Great, thanks. I couldn't last more than 20 minutes when I
  started but my .... has really improved. You should
  come along.
  A: Sorry but I can't even hit a ball. My .... is awful.

4 A: The new teacher is much more .... than the old one.
  She made us work an awful lot harder.
  B: Tell me about it. I worked up a .... in seconds!

5 A: I'm so unfit. I really need to get back into ....
  B: Why don't you try salsa dancing? It's great fun.
  A: I think I'm too .... for that. In fact, my boyfriend says
  I've got two left feet.

6 A: Can we slow down a bit? I'm getting out of .... running
  up this hill.
  B: Sorry, but we need to keep going. .... is important if
  you want to get really fit.

DEVELOPING CONVERSATIONS
Checking what you heard

Write questions for each of the statements.
1 I've just taken up fencing. *You've just taken up what?*
2 My new football boots cost nearly £200.
  ....
3 We didn't get home until two in the morning.
  ....
4 I'll be teaching my Pilates class later this evening.
  ....
5 My parents are going on a trek across the Sahara.
  ....
6 I've just heard from Anna for the first time in ages.
  ....
7 It took my sister under an hour to complete the race.
  ....
8 I ran 25 km last night.
  ....

READING

**A Read the title and first paragraph of the article
opposite. What is the main content?**
  a a report on the trend of working for yourself
  b profiles of people who have set up a business
  c tips on how to turn your hobby into a career

**B Read the first line of paragraphs 2, 3 and 4. Match
the names of the entrepreneurs to the photos.**

**C Read all of the article. Write M (Marcus), R (Ricardo)
or V+H (Valeria and Helen).**
  Who
  1 is going to develop a new product/business? ☐ ☐
  2 used to work in a completely different field? ☐
  3 felt very depressed before setting up the business? ☐
  4 provides a service in a local area? ☐
  5 has an inherent talent? ☐
  6 didn't do training in order to get a job? ☐
  7 wished he/she had completed a course? ☐
  8 was told by other people that there was a need for
    the business? ☐ ☐
  9 started with very simple equipment? ☐

How many of us have thought, 'Why don't I just quit my day job and set up a business on my own?' For most of us it remains a dream, but for some who take the plunge, it's a dream come true. We look at four keen
5 entrepreneurs who have turned their hobby into a new career.

Lifelong cyclist and fitness fanatic Marcus King has a small but successful business selling cyclewear. But the road to business hasn't been easy. Three years ago Marcus was
10 made redundant from a construction company where he had worked for eight years. 'It came as a dreadful shock. I just didn't know what to do with myself. I felt completely let down and useless. To get out of the house, I used to go on long bike rides. Then the idea came to me –
15 what cyclists need is well-designed, easy-to-wear tops and shorts. I chatted to some cyclist friends and they all agreed there was a gap in the market.' Now Marcus sells his range through his website and selected stores around the country. There are plans to add a range for children in
20 the near future. 'I should have done it years ago. Making a living out of cycling is just the best thing.'

Ricardo Cerruti's life is music. Ever since he started DJ-ing at the school disco, he's been fascinated by it. 'I learnt how to mix in my own bedroom on a really basic
25 little system. Very different from what I use now. When I was a teenager, I would DJ at friends' parties or even in the street, just for fun.' Ricardo has just come back from South America where he was working in the top clubs. 'I still have to pinch myself to believe it's true. I never really
30 trained for this job. I guess it just comes naturally. And I don't have many formal qualifications, I dropped out of college in the first year, which I regret now. So I need help with the business side of things. I'm setting up my own record label just now and I hope to help young kids who
35 are into music get a foot on the ladder.'

From hobby to job

An interest in holistic therapies and a desire to help people lead Valeria Diaz and Helen Lee to set up Stressbusters – an on-site massage service for local businesses. 'After talking to family and friends, it was
40 clear that half the local workforce was suffering from stress and tension. People work such long hours that it's hard for them to fit in an appointment in a clinic. So then we had the brainwave of taking the therapies to them, at their desks,' Helen explained. Valeria and Helen
45 met at evening classes and hit it off straightaway. Valeria continued, 'We were both doing the courses just out of interest. We got the qualifications but never expected to make a living out of our hobby. But more and more people came to us complaining about being at a desk
50 all day, so we decided to turn it into a business.' These businesswomen plan to take on more therapists once Stressbusters is established.

Glossary

cyclewear: clothes and accessories worn when cycling
to mix: to combine sounds from CDs or records to create different musical sounds
holistic therapies: treatments that take care of the body and the mind

D **Look at these expressions in context. Choose the correct meaning.**
1 take the plunge (lines 3–4)
  a take a bold and important step   b take up a hobby
2 I have to pinch myself (line 29)
  a I can't believe what people say.   b I can't believe it's really happening.
3 get a foot on the ladder (line 35)
  a make a start in business   b work harder
4 had the brainwave (line 43)
  a had the idea   b had the time
5 hit it off straightaway (line 45)
  a formed a business immediately   b liked each other immediately

Learner tip

Don't panic when you come across new vocabulary! Remember to use the context around the word or phrase to help you understand. Also use the wider context of the situation and the relationships between people.

VOCABULARY Football and life

A Choose the correct words.

A: What was the match like?

B: We ¹ *thrashed / bashed* them 6–1. You should have been there. It was the most amazing final. We scored in the first minute – it went straight past the ² *manager / goalkeeper* into the back of the net. Then the captain ³ *fouled / filed* Richards and he got sent ⁴ *out / off*, and we scored again from a free kick. Mind you, there was a bad moment when Mitchell tackled and their defender ⁵ *dropped / dived*, but the ref allowed play to go on. Then they scored their only goal. They had a couple more chances that hit a ⁶ *stick / post* and the ⁷ *bar / frame*, but then we got four more goals, one after the other. Heaven.

B Add each word in the box to the group of words it can go with.

substitute	disallowed
fixed	tackle
greedy	close
promoted	sack

1 Do you think the team / the sales rep / Lisa / will be .... soon?
2 They had to .... the captain / the original for a copy / some of the ingredients.
3 Unfortunately, the goal / access to the website / the expenses claim has been ....
4 He's such a .... player / eater / person / child.
5 The decision was taken to .... the manager / the whole team / the captain for poor performance.
6 It was a really .... game / decision / contest / election.
7 It became apparent that the game / the election / the match / the result was ....
8 He tried hard to .... the problem / the striker / the situation / the shortage.

Learner tip

Practise your English through your interests, e.g. listen to music and sports commentaries in English, join online clubs and forums with people in other countries, read sports/hobby magazines in English, etc.

GRAMMAR *should(n't) have, could(n't) have, would(n't) have*

A Write sentences for each situation. Use *should've / shouldn't have* and the verbs in the box.

give up the gym	apologise for swearing at the referee
miss so many sessions	take on so much work
set off earlier	score in the first half

1 We lost the game by just two points.
We ....
....
2 I didn't go to many of my German classes.
I ....
....
3 They missed the start of the play.
They ....
....
4 I'm really out of shape.
I ....
....
5 We didn't get any time off last summer.
We ....
....
6 They were both sent off.
They ....
....

B Match the comments (a–f) to the sentences you wrote in exercise A.

a Then they would never have been banned from the next match.
b Then I wouldn't have put on so much weight.
c Then we could've gone away for a couple of weeks.
d Then they wouldn't have disturbed everyone in their row of the theatre.
e Then I would've got by better when trying to make conversation on holiday.
f Then we might've won the tournament again this season.

C Choose the correct forms.

1 We didn't win, but it *would've / could've* been worse. We *could've / might never have* come last.
2 I *would've / wouldn't have* called you before, but my battery was dead. I *would've / should've* charged my mobile before I left.
3 We *should've / would've* loved to have come to the party but the twins were both ill.
4 I *would've / wouldn't have* normally complained but the waiter was just so rude.
5 I missed the flight, but it *should've / could've* been worse. It *could've / would've* been the last one.
6 I *would've / wouldn't have* bothered you but it seemed like an emergency.

DEVELOPING WRITING
A report – evaluating proposals

A **Read the report on proposals to improve facilities in a residential area. Circle the five aspects that apply to report writing.**
passive forms
long paragraphs
clear language and layout
essay format
headings
numbered points
descriptive language
fairly impersonal style

B **Choose the correct words in the report.**

C **Rewrite the sentences using the words in brackets. Make any necessary changes but don't change the word in brackets.**

1 The leisure centre will give the city more options (provide)
   The leisure centre ....
   ....

2 People could see a range of shows in a state-of-the-art theatre. (allow).
   A state-of-the-art theatre ....
   ....

3 The majority of people will like the sports centre. (appeal)
   The sports centre ....
   ....

4 It's a good proposal to build a theme park. (worth)
   A theme park ....
   ....

5 Building a new library would benefit the area. (improvement)
   Building a new library ....
   ....

6 You can have conferences at the leisure centre. (held)
   Conferences ....
   ....

D **Write a report (150–190 words) based on the task below.**

> Your local council is planning to build either a library or a concert venue. Write a report, describing the benefits of each project and saying which one you would choose, and why.

Current situation
[1] *Actually / Currently*, the area has neither a sports centre [2] *not / nor* a cinema. The council has the budget to provide just one of these facilities. The [3] *reason / purpose* of this report is to assess the two proposals and decide which would be more beneficial.

A sports centre
This would [4] *benefit / provide* the area in the following ways:
1 It would [5] *let / allow* people of all ages to take part in a range of sporting activities in their free time.
2 The facilities could be used by schools and other organisations as part of the [6] *generally / overall* leisure provision in the area.
3 It would create a number of new jobs and [7] *bring / take* in valuable revenue to the area.

A cinema
This would offer the following [8] *pros / advantages*:
1 It would provide a family-friendly form of [9] *leisure / entertainment* and a cultural destination.
2 It could be used for providing training for students of media and film studies.
3 It would [10] *get / attract* other businesses to the area, including restaurants and shops.

Recommendation
While a cinema could offer benefits, it would only appeal [11] *for / to* certain sections of the community. In my opinion, the council should build a sports centre because it could offer more facilities to a bigger range of people. It would also provide greater job [12] *opportunities / vacancies*.

GRAMMAR
Present perfect continuous / simple

A Match the sentence beginning to the correct ending, a or b.

1 I can't find my pen. What on earth
   a have I done with it?
   b have I been doing with it?
2 She should be good at German by now. She's
   a learnt it for years.
   b been learning it for years.
3 What's the delay with this train? We've
   a hung around for ages.
   b been hanging around for ages.
4 Can we try Cuba for a holiday? I've
   a been fancying that for years.
   b fancied that for years.
5 There's no more snow, so I don't know why they haven't
   a opened the road yet.
   b been opening the road yet.
6 Serve this lady next. She's the one who's
   a been waiting the longest.
   b waited the longest.

B Find and correct three tense or time expression mistakes in each conversation

1 A: I didn't know you were keen on horse-riding. How long do you do that?
   B: Since a year on and off. I'm not very good but I enjoy it. I've just been signing up for classes at the Miller Stables.
   A: You're kidding! I've been working there part time since March.
2 A: You're into windsurfing, aren't you? I never tried it in my life. What's it like?
   B: Amazing. I've already been going to the coast twice this month. Come with me next time if you like.
   A: I need to get back in shape first, I think. I've joined the gym and I've still lost a few kilos.
3 A: Sorry, have you waited long? My bus was late.
   B: No, don't worry. I've only already got here.
   A: OK, have you ever decided which film you want to see?
4 A: Where have you been? I've been trying to call you for all morning.
   B: Sorry, I've been at the dentist's since hours.
   A: Oh, are you OK?
   B: Yes, but my tooth has hurted since last night.

VOCABULARY Lucky escapes

Complete the conversations with a phrase from box A and box B. Sometimes there is more than one possible answer.

A		
had a hairline fracture	sprained my knee
passed out	twisted my ankle
was paralysed from the waist down	banged her head

B		
might've torn the ligaments	could've broken it
might've knocked herself out	could've been killed
could've drowned	might've broken it

1 A: I had to walk with a stick for a few days after I
   sprained my knee.
   B: I bet that was painful. But, it could've been worse. You *might have torn the ligaments*, falling on the ice like that.
2 A: She's pretty shaken up after falling in the river. She
   .... and she didn't come round for a couple of minutes.
   B: I think she had a lucky escape. She ....
3 A: They X-rayed it and Alex .... after he landed awkwardly on his leg.
   B: That sounds painful but maybe he had a lucky escape. He .... completely.
4 A: They had a terrible accident. He .... and they say he'll never walk again.
   B: That's so awful, but, if you think about it, I suppose he ....
5 A: Amy .... really hard when she fell off her bike. And she wasn't wearing a helmet.
   B: Sorry to hear that but it could've been worse. She ....
6 A: I .... when I slipped down the stairs. My whole foot is bandaged up.
   B: Poor thing. Still, it could've been worse. You ....

LISTENING

A 🔊 **5.1 You are going to hear a sports programme about a relatively new sport. Listen and complete the information about touch rugby.**

Touch rugby

Sport profile

Can be played in men's, women's and ¹ .... teams

Getting more popular ² ....

Started in ³ .... in the 1960s as a ⁴ .... game for players of traditional game

Little equipment needed: just a ball, ⁵ .... and a group of friends

Aim

Each team to score touchdowns and prevent ⁶ .... from scoring Play similar to traditional game but less physical ⁷ .... and exciting

Benefits

⁸ .... levels improve, quickly gets heart pumping and burns off excess weight develops ⁹ ...., ball skills and ¹⁰ .... coordination

Player profile

Anybody: all shapes, sizes, and ¹¹ ...., can play at own ¹² ....

Reasons for taking up the sport

Simon: to get back in ¹³ ....

Angie: to find a sport she could do with ¹⁴ ....

PRONUNCIATION
Not pronouncing sounds

Language note not pronouncing sounds

Remember that some sounds are not pronounced in connected speech, especially when a final consonant in a word is followed by another consonant.

... *if you don't mind me saying* ...

A **Mark where you think the sounds disappear in these sentences.**

1 You can play in men's, women's and mixed teams.
2 It's similar to rugby but without the tackling.
3 We get people of all shapes, sizes, and ages.
4 It's so simple that after two to three games you get the basic skills.
5 It's up to you to keep playing and develop your game.
6 I used to travel a lot for work.
7 I couldn't find the time to exercise.
8 I wanted something my husband and I could do together.

B 🔊 **5.2 Listen and check. Then practise saying the sentences.**

Vocabulary Builder Quiz 5 (*OVB* pp18–20)

Try the *OVB* quiz for Unit 5. Write your answers in your notebook. Then check them and record your score.

A **Which is the odd one out in each set?**

1	sew	thread	post	cloth
2	dive	serve	double fault	forehand
3	fanatic	tackle	volunteer	substitute
4	foul	penalty	free kick	comic
5	paralysed	sprained	disallowed	twisted

B **Which word do you need to complete the sentences in each set?**

1 Wait! I need to get my .... back. / He gets very short of .... after walking. / How come you're out of .... already?
2 How can I build up my .... ? / You have a high level of physical .... / Regular exercise maintains ....
3 What can I do to get in .... ? / I'm so out of .... after my accident. / Walking helps keep you in ....
4 I've been a bit of a .... / She made such a .... of herself. / They made a real .... out of everyone.

C **Complete the sentences with words that start with *self-*.**

1 He's left his job and has gone ....
2 Staying in a hotel is too expensive so we always have a .... holiday.
3 He's never had a guitar lesson. He's completely ....
4 She needs something to boost her confidence. She has really low ....
5 I'm so .... I always go red when I meet people.
6 If you're nervous walking home at night, why don't you take up .... classes?

D **Which preposition can complete the sentences in each pair?**

1 Why was he sent .... after only 10 minutes?
I shouldn't have put .... paying my credit card bill.
2 Why are you so stressed? Just chill ....
It was so hot I nearly passed ....
3 I bumped .... the table and bruised my knee.
How did he get .... politics?
4 It was hard to keep .... with the others in the class.
They've been thinking of taking .... Italian.

E **Correct one letter in the underlined words.**

1 Is there anything interesting at the craft <u>fail</u>?
2 We spent aged <u>wondering</u> around the market.
3 It was really <u>clone</u> but we scored in the last minute.
4 The trainer was arrested because the race had been <u>filed</u>.
5 Why did they give her the <u>lack</u> from her job?
6 The report of the <u>browning</u> hit the town very hard.

Score ____ /25

Wait a couple of weeks and try the quiz again.
Compare your scores.

VOCABULARY Where you stayed

A Complete the opinions with the words / phrases in the box.

| unbearably hot | facilities | weather | incredible |

1 We usually stay in a hotel so that we don't have to bother cooking. But the .... in this place were just .... – it had every gadget you could think of. As it turned out the .... was .... , so we took it in turns to make a salad and ate out on the terrace.

| a bit of a dump | middle | nowhere |

2 We've used the network all over the world and most of them are really good value if you're on a budget. But this one was in the .... of .... , miles from the nearest town. And it was quite run down ... in fact, ... to be honest.

| filthy | muddy | overlooked |

3 Being able to travel around was supposed to take us to beautiful areas, but the first place we went to .... a building site. And the field was all .... and we got absolutely .... every time we stepped outside. Then we broke down on the way home. Never again!

| beaches | stunning views | deserted |

4 I'd never stayed anywhere so luxurious. Everything was so stylish and we had some .... from our window. It was great to be away from the crowds, too. The local .... were .... so we had the place to ourselves.

| whole | incredibly welcoming | spotless |

5 I'm not one for expensive hotels so we tend to stay somewhere smaller. We booked for a couple of nights on a farm. The owners were .... and the .... place was lovely and clean, just .... And after breakfast, we didn't need to eat again until dinner!

B Match the opinions in exercise A with the places (a–f). There is one place you don't need.

a a bed and breakfast   d a tent
b a self-catering apartment   e a camping van
c a youth hostel   f a posh hotel

GRAMMAR Modifiers

A Choose the correct word / phrase in brackets and write it in the correct place.

1 The room was spacious, considering the price we paid. (quite / a bit / absolutely)
2 I've never met him but people say he's a joker. (a bit too / a bit of / a bit)
3 The main square was packed with tourists all weekend. (very / absolutely / a bit)
4 The tenants left a mess everywhere. (rather / completely / really)
5 The food was spicy for my liking. (a bit too / not very / a bit of)
6 Rents in this area are high just now. (absolutely / very / hardly)
7 The trip was a disaster from start to finish. (very / complete / extremely)
8 I thought the area around the flat was nice. (a bit / completely / quite)

B There is one word missing in each sentence. Write it in the correct place.
1 What's the matter? You're in a bit of bad mood today.
2 There was hardly to do at the resort. The kids were really bored.
3 The place was deserted. There was anyone staying at the hotel.
4 I'm going to be a late, but only about five minutes.
5 I'm going to send this steak back. It's very nice.
6 There are hardly vacancies during the summer.
7 Turn the TV down. It's a bit too.

C Rewrite sentences 1–4 to make them weaker and 5–8 to make them stronger. Use the words in brackets and add any necessary words.
1 The area down by the station is really filthy. (rather)
   The area down by the station is rather dirty
2 The hotel was a complete rip-off. (a bit too)
   ....
3 The campsite was a nightmare. (bit)
   ....
4 The hotel room was really cramped. (not / particularly)
   ....
5 The food was quite tasty. (absolutely)
   ....
6 The weather wasn't great. (completely)
   ....
7 The campsite wasn't very attractive. (right)
   ....
8 The view was quite interesting. (really)
   ....

DEVELOPING CONVERSATIONS
Negative questions

Match the statements (1–6) and the questions (a–h). There are two questions you don't need.
1 We'd better be going now.
2 We're going to ask for our money back.
3 We've just booked a fortnight in Spain.
4 We were burgled last month.
5 We came back off holiday early.
6 We're thinking of moving abroad.

a Really? Wasn't the meal very good?
b Why? Didn't you like the resort much?
c Oh, haven't you had a holiday yet?
d You're kidding! Aren't you very happy here any more?
e Honestly? Couldn't you rent a flat for a while?
f No way. Aren't things in this area going down hill?
g Oh, can't you stay a bit longer?
h Why not? Isn't it satisfactory?

LISTENING

A 🔊 6.1 You are going to hear three conversations. Listen and choose the correct information about each situation.
1 two friends *on the beach / in a field* looking for their *tent / camping van*
2 a couple in *their own home / a flat for sale* talking to *an interior designer / a TV presenter*
3 *two chambermaids / a chambermaid and a manager* in a *posh hotel / bed and breakfast*

B Listen again. Are these statements true or false?
1 Phil thought he knew where they were going.
2 Lisa disturbed someone who was sleeping.
3 Lisa complained of getting dirty.
4 The TV team had changed the heating and lighting.
5 The walls were covered in lots of different colours.
6 The presenter agreed that the makeover wasn't very good.
7 Magda had worked more slowly than usual.
8 The guests in room 129 didn't leave it very tidy.
9 Helen wasn't very sympathetic to Magda's complaints.

Language note diphthongs
- -
A diphthong is a sound formed by the combination of two vowels in a single syllable:
coin /ɔɪ/   dear /ɪə/   place /eɪ/   buy /aɪ/
There are eight diphthongs in English
(see also Workbook page 47).

PRONUNCIATION Diphthongs

A 🔊 6.2 Listen to these sounds.
/eɪ/   /ɪə/   /aɪ/   /ɔɪ/

B Match the symbols to the underlined words.
1 We're tr<u>y</u>ing to sleep.
2 J<u>oi</u>n us again ...
3 Sorry to h<u>ear</u> that.
4 Go and have a br<u>ea</u>k.

C Which letters in bold have a different sound?
1 b**oy**   n**ow**adays   sp**oi**lt   empl**oy**ment
2 s**i**te   f**i**xed   q**ui**te   h**ei**ght
3 l**i**ar   w**ei**rd   id**ea**   b**ee**r
4 l**ea**der   self-c**a**tering br**ea**kdown   tr**ai**ning

D Listen and check. Practise saying the words.

GRAMMAR *have / get something done*

Complete the sentences for each cartoon using the verbs in the box.

get a tattoo / do	just have his motorbike / stolen	get her ears / pierce
should / have the roof / check	have to / get her shoe / repair	have / central heating / install

She's going to ....
....

She wants ....
....

They ....
.... of each other's names.

He needs to ....
....

They ....
.... before they bought it.

He...
....

VOCABULARY Understanding idioms

Complete the conversations with the idioms.

costs an arm and a leg	make ends meet
taking the mickey	finding my feet
having a whale of a time	out of pocket
through rose-coloured glasses	in small doses

1 A: Look at the children having fun in the pool.
   B: I know. They look like they're ....
2 A: Doesn't Millie dominate the conversation all the time?
   B: Tell me about it. I enjoy her company but only
      ....
3 A: How's Max getting on at college?
   B: His studies are going great but he's short of money all
      the time.
   A: Couldn't he get a part-time job to help .... ?
4 A: I don't think Tim understands how serious the
      situation is. We're way behind schedule.
   B: I know but he always looks at things ....
5 A: What was the festival like?
   B: The bands were great but I've come back completely
      broke.
   A: I know what you mean. Everything .... at these
      things.

6 A: Are you enjoying your new job?
   B: Yes, thanks, but I don't really understand all the systems yet.
      I'm still ....
7 A: You should get a pair of those leopard-skin leggings. They'd
      look great on you.
   B: Stop .... I'd look awful!
   A: Sorry. I was only teasing.
8 A: How come you ended up paying the hotel bill?
   B: Kim paid for the flights but they were real a bargain. The
      hotel cost double so I'm completely .... now.

DEVELOPING WRITING An email – giving news

A Read the email quickly. Match the opening sentences to the paragraphs.
a We are slowly finding our feet.
b Hello to all of you back home.
c I don't start work properly until next week.
d Everyone in the block seems pretty friendly.
e Well, we're finally here after all that planning.

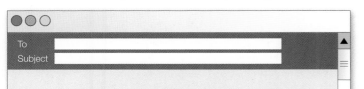

```
●●●
To      [                    ] ▲
Subject [                    ] ≡
```

¹ ...... Sorry I haven't had time to contact each of you but it's all been a bit hectic.

² ...... We had a few problems on the journey and there was no-one to meet us when we landed in Rio. A great start! In the end my boss came to pick us up. I'd only met her once before but she was fine about it and the kids helped to break the ice.

³ ...... We spent the first week in the company flat, which was OK but very impersonal. I must admit both Elena and I felt a bit homesick. Then we found a furnished flat last week, which was a relief. All our boxes arrived safely on the removal van and having familiar stuff here has made us feel more at home.

⁴ ...... Needless to say, it's the kids who've made the biggest connection with the locals. They think it's a big adventure and don't seem to miss home too much.

⁵ ...... I feel a bit nervous about it but that's why we're here after all. I'll let you know how I get on.

Cheers for now.
Luke

B Read the email again and circle the topics that Luke mentions.

the weather	the cost of living
the journey	accommodation
getting to know people	work
learning a new language	food

C Replace the underlined words and expressions with the language in the box.

hectic	break the ice
missing	feel homesick
locals	find our feet
we get on	it was a relief

1 We'll let you know how <u>successful we are</u> at finding a flat.
2 I must admit I haven't had time to <u>be sad about not being at home.</u>
3 My work schedule has been so <u>busy</u> I haven't had a minute to call home.
4 Esme is really <u>sad because she can't see</u> her grandma, but I think she'll be fine.
5 The <u>people in the area</u> have been so kind and helpful.
6 I was feeling worried about the first day in the new office but my boss helped to <u>ease the tension.</u>
7 <u>We felt more relaxed and happy</u> when we'd landed safely in Vancouver.
8 It's taken a while but we're starting to <u>feel confident</u> in our new surroundings.

D Match the sentence halves.
1 It was hard at first but we're slowing picking
2 Everyone at the office made me
3 The hardest thing was moving across time
4 We've finally got our stuff
5 I forgot to bow to the boss – the worst cultural
6 We had to have the whole house
7 You couldn't believe the prices – you can get

a zones and dealing with the jet lag.
b shipped over from the UK to here.
c by on about $10 a day!
d gaffe you can make!
e cleaned before we could move in. Charming!
f feel very welcome from day one.
g up the local language.

E Imagine you have just relocated to a new country. Write a general email (150–190 words) to update your friends and give your news. Include three or four of the topics in exercise B.

READING

A Read the article quickly. What is the main topic?

a how to deal with the problems faced by the children of immigrants

b how art was used to help Bangladeshi children's home life

c how Bangladeshi children see home

B Read the article again. Are these statements true, false, or doesn't the text say?

The researchers

1 had already done a lot of research with young children. ☐

2 understood the children's ideas by asking them to write and make things. ☐

3 had expected to find a difference in how the children saw 'home' and 'away'. ☐

4 asked the children to categorise their work according to country. ☐

The children

5 preferred shopping in Bangladesh because it was cheaper. ☐

6 had problems with the two aspects of their identity. ☐

7 tended to think of Bangladesh as a place for a holiday. ☐

8 only ever ate Bangladeshi food. ☐

9 didn't relate distance with the closeness of a relationship. ☐

C Look at the words in bold in the article. What do they refer to?

D Write the missing prepositions. Look back at the article if you need to.

1 come up .... interesting findings / a good idea / a possible solution

2 set .... a research project / a small business / a roadblock

3 take part .... an art workshop / a reality TV programme / a sports tournament

4 divide .... two categories / equal portions / groups of three

5 work .... what 'home' meant / the correct answer / the final amount

---

Language note collective nouns

A collective noun is a word that represents a group, e.g. *committee, team, family, police,* etc. We often use a plural verb even though the noun is singular:
*Home is simply where the **family are**.*
***Leeds are** winning: they have just scored.*

Home is where

Work with British-born Bangladeshi children by researchers from the University of Sussex came up with some interesting findings.

The researchers set up the project after finding that little work had been done with children whose families had moved to Britain from another country. Their research was in schools in East London, **where** there is a large south Asian community who regularly visit family in Bangladesh. The main themes of the research were 'home' and 'journeys', and the children took part in art workshops and diary-writing tasks.

The children were given art materials to use in painting and model-making. In one task, the nine- and ten-year-olds divided the art they had made into two categories – 'home' and 'away'. When the researchers looked at the art, they said they found it wasn't immediately clear **which piece** referred to which place.

Dr Kanwal Mand, one of the researchers, explained that the children were asked to do prints or pictures and that they used colour categories to indicate 'home' (blue) or 'away' (red). **They** avoided naming the categories as Bangladesh or Britain, as they wanted the children to work out what 'home' and 'away' meant to them.

the heart is

Her colleague, Dr Katy Gardner, explained that when the children compared 'home' and 'away', there were some surprising results. Some images, like **those** showing the Asian tradition of painting hands, were found in both the 'home' and 'away' piles. Other pictures showed images of Mecca next to Big Ben and other London landmarks. Gadgets and consumer goods such as Nintendos, mobile phones and football shirts were linked to Bangladesh. Dr Mand suggested that this might be because the children could afford to buy such objects **there**.

The children did not appear confused by the two sides of their identity and were not suffering from any clash of culture. They were well adapted to living in London and were skilled translators. Dr Gardener said that the children often thought of Bangladesh as other Londoners might. They complained about the heat, mosquito bites, and the spiders and frogs. Many of **them** saw Bangladesh also as a tourist destination and talked about **its** shopping malls and fun fairs.

In one workshop, the pupils drew circular diagrams of what is important to them, where people, places or objects they didn't like were furthest from the centre. Dr Gardner explained that the people the children thought of as closest were not necessarily **those** who lived near them. Some of their relations in Bangladesh were positioned really close to the children in the diagram, while cousins who lived nearby were positioned further away. Things that the children liked and related to were quite close, for example, Manchester United, and things they didn't like such as Brussels sprouts were positioned far away.

She added that if the children had family in Bangladesh they saw **that** as home, and if they had relations in London they saw that as home, too. It seems that people view home through family. Home is simply where the family are.

Glossary

workshop: a meeting to discuss / perform practical work in a subject or activity
Mecca: the holy city of Islam
Brussels sprouts: small cabbage-like vegetables

Vocabulary Builder Quiz 6 (*OVB* pp22–24)

Try the *OVB* quiz for Unit 6. Write your answers in your notebook. Then check them and record your score.

A Read the statements. Was each experience positive (✓) or negative (✗)?
1 The place was a real dump.
2 There were the most amazing facilities everywhere you looked.
3 The site had the most stunning views.
4 It looked quite grand from the outside, but the rooms were filthy.
5 Everything we ate was either bland or greasy.
6 The owners were incredibly welcoming.

B Which word is missing from each the sentence?
1 The guy next door was playing music at full ....
2 How long will it take to get .... the operation?
3 She's .... up with a nice girl at uni.
4 The hotel prides .... on the quality of its food.
5 I'm getting sick of his continual ....-downs.
6 We've been slaving .... on this for weeks.

C Add the missing prefix or suffix.
1 Why are you so rest.............? Just chill out.
2 The beaches were complete desert............., not another person in sight.
3 Our hotel room ....looked a quiet bay.
4 It took ages to scramble up the wind............. path.
5 We didn't go out in the day as it was ....bearably hot.
6 The area has undergone a complete ....formation.

D Replace the underlined words with a more descriptive verb from *OVB* Unit 6.
1 The drunk <u>walked</u> out of the pub.
2 There were so many people it took ages to <u>find</u> him in the crowd.
3 He <u>looked at me angrily</u> when I told him I was leaving.
4 After twisting her ankle, she <u>walked in pain</u> off the pitch.
5 I was <u>walking in a relaxed way</u> through the park when I ran into my old friend.
6 I didn't read the whole report. I just <u>looked quickly</u> at the summary.
7 Sorry I can't stop. I'm <u>going quickly</u> to work.

Score ____ /25

Wait a couple of weeks and try the quiz again. Compare your scores.

07 NATURE

VOCABULARY
Weather and natural disasters

A Complete the names for natural disasters. Then choose the correct answer.

Questions, questions ...

1 What language does the word ts _ _ _ _ _ come from (literally 'harbour wave')?
  a Chinese
  b Japanese

2 What is more likely to cause a fo _ _ _ _ f _ _ _?
  a human carelessness
  b the heat from the sun

3 A t _ _ _ _ _ _ is a vertical column of spinning air. Which country is a major hotspot for this type of storm?
  a Japan
  b the USA

4 Which crop failed in Ireland, leading to the f _ _ _ _ _ of the 1840s?
  a wheat
  b potatoes

5 Which country has an extensive system to control f _ _ _ ds?
  a the UK
  b the Netherlands

6 In which country did the strongest ea _ _ _ _ _ _ _ _ on record (9.5 on the Richter scale) occur?
  a Chile
  b Indonesia

7 Approximately how many v _ _ _ _ _ _ es are still active and so may erupt in the future?
  a about 1,900
  b about 500

8 Which desert has experienced the longest d _ _ _ _ _ t?
  a the Sahara, in north Africa
  b the Atacama, Chile

B Choose the correct words.
1 A: Wasn't that *storm / tornado* incredible yesterday? The thunder was so *strong / loud*, I jumped right out of my chair. And the *lightning / lighter* lit up the whole sky. It was amazing!
  B: Actually, I didn't think it was much fun. I got absolutely *wet / soaked* and it took me all day to dry *up / out*.
2 A: I can't stand this weather. It's so cold I nearly *freezing / froze* to death on the bus to work.
  B: I know what you mean. And I don't think the snow is due to *fall / melt* for days yet.

3 A: Did you enjoy the view from the top?
  B: Actually, it wasn't very clear when we got up there. A light *misty / mist* was forming over the fields.
  A: That's pretty common. Some days we get really *strong / thick* fog. You have to wait ages for it to *lift / rise*.
4 A: I wasn't that keen on Florida. The *heat / hot* was unbearable and it was so *wet / humid* I needed a shower every hour.
  B: When we were there, the wind was really *boiling / blowing*. It was so *strong / tough* we hardly went out all week.
5 A: Is it still *pouring / spilling* down near the beach? It was awful earlier on.
  B: No, it's *cleared / eased* off quite a bit over here. It's only really *spitting / dripping* now. And there's only a *slight / slim* breeze. We should be OK for a walk.

GRAMMAR Narrative tenses

A Complete the text with the correct form of the verbs. Use the past simple, past continuous, present perfect or past perfect.

I ¹ .... (watch) this documentary the other night about tornadoes. ² .... (never / see) anything like it before. It ³ .... (film) in 'Tornado Alley' in the US – states like Oklahoma and Kansas, which are major hotspots for tornadoes. The programme ⁴ .... (show) a tornado that ⁵ .... (form) just outside a small town in South Dakota. There was a family who ⁶ .... (not realise) that the storm ⁷ .... (come) and had just minutes to get into their truck and set off in the opposite direction. Then there was this guy who ⁸ .... (work) as a storm chaser for years, a professional scientist whose job is to plant sensors into the path of the wind. I ⁹ .... (not believe) anyone would do this! While he and his friend ¹⁰ .... (speed) along in an ordinary car, one of the biggest tornadoes of that year ¹¹ .... (move) right towards them. It ¹² .... (be) like something out of a movie. They ¹³ .... (manage) to plant the sensor and then the tornado just ¹⁴ .... (die) away. Apparently, they don't last that long and they only travel like 10 km – far enough though if you live in 'Tornado Alley'.

B **Match the sentence halves.**
1 Typical! The weather only turned bad after
2 It was so beautiful to see a rainbow just after
3 The fog was so thick I couldn't see a thing as
4 We decided to shelter under some trees until
5 My friend from South Africa had never
6 It started to pour down just as we

a the rain eased off and the sun came out.
b the storm had passed.
c seen snow until she came to Scotland.
d I'd booked a week's holiday.
e were walking back from the beach.
f I was driving along the motorway.

DEVELOPING CONVERSATIONS
Exaggerating

Choose the correct lines from the box to complete the conversations.

a but every time I see her she's wearing a different pair!
b It was like twice the price of any other laptop.
c but they were very slow.
d It's the best CD I've ever heard, by miles.
e They've got like ten houses around the world.
f but she did keep me waiting a long time.

1 A: I must have waited an hour for my main course.
   B: Really?
   A: Well, maybe I'm exaggerating a bit, ...
2 A: ....
   B: Really?
   A: Maybe I'm exaggerating a bit, but it was pretty expensive.
3 A: ....
   B: Really?
   A: Maybe I'm exaggerating a bit, but they are very wealthy.
4 A: She must have hundreds of pairs of shoes.
   B: Really?
   A: Maybe I'm exaggerating a bit, ...
5 A: ....
   B: Really?
   A: Well, maybe I'm exaggerating a bit, but it is pretty good.
6 A: Annie never, ever arrives on time.
   B: Really?
   A: Maybe I'm exaggerating a bit, ...

LISTENING

A 🔊 **7.1 Listen to Eddie and Jan talking about a new cloud formation. What's the relationship between them?**
a a scientist and a reporter
b a lecturer and student
c two friends

B **Listen again and write the correct letter E (Eddie) or J (Jan).**
Who ...
1 already knew about the cloud? ☐
2 thought the other person was taking the mickey? ☐
3 finds more information to support his / her argument? ☐
4 gives descriptions of the clouds? ☐
5 suggests they find out more about the Cloud Appreciation Society? ☐
6 is pleased by the other person's change of attitude? ☐

PRONUNCIATION Intonation

Language note intonation
- -
Intonation is the changes in sound produced by the rise and fall of the voice. English tends to use quite a wide voice range, particularly when expressing surprise, interest or enthusiasm. A flat intonation can give the impression that you are not interested, especially when talking to native speakers.

A **Practise saying these sentences.**
1 A new type of what?
2 Eddie, are you winding me up? It's not April Fools' day, is it?
3 No way! You're kidding. Let me see that.
4 Wow! You're right. Those photos are amazing.
5 Wow, you've really got in to this, haven't you?
6 Who would've thought a cloud could create so much interest?

B **Listen and check. Practise again and try to imitate the intonation.**

GRAMMAR Participle clauses

A Complete the sentences about challenges to the natural world with the correct form of the verbs in the box.

reach	live	recycle	affect
become	cut down	invest	pollute

1 The number of people .... their carbon footprint isn't rising fast enough.
2 The percentage of people .... everyday materials hasn't risen by much.
3 Few of the agreements .... on climate change are having a real effect.
4 The number of species .... extinct worldwide shows no sign of slowing.
5 The amount of money .... into green technology is too low.
6 Seas and rivers .... by industry are never fully cleaned up.
7 Many of the people most .... by climate change have little political influence.
8 The percentage of the population .... to over 80 is rising.

B Choose the correct form. Then complete the sentences to make them true for your town/city.

1 The percentage of young people *going / gone* to university ...
....
....
2 The amount of affordable housing *building / built* ...
....
....
3 The job opportunities *creating / created* for young people ...
....
....
4 The percentage of people *lived / living* alone ...
....
....
5 The amount of money *invested / investing* in transport ...
....
....
6 The number of tourists *visited / visiting* ...
....
....

READING

A Read the webpage opposite quickly. Who wrote it and why?
a a science writer to reply to requests for information
b a travel writer to recommend places to see
c a traveller to describe places he / she has visited

B Read the webpage again and match the opinions to the places. There is one opinion you don't need.
1 'I never knew they came in so many colours. And seeing them move around their native habitat in such numbers was such a joy.'
2 'We weren't sure it was going ahead so it was such a treat when we saw the first streak of colour appear. I thought I was going to cry.'
3 'I never thought I would get so close to one. To see it erupting was the most awe-inspiring thing I've ever seen.'
4 'I had to pinch myself on the first day. I couldn't believe I was up-close and personal with these incredible animals.'
5 'I must have taken hundreds of photos. The shapes and colours were just so different from what we have at home.'

C Which place / activity
1 is a long distance from a town / city?
2 has an attraction that may or may not appear?
3 has official status as an important natural area?
4 is a destination for people with a particular hobby?
5 involves close contact with animals?
6 occurs in different parts of the world?
7 has animal life in a spectacular range of colours?
8 includes a well-known landmark?

D Write the missing verbs. Look back at the webpage if you need to.
1 If you're into marine life, ... no further than the waters off the south coast.
2 The forest .... an incredible range of wildlife and plants.
3 Go up to the top of the hill. The view will .... your breath away.
4 The site was just beautiful, ... by huge mountains and dense forest.
5 Hours waiting and we didn't even .... a glimpse of a bird or animal. It was such a waste of time.
6 These waters .... the perfect habitat for dolphins.

Natural Wonders Not To Be Missed

If you want to see something that will take your breath away, forget the Sydney Opera House, Golden Gate Bridge or even the Great Wall of China. Look no further than the natural world for inspiration. Here's a selection of must-see places and must-do activities from around the globe.

A The best light show on earth

Aurora Borealis or the 'Northern Lights' is the name given to the extraordinary natural phenomenon of coloured lights seen in the skies of the northern regions of Scandinavia, Alaska and Canada. Often described as the most spellbinding natural firework display, the lights fill the sky with dancing streams of red, yellow, green and violet. Never the same twice, the appeal of the lights is made all the stronger in that their appearance is not guaranteed. The right combination of conditions has to be in place for this magic show to start.

B A plant–lovers' paradise

If plants are your passion, then look no further than South Africa, which is home to about 10 per cent of all known species on earth. The Western Cape includes the fynbos – a unique type of vegetation consisting of thousands of plant species native to the area. So special is the vegetation here that it has been designated as one of the earth's six plant kingdoms. The Cape Floral Region, which includes the iconic symbol of Cape Town – Table Mountain, became a Unesco World Heritage Site in 2004. Among this glorious floral spectacle, one of the highlights must be the 130 species of protea, which come in all shapes, sizes and colours.

C Brilliant bird life, spectacular setting

If your idea of bird watching is waiting for hours on a rainy day to catch a glimpse of a dull, brown bird, think again. The small central American country of Guatemala boasts an incredible range of bird life, all in glorious technicolour. Among the birds is the elusive Resplendent Quetzal, whose courtship and nesting behaviour attract birdwatchers from around the world. And the national parks and nature reserves around Lake Atitlán provide the perfect habitat for the 320 species recorded in the area. The shimmering waters of the lake are surrounded by forests and dominated by the impressive cones of three dormant volcanoes.

D Lend a hand to the elusive panda

If you've only ever seen a giant panda on a TV wildlife documentary, take the opportunity to live alongside one of the world's rarest and most adored animals. Set in the majestic surroundings at the foot of the Qinling mountains, the Shaanxi Province Rescue and Breeding Research Center near Xian in China welcomes volunteers to work with these fascinating creatures. The tasks include monitoring the animals' behaviour, preparing the bamboo which is their staple diet, and keeping their pens clean. Not for the average tourist as the location is pretty remote, but animal lovers could find themselves working with some of the other amazing species indigenous to China such as the Golden Monkey or Crested Ibis.

Glossary

phenomenon: a fact or event, especially in nature
courtship: animal behaviour to attract a mate
ibis: a species of bird with long legs and a long neck

VOCABULARY Plants and trees

Complete the texts with the words in the boxes.

stem	herbs	palm tree	leaves	roots

I'd always thought of gardening as a hobby for older people, but having my own little area of earth has changed me. I now find the whole process of growing plants fascinating. It amazes me that when you plant dry, brown ¹ .... , a few weeks later you get a strong ² .... , green ³ .... and maybe beautiful flowers. From the smallest patch of ⁴ .... to add to cooking to the largest ⁵ .... to sit under on sunny days, growing plants is like a tiny miracle.

oak	flower	weeds	seeds	bushes

I've just joined a group of guerrilla gardeners – a group of volunteers whose mission is to green up abandoned areas of land. We're working on a big area down by the station. We cleared the whole site of ⁶ .... and planted thousands of ⁷ .... When they ⁸ .... next spring, the whole area will be transformed. Our proudest moment was when we planted native ⁹ .... and ¹⁰ .... trees in an area that was going to be made into a car park.

DEVELOPING WRITING
A story – using the first line

A **Complete the story with the time expressions in the box.**

when	just	suddenly	within seconds
while	before	later	on this particular night

I'd never been so terrified in all my life. It all happened on a flight from New York to London, ¹ .... the plane flew into a storm. I'd done that overnight trip hundred of times ² .... and never even noticed the weather. ³ ...., there was nothing eventful about the start of the journey. It was a relatively quiet flight and we took off more or less on time.

⁴ .... the crew was talking us through the safety drill, I flipped through the in-flight magazine and then tried to sleep. A couple of hours ⁵ ...., I was woken by the pilot's announcement about turbulence. ⁶ .... two of the flight attendants were hurrying up and down the plane, checking safety belts.

Then ⁷ .... I got the fright of my life. There was an incredibly loud bang and the plane shook violently. It dropped through the air for what seemed ages and I thought my time was up. I could hear the others passengers screaming. Then pilot explained that we'd been hit by lightning but that we'd ⁸ .... come through the storm and there was nothing to worry about. It was such a relief when we landed in London safe and sound.

B **Choose the correct words.**
1 I got the *frightened / fright* of my life.
2 I was *afraid / scared* stiff.
3 I was almost scared to *death / die* by it.
4 We were all thrown into a *panic / panicked*.
5 I was shaking with *fear / scare*.

C **Match 1–6 and a–f.**
I could hear …
1 the waves   a snorting and stamping.
2 the flames   b thumping in my ears.
3 the horse's hooves   c thundering towards me.
4 the dog   d crackling as the fire got nearer.
5 my heart   e growling and snarling.
6 the bull   f crashing against the side of the boat.

D Complete the sentences with the correct form of the verbs in brackets.

1 The weather .... (be) beautiful all morning but then clouds suddenly .... (appear) out of nowhere and the rain .... (start) to pour down.

2 We .... (walk) round in circles for hours before I .... (realise) we were completely lost. If only I .... (remember) to bring a map.

3 I .... (just settle) down to sleep in the tent when I .... (hear) a loud roar. I .... (no dare) look outside for fear of what I might see.

4 The sea .... (turn) from gentle waves into a wild storm in what .... (seem) like seconds. I .... (never need) so much strength to control the boat.

5 I watched the snow .... (fall) silently and steadily out of the window of the tiny cabin. It suddenly .... (dawn) on me that I .... (not tell) anyone where I was.

6 As I .... (stroll) along the deserted trail, I .... (hear) a hissing sound. Seconds later, the biggest snake I .... (ever see) was right in front of my face.

7 The smoke .... (become) so overwhelming I .... (can) hardly breathe. Then the sound of the helicopter filled the area and I knew I .... (going to) be OK.

8 Although I .... (explore) this area hundreds of times before, I .... (never experience) such ferocious weather conditions. I thought I .... (will never) get off the mountain alive.

Learner tip

Before you write a story, think about the background to the setting and character(s). Ask yourself: *Who? When? Where? What? Why?* and make notes on the key events before you start.

E Write a story (150–190 words) for the short story competition below. Use one of these ideas if you want to.

- being caught in bad weather
- being chased/bitten by an animal
- getting lost in a remote place

You have decided to enter a short story competition in an English-language magazine. The story must begin with the words:

I'd never been so terrified in all my life.

Vocabulary Builder Quiz 7 (*OVB* pp26–28)

Try the *OVB* quiz for Unit 7. Write your answers in your notebook. Then check them and record your score.

A Which is the odd one out in each set?

1	drought	earthquake	famine	shade
2	melt	fog	hail	mist
3	estate	will	subsidy	inheritance
4	bush	breed	seed	stem
5	water	invasive	weed	flower

B Which words can complete both these sentences?

1 Did you hear that clap of .... ?
Lorries .... past the house every few seconds.

2 My memory of the accident is a bit ....
It was so .... you couldn't see your hand in front of your face.

3 Racing drivers need .... reactions.
A flash of .... lit up the sky.

4 The crowd .... into the stadium before the match.
Huge areas of the river bank have been ....

5 There was a cool .... blowing across the beach.
Passing my driving test was a ....

C Choose the correct words.

1 This weather is awful. We'd better pull *out / over* to the side of the road.

2 A good diet is often associated *with / to* living a long time.

3 His decision *deemed / was deemed* to be unacceptable.

4 She's just been made a board *owner / member* of the company.

5 I *dare / contest* you to eat this chilli.

6 The teacher's help was *significance / invaluable* in helping the students pass.

7 We can go out as the rain is easing *off / down* a bit.

8 The judge decided she was the *rightfully / rightful* owner.

D What form of the words in brackets do you need to complete the sentences?

1 It's no (exaggerate) to say the flood has been devastating.

2 We need to provide for an (age) population.

3 The problem of witness (harrass) is rising.

4 The officials reported several cases of voter (intimidate).

5 Strike leaders have agreed to the (resume) of talks with management.

6 Farming continues to be heavily (subsidy).

7 They were found to be in (violate) of the law.

Score ___/25

Wait a couple of weeks and try the quiz again. Compare your scores.

VOCABULARY Crimes

A Choose the correct words.

1 It's pretty rough round here now. The number of street *robberies / burglaries* has gone up a lot.

2 It turned out it wasn't a *disappearance / kidnapping*. The girl had just decided to run away.

3 They were convicted of *fraud / identity theft* after selling shares in companies that didn't exist.

4 If you kill someone when you are *racing / speeding*, to me it's still *murder / death*.

5 The city was in crisis for days after a series of *bombings / bombers* and then *violent / riots* in the streets.

6 The council was involved in a *bribery / blackmail* scandal after they were accused of accepting money for giving contracts to local businesses.

B Complete the conversations with the verbs in the box.

was killed	had just gone off	had set fire

1 A: So, what actually happened?
B: Well, I saw the flames and at first I thought someone
¹ .... to the building. Then a passerby explained that a bomb ² .... It was a miracle that no-one ³ ....

was only doing	've gone	got caught

2 A: I ¹ .... on camera last week. I've just paid a £70 speeding fine and now I ² .... a hundred pounds overdrawn. I wouldn't mind but I ³ .... 34 miles in a 30-mile zone.
B: What are you complaining about? You shouldn't have been speeding in the first place.

vanished	was held captive	'd been seized

3 A: Did you hear about that guy who ¹ .... by a gang for over two years?
B: No, what was that?
A: Apparently, he'd been working abroad and then he just ² .... No-one knew where on earth he was. Then it turned out he ³ .... by this gang. They wanted publicity for their cause but they released him after negotiating with the government.

hadn't stolen	'd smashed	'd never been broken into

4 A: Maddie told me about the burglary. You poor things.
B: Yeah, we ¹ .... before so it was a real shock. They ² .... the window in the back door to get in. I reckon they must've been disturbed because they ³ .... much – just a bit of Maddie's jewellery.

's found dead	never comes back	'd been stabbed

5 A: What's your book about?
B: Oh, it's a crime story. It's about a kid who goes out to meet his mates but .... Then he .... in a back street. He .... to death.
A: How can you read that stuff? It sounds awful, just really upsetting.

'd got hold	came up to	d grabbed

6 A: So how did it happen?
B: I was just texting my friend and this guy .... me to ask the time. Next thing I knew, he .... my bag and disappeared into the crowd.
A: What a nightmare. You must've been terrified.
B: To be honest, I was more worried about identity theft. He .... of all my details.

DEVELOPING CONVERSATIONS
Comments and questions

A Correct one mistake in each reply.

1 A: We had our car stolen last weekend.
B: What shame!

2 A: My dad has been a victim of identity theft.
B: Oh, you joke!

3 A: We had to come back off holiday early because there were riots in the capital.
B: You must been a bit scared.

4 A: They closed the airport due to a bomb scare.
B: That's very dreadful!

5 A: The band's singer was caught speeding on the motorway.
B: That awful!

6 A: Some kids broke into the local sports centre.
B: Oh, not!

B Match the follow-up questions (a–h) to B's reply (1–6). There are two questions you don't need.

a What were they protesting about?
b How fast were you going?
c What kind of example does that set to their fans?
d How did they get hold of all his details?
e Did they get away with much stuff?
f Are the insurance company sorting it all out for you?
g When did they release him?
h Did they find a device anywhere nearby?

GRAMMAR
Modals + present and past infinitives

A Choose the correct forms.

1 He *can't / mustn't* be very sorry because he keeps on committing crimes.
2 You *should've / must've* reported the break-in straightaway.
3 His family *can't / must* be desperate, not knowing when he'll be released.
4 You can't *be feeling / feeling* very happy in the house after the burglary.
5 The police think the gang *mustn't / can't* have got far as they have set up road blocks.
6 The police must have *investigated / been investigating* the case for months.
7 You *might / should* get your identity stolen if you leave personal details lying around.
8 They shouldn't have been *doing / done* that speed in a residential area.

B Rewrite the sentences using the correct form of the verbs in brackets.

1 It was a better idea for me to report him to the police. (should)
   .... *I should've reported him to the police.*

2 I feel sure you were shocked by the robbery. (must)
   ....
   ....

3 It's possible he was at the scene of the crime. (might)
   ....
   ....

4 It was a better idea for you to protect all your personal information. (should)
   ....
   ....

5 I feel sure she isn't guilty of fraud. (can't)
   ....
   ....

6 Perhaps she isn't living in this area anymore. (might)
   ....
   ....

7 It was possible for there to be a nasty accident. (could)
   ....
   ....

8 I feel sure the burglar wasn't more than 15 years old. (couldn't)
   ....
   ....

LISTENING

A 🔊 8.1 Listen to Part 1 of a radio programme. What is its main purpose?

a to talk about a popular type of fiction
b to tell a detective story
c to interview a crime writer

B Listen to Part 2. Are these statements true or false?

1 Crime stories and thrillers account for less than half of general fiction books.
2 Victoria's company has never published anything but crime stories.
3 Her company has published two award-winning authors.
4 She thinks the storyline is the most important thing in a crime novel.
5 There is a big variety of places and time periods in crime fiction.
6 Victoria thinks crime fiction is more popular with men.
7 Victoria doesn't care about whether a writer is a man or a woman.

PRONUNCIATION Diphthongs

> **Language note** diphthongs
> --
> Remember there are eight diphthongs in English.
> (See also Workbook page 35)

A 🔊 8.2 Listen to these sounds.

/aʊ/	f**ou**nd	/əʊ/	hell**o**
/eə/	r**a**re	/ʊə/	c**u**re

B Match the sounds to the underlined words.

1 even r<u>u</u>ral parts of Scandinavia
2 we started to f<u>o</u>cus on just crime
3 a multi-million p<u>ou</u>nd industry.
4 some people enjoy being sc<u>a</u>red

C Which letters in bold have a different sound?

1 kn**ow** cr**ow**n th**ou**sand surr**ou**nd
2 alth**ough** prom**o**te c**ou**rt thr**oa**t
3 pl**u**ral t**ou**r c**u**re s**ou**r
4 dr**ea**dful w**ea**r million**aire** pr**ay**er

D 🔊 8.3 Listen and check. Practise saying the words.

VOCABULARY
Agreeing and disagreeing

A **Cross out one extra word in each reply.**

1 A: The police have a really difficult job.
   B: I'm with you on ~~to~~ that.
2 A: People who break the speed limit should lose their driving licence.
   B: I couldn't agree with more.
3 A: The council should install more cameras in public places.
   B: That's not a very bad idea.
4 A: I think he was bound to fall into a life of crime.
   B: I don't really see it like that for myself.
5 A: People often think the crime rate is worse than it really is.
   B: I know what you do mean.
6 A: Demonstrators should pay towards the cost of policing their march.
   B: Well, that's a one way of looking at things.
7 A: I think burglary is one of the worst crimes in modern society.
   B: That's a complete rubbish!
8 A: Putting people in prison for long sentences just doesn't work.
   B: I am agree with you up to a point.

B **Write your own responses to agree or disagree with these opinions.**

1 Sentences for serious crimes should be longer than they are at the moment.
   ....
2 In general, society is much safer than it was 20 years ago.
   ....
3 Prisons just teach young people how to commit crime.
   ....
4 Police officers should be among the highest paid workers in society.
   ....
5 Sentences for female criminals should be shorter than for males.
   ....
6 Criminals should be made to apologise to their victims.
   ....
7 Young offenders need help to improve their behaviour, not punishment.
   ....
8 The development of the internet has led to an increase in crime.
   ....

GRAMMAR
Nouns and prepositional phrases

A **Complete the sentences with the words in the box and add the correct preposition.**

excuse	involvement	damage	quality
need	return	focus	~~point~~

1 I can't see the ...*point in*... speed cameras. People just speed up again after them.
2 It's time we put the .... preventing crime.
3 I think there's a .... more police out on the streets.
4 She didn't have an .... her bad behaviour.
5 We don't want a .... the high crime rates of the past.
6 A safe environment hugely improves people's .... life.
7 Was there much .... your car in the accident?
8 How can we increase people's .... the local community?

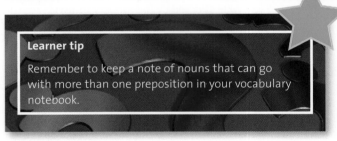

Learner tip

Remember to keep a note of nouns that can go with more than one preposition in your vocabulary notebook.

B **Complete the sentences. Use a different preposition in each pair.**

1 a There's a problem .... my computer.
   b I don't want to create a problem .... you.
2 a I've earned hardly any interest .... my savings.
   b Do you have much interest .... modern art?
3 a Older people need to set an example .... teenagers.
   b This is an example .... his best work.
4 a The law didn't have much impact .... crime rates.
   b The impact .... the changes won't be known for many years.
5 a There's a strong argument .... educating prison inmates.
   b They had an argument .... the person who caused the accident.

DEVELOPING WRITING An online forum – giving opinions

A Read the opinion on an online forum opposite quickly. Choose the best heading.
- a It feels like a police state
- b Cameras are a necessary evil

B Choose the correct words.

```
○○○
```

Modern cities are full of cameras – on the high street, in shops and banks, and more recently even in schools. People say they want a return ¹ *for / to* the 'good old days' when they could walk down the street without ² *watching / being watched*. I don't think this time ever really existed but it's right that people are concerned ³ *about / of* the surveillance society. In an ideal world, we ⁴ *would've / would* all live without any forms of control, but the ⁵ *true / truth* is that people break the law every day. Reports of burglaries, car theft, assaults and damage ⁶ *on / to* property fill the news. In fact, I was the victim of an unprovoked attack in the city centre last year. I wasn't badly hurt but thanks ⁷ *of / to* the cameras in the area, the gang was identified and caught quickly. Without CCTV, there was no ⁸ *luck / chance* they would've been caught. Walking around any city now and seeing cameras in place makes me feel more secure, it's as simple as that. And there's just one question to the people who say they are worried about their ⁹ *freedom / free* – what have you got to worry about if you haven't ¹⁰ *done / made* anything wrong?

Posted by rikki2 at 20.42 17 comments 💬

I couldn't understand why last month cameras went up on the streets along my route to work. There

C Complete the sentences with the words in the box.

go on	role	drop	far
research	nothing	lack	case

1 If you have .... to hide, you shouldn't worry about being on camera.
2 .... suggests that having cameras in one place just moves the crime to a different area.
3 Installing cameras in schools is just going too .... Where will it all end?
4 Having cameras everywhere leads to a .... of trust in society.
5 Cameras have a .... to play in places like airports, police stations and banks.
6 The money spent on cameras should .... improving run-down areas and installing good street lighting.
7 There's a .... for using cameras in schools as they help reduce bullying and vandalism.
8 Residents reported a .... in street crime after the installation of a network of cameras.

D Which sentences in exercise C are pro cameras and which are anti?

E Write a reply (150–190 words) to the opinion in exercise B. Include your overall opinion on CCTV (closed circuit TV), reasons for your opinions and examples from your own experience.

Language note talking in general
- -

Remember that we don't use an article when talking about things/people/situations in general, e.g.
Modern cities are full of cameras. (not *The modern cities* ...)
People break the law every day. (not *The people break* ...)

READING

A **Read the article opposite quickly. What tone has the writer used?**
a critical of Shaun Greenhalgh
b slightly unbelieving of the facts of the story
c purely factual

B **Read the article again. Choose the correct person for each question.**
Who ...
1 never attended art college?
2 approached potential buyers of the artworks?
3 became aware that an artwork was fake?
4 found ways of proving that the artworks were authentic?
5 didn't like being the centre of attention?
6 didn't deny his/her guilt?
7 checked a fake from Ancient Egypt?
8 took a long time to prepare before deciding on what to copy?

C **Complete the text with the correct form of the words in brackets.**

So what motivated Shaun Greenhalgh to enter into a ¹ .... (conspire) and ² .... (fraud) the art world of thousands of pounds? It appears that it wasn't for the money because the family continued to live a modest lifestyle even when they had acquired a small fortune. There's no question that Shaun was an ³ .... (accomplish) artist, but also an ⁴ .... (assume) character, so why create so many ⁵ .... (forger) and risk ⁶ .... (prison)? Police ⁷ .... (enquire) suggested that Shaun resented the legitimate art market because it hadn't recognised his talent. His lawyer, however, said the he made the copies to 'perfect the love he had for such arts'.

The fine art of forgery

Meet Shaun Greenhalgh, painter, sculpture, wood carver ... and criminal. Over a period of 17 years, until his imprisonment in November 2007, Shaun created over 120 breathtaking works of art, not from an inspiring and well-equipped studio, but from his garden shed in Bolton, Greater Manchester. This unassuming man of 47, who had never had an art lesson in his life, became one of the most accomplished art forgers in Europe.

The inspiration for his work came from library books, which detailed lost masterpieces from around the world. Shaun undertook meticulous research and learnt a staggering range of techniques to be able to create his copies, everything from pastels and watercolours, to ancient and modern sculpture, and metalwork. Both the tools he used from the local DIY store and his methods of ageing his work were fairly rudimentary, but Shaun and his accomplices managed to fool all areas of the art world including dealers, auction houses, museums and private collectors.

So who else was in this gang? A network of wealthy and well-connected fraudsters? In fact, Shaun's 'gang' turned out to consist of himself, and his elderly mum and dad, who all lived together in their small and somewhat shabby council house. While Shaun worked away in his shed recreating 'lost' art treasures, his father, George, was the salesman in the team. He made up colourful stories about each of the fakes to explain the provenance of each item. Working together with his wife, Olive, they even acquired catalogues for antique sales to further authenticate Shaun's work. It is estimated that they made up to £850,000 in their 17-year collaboration.

By far their most daring forgery was The Armana Princess – a statue thought to represent of the daughter of Pharaoh Akhenaten and Queen Nefertiti, the mother of King Tutankhamun. The original would have been over 3,000 years old while Shaun's version was created in about three weeks using basic tools, and aged using a mixture of tea and clay. George's role was to approach Bolton Museum with a simple enquiry about the statue.

He claimed it had been passed down the generations in his family for about 100 years and that he thought it might be worth a few hundred pounds. Experts from the British Museum and auction house Christie's assessed the authenticity and potential value of the statue. On their recommendation, Bolton Museum offered George £440,000 for the statue, which of course he gladly accepted.

Finally, in November 2005, the family's luck ran out. They tried to sell three 'Assyrian' stone tablets, which were supposed to date back to 681BC, at a value of about £500,000. George maintained they had been in his family since he was a child. An expert at the British Museum spotted a mistake in the hieroglyphic-style writing on one of the tablets. The Museum informed the police, who raided the family home and found a huge collection of fakes, including Shaun's three previous attempts at The Armana Princess. All three admitted conspiracy to defraud and Shaun received a prison sentence of just under five years.

Glossary

forger: a person who makes illegal copies of something
council house: a house owned by the council and rented to tenants
provenance: a record of ownership of a work of art or antique
tablet: a piece of stone, clay, or wood on which an inscription is written

Vocabulary Builder Quiz 8 (*OVB* pp30–32)

Try the *OVB* quiz for Unit 8. Write your answers in your notebook. Then check them and record your score.

A Complete the missing part of each word.
1 He was arrested for the burg............ of several properties.
2 They started ....mailing him after they found out about his affair.
3 She lost her job when they found out about her fraud............ activities.
4 The kidnap............ were arrested when they released their hostages.
5 Street rob............ is rising in most big cities.
6 We saw the man behaving suspic............ and called the police.
7 The tourists were drunk and their behaviour was appal............ .
8 There are several schemes in place for offender rehab............ .

B Form the nouns for people / things from the verbs. Put them in the correct list (-or or –er).

| dictate | defend | project |
| labour | inspect | contain |

-or	-er

C Match the sentence halves.
1 The kidnapping took place in broad
2 How on earth did they get
3 She isn't even the boss but she's always laying
4 No-one ever punishes these kids. They get
5 Despite appeals for help, no-one came
6 She was sentenced to community

a away with murder.
b forward with information.
c down the law.
d daylight on a busy street.
e service as it was a first offence.
f hold of my bank details?

D Write the missing word in the correct place.
1 The house has been broken three times in a year.
2 How long have they held captive?
3 I couldn't believe I'd overdrawn by £500.
4 I've always opposed to the death penalty.
5 He vowed never commit a crime again.

Score ___/25

Wait a couple of weeks and try the quiz again.
Compare your scores.

VOCABULARY Working life

A Complete the sentences with the correct form of *get* and the words and phrases in the box.

promoted	a raise	made redundant
on-the-job training	the hang of everything	

1 My brother .... six months ago and he hasn't found another job yet.
2 I didn't have a clue what I was doing in the first few days, but I .... now.
3 We .... every year in my firm. Instead, we have a system of bonuses if we meet targets.
4 We .... at the moment. It's great. I'm learning loads of new skills.
5 I've worked for them for nearly three years but I .... yet. I'm not sure what to do to get to the next level.

Language note 'empty' verbs

Verbs like *get, make, do, have* and *take* are sometimes called 'empty' verbs because their meaning can change according to what follows, e.g. *get up / a raise / fired / to work*, etc. Keep a note of useful collocations with these verbs in your vocabulary notebook.

B Match the sentence halves.

How's your new job going?
1 Don't ask. My boss is driving me mad. She's a
2 Great, thanks. I love helping young kids. I'm
3 Not great, I'm afraid. I'm struggling
4 Awful, to be honest. I nearly handed
5 I had no idea nursing would be so hard, I'm
6 It's great, just really stimulating. I feel
7 It's not rocket science. In fact, the work

a I'm really stretching myself.
b in my notice last week.
c finding it emotionally draining.
d is pretty menial.
e finding it very rewarding.
f to cope with working shifts.
g complete control freak.

GRAMMAR Conditionals with present tenses

A Find and correct a mistake in each sentence.

1 If you haven't taken all your holiday by the end of the year, you won't carry it over.
2 Staff get promotion if they have been achieving all the goals outlined by their line manager.
3 If employees are feeling demotivated, we gave them on-the-job training.
4 The reps get a bonus if they will reach their sales targets.
5 If you don't miss a deadline, you lose ten per cent of your marks.
6 Students get better results if they having control over their work.

B Choose two of the three verbs to complete the sentences.

1 What .... to do if you .... your finals? (don't pass / won't pass / are you going)
2 If nothing .... wrong, I .... college soon. (will happen / goes / 'll be starting)
3 If I .... promotion this time, I .... in my notice. ('ll hand / might not get / don't get)
4 If all else .... , I .... get a part-time agency job. (won't be able to / fails / 'll have to)
5 Just .... me a ring if you .... any more queries. (have / give / 'll have)
6 We .... for work abroad if I .... a job soon. (might look / won't get / don't get)
7 If the worst .... to the worst, I .... redundant. (comes / 'll be made / gets)
8 You .... him if he .... other students. (should report / will bully / 's been bullying)

DEVELOPING CONVERSATIONS
Feelings about the future

A Cross out one response that doesn't fit.

Do you think you'll ever live abroad?
1 *I'm bound to. / Probably not. / Definitely.* I'm learning English so I can move to Australia.
2 *Definitely. / Hopefully not. / I doubt it.* I would miss my family too much.
3 *I doubt it. / Probably. / Hopefully.* It's good to experience new things.
4 *I might. / Hopefully. / Definitely.* It would depend on the job opportunities.
5 *Definitely not. / I'm bound to / I doubt it.* I can't see myself leaving my home town.

B Give your own answer and a reason, to questions 1–5.

Do you think you'll ever ...

1 learn another language apart from English?

....

2 meet your hero / heroine?

....

3 be famous?

....

4 give up your worst habit?

....

5 travel round the world?

....

LISTENING

A 🔊 **9.1 You are going to hear three teachers talking about streamlining the curriculum. Listen and match the teachers (1–3) to the subjects they would cut (a–c).**

1 Martine
2 Greg
3 Wendy

a PSHE and modern foreign languages
b RE and ICT
c RE and PE

B 🔊 **9.1 Listen again and choose the correct answers.**

1 What is Martine's opinion about sport?
   a It shouldn't be taught in a state school.
   b Let students who like it do it outside normal class time.

2 Greg thinks sport
   a should be taught for more than one hour a week.
   b can teach about competition and stop students misbehaving.

3 Greg suggests
   a computer studies should be part of all lessons.
   b all students need a computer at home.

4 Wendy strongly disagrees with Greg about ICT because
   a students don't learn useful computer skills at home.
   b buying a home computer is expensive.

5 Martine say languages are important
   a to her students who are good at French.
   b for more than just communication.

6 All three teachers agree to cut
   a PSHE.
   b Science.

Language note stress on abbreviations

- -

In abbreviations with a series of letters that are read separately, the stress is on the last letter.

PRONUNCIATION
Stress on abbreviations

A 🔊 **9.2 Try reading these sentences with the correct stress on the abbreviations. Then listen and check.**

1 I think PE and RE.
2 I'm not with Greg on ICT.
3 I would do away with PSHE.

B 🔊 **9.3 Now practise staying these common abbreviations. Then listen and check. What does each one stand for?**

BBC	UCLA	ATM	VAT	UN
FBI	IMF	PC	SMS	ISP

GRAMMAR
Conditionals with past tenses

A Complete the sentences with the pairs of verbs in the box.

could drop / 'd choose	give up / didn't have to
had / lent	'd get / pushed herself
would make / were	was made / wouldn't bother
wasn't / 'd get	didn't work / might sign up

1 I'd .... work tomorrow if I .... pay my mortgage.
2 I'm retiring soon, if I .... redundant, I .... looking for a new job.
3 I'm sure she .... promotion if she .... a bit more.
4 If I .... shifts, I .... for an evening course.
5 If one person .... a deadline to meet, the whole team .... a hand.
6 I think students .... more progress if class sizes .... smaller.
7 If my boss .... such a control freak, we .... more work done.
8 If I .... a school subject, I think I .... Art. I'm just hopeless at it.

B Make a sentence with *if* for each situation.

1 I didn't get promoted. I didn't meet my targets.
   If I'd met my targets, I'd have got promoted.

2 I wasn't good at Music. I dropped it when I was 14.
   ....

3 You didn't get any redundancy pay. You didn't work for them for more than one year.
   ....

4 My parents didn't go to university. They didn't have the opportunity.
   ....

5 I'm working in a factory. I haven't been able to get a job in my field.
   ....

6 She didn't get the hang of the job quickly. The boss didn't help her.
   ....

7 I was working really long hours. I got ill.
   ....

8 My school didn't teach modern languages. I didn't take up Spanish.
   ....

READING

A Read the article opposite quickly. Which part of a newspaper do you think it would appear in?
a economy
b general news
c travel

B Seven parts of the article have been removed. Write the correct letter (a–h) in the gaps in the article. There is one extra sentence that you do not need to use.
a The post requires him to live on and write a blog from Hamilton Island
b The other candidates seemed very pleased for him,
c In addition to preparing a blog and video updates to attract tourists to the area
d The final selection process took the form of a four-day trip to Hamilton Island
e what impressed the executive director of Tourism Queensland was his self-motivation,
f which had suffered a decline in tourism due to worldwide economic recession
g The job description read quite simply,
h They had just 60 seconds to get across their creativity and skills.

C What do these numbers in the article refer to?
1 34,000 (line 2)
2 six-month (line 6)
3 1.7 million (line 18)
4 16 (line 36)
5 15 (line 37)
6 hundreds (line 61)

D Which five adjectives would you use to describe Ben?

adventurous	fit	arrogant	articulate
dull	bright	outgoing	cautious

E Match the sentence halves
1 I was very glad to be shortlisted
2 What will be involved in the selection
3 No-one thought he would be
4 They're advertising a post that
5 Would it be possible to submit
6 Although I didn't get the job, they gave

a my application online?
b me credit for my skills at interview.
c appointed as managing director so quickly.
d requires a huge range of qulifications.
e from the hundreds of people who applied.
f process – tests as well as an interview?

BRITISH MAN WINS 'WORLD'S BEST JOB'

Ben Southall, a 34-year-old charity worker, has beaten more than 34,000 other applicants in a most unusual employee selection process.

Ben has just been appointed as caretaker of a tropical Australian island, a six-month contract for what has been described as 'the best job in the world'. [1] .... on Queensland's Great Barrier Reef in return for a salary of over £70,000, a rent-free three-bedroomed villa complete with pool, and a golf cart. His bosses are the officials of Tourism Queensland, who advertised the job in January 2008. Their aim was to create publicity for north-eastern Queensland, [2] .... The post is part of a campaign costing 1.7 million Australian dollars and it's been called 'the most successful tourism marketing campaign in history.'

No formal qualifications were specified for the job but candidates needed to be experienced in a range of water sports. [3] .... 'Excellent communication skills, good written and verbal English skills, an adventurous attitude, willingness to try new things, a passion for the outdoors and good swimming skills, and enthusiasm for snorkelling and/or diving.'

Prospective candidates were invited to submit online video applications. [4] .... Unsurprisingly, the advert generated a huge response, causing the website to crash. The 34,000 hopefuls who did manage to register their application had to be shortlisted to just 16 finalists from 15 different countries.

[5] .... , where the candidates were interviewed, took swimming tests and had to demonstrate their blogging abilities. Ben was announced as the winner in a reality TV-style ceremony organised by Tourism Queensland. On hearing his name, he looked rather taken aback that he'd been selected but he quickly went on to give credit to the other finalists he'd been up against. 'Wow ... to all of the candidates that stand behind me – every one there is an absolute winner,' he said.

For the duration of his contract, Ben's place of work will include the spectacular scenery, warm waters, and soft sands of the island. His work uniform will be mainly wetsuit and flippers. [6] .... , his duties also include feeding some of the hundreds of species of fish that live around the island, and collecting the island's post. In his video application, there was footage of him riding an ostrich, running a marathon, and trekking through Africa. His appraisal of himself was as 'the adventurous, crazy, energetic one'. However, [7] .... calling him 'a level-headed, well-grounded bloke'.

Whatever his qualities, not many people can say they've done the best job in the world and mean it.

Glossary

wetsuit and flippers: equipment used in diving
well-grounded: sensible
bloke: informal word for *man*

VOCABULARY Starting presentations

A Choose the correct words.

1 What I'm going to try and do today is *tell / say* you a bit about the latest equipment. I'd like to begin by giving you an *oversight / overview* of the changes to the new model and then after that I'll move on to *make / do* some recommendations about how you can get the best effects in your own images.

2 What I'm going to try and do today is *talk / talk to* you about the way styles changed across the 15th and 16th centuries. I'd like to begin by *outlining / focusing* the main trends in portraiture at the start of the period and then after that I'll move on to *comment / consider* why these changes took place.

3 What I'm going to try and do today is *summarise / summary* the main reasons for the decline in local species. I'd like to begin by *reviewing / revising* what the latest figures have to say and then after that I'll move on to *heighten / highlight* some of the specific problems in this area.

4 What I'm going to try and do today is *take / make* a look at the proposed changes to the road layout. I'd like to begin by *presenting / commenting* on the current situation and then after that I'll move on to *highlight / focus* on why these plans have been drawn up.

B Match the introductions (1–4) to the correct audience (a–d).

a a wildlife group
b a photography club
c a group of local residents
d a group of art students

C Correct three mistakes in each introduction.

1 What I'm going to try and do today is tell to you about the best ways to look after your collection. I like to begin by showing you a short video and then after that I move on to the main do's and don'ts.

2 What I'm going to try and do today is summarise about the changes in sales patterns in our new markets. I'd like to begin by reviewing of the main trends and then after that I'll move on to make up some recommendations for future growth.

3 What I'm going to try and do today is take a looking at the history of the car industry in the area. I'd like to begin by comments on why this area has always been synonymous with cars and then after that I'll move on to highlight on some of the most successful models.

DEVELOPING WRITING A personal statement – varying sentence structure

A Read the personal statement opposite from an applicant for a summer job. What type of work is involved?

a working in a local activity centre for young people with learning difficulties
b giving advice to international visitors in a tourist office
c working with English-speaking teenagers in a summer school

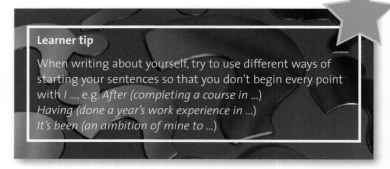

Learner tip

When writing about yourself, try to use different ways of starting your sentences so that you don't begin every point with *I ...*, e.g. *After (completing a course in ...)*
Having (done a year's work experience in ...)
It's been (an ambition of mine to ...)

B Complete the personal statement with the sentence openers a–g.

a Before starting university
b As well as being
c Having successfully completed
d When not working or studying
e For the last three years
f In addition to volunteering
g Reaching upper-intermediate level

¹ .... my university entrance exams and gained a place on a teacher training course, I am keen to get as much experience of working with young people as possible.

² .... in my English studies has been a great achievement and has given me confidence in both speaking and writing. Recently, I have also taken up Spanish and I am enjoying the challenge of learning another language.

³ .... , I have run an activity day for local teenagers. This involved organising a range of activities such as rollerblading and judo, and crafts like clay modelling and painting. ⁴ .... great fun, it also improved my organisational and communication skills.

⁵ .... with young people, I have also worked part time in a small local theatre. This has helped me work as a team and also try out ideas for marketing.

⁶ .... , I spend my time playing the guitar, writing songs and keeping in touch with friends across Europe via my computer.

⁷ .... , I look forward to the opportunity of meeting new people and getting some more work experience.

C Match each of the sentence openers (1–5) with two possible endings (a–j).
1 In order to get some practical experience, I
2 It's been an ambition of mine to
3 Being involved in the local orchestra
4 In terms of personal skills, I
5 My interests include

a cooking and making clothes.
b would say I'm reliable and creative.
c did some voluntary work in my local area.
d travel and use my language skills.
e gave me self-confidence when performing.
f took a part-time job as a classroom assistant.
g creative writing and playing in my band.
h see myself as sociable and a team player.
i work with young people.
j improved my own music skills.

D You want to apply for a summer job working with English-speaking teenagers in the USA. Write a personal statement (150–190 words) as part of your application.

Vocabulary Builder Quiz 9 (*OVB* pp34–36)

Try the *OVB* quiz for Unit 9. Write your answers in your notebook. Then check them and record your score.

A Match 1–5 and a–e.
1 have a knock-on   a freak
2 be a control   b brief overview
3 give a   c effect
4 be awarded   d after your aunt
5 be named   e credits

B Add the missing prefix or suffix.
1 A long daily commute can be very drain............. .
2 There's concern about the threat of redundan............. .
3 She says she isn't badly behaved, just ....understood.
4 The afford............. of housing is an ongoing issue.
5 They want to ....centralise in favour of regional power.
6 We've just been ....structured into new divisions.

C Complete the words that begin with *under*.
1 If you under............. your staff, you won't keep them.
2 The legal limit is 18 but teenagers still drink under............. .
3 Under............. countries need trade not aid.
4 We're under............. because 10 people are off sick.
5 It would be a mistake to under............. the competition.

D Which word do you need to complete the sentences in each set?
1 I'll bear it in .... / It never crossed my .... / It's been preying on my ....
2 She played a crucial .... in the decision. / He's taking on a managerial .... / It's my .... to set up the project.
3 His boss has a lot of .... over him. / She used her .... with the board to change the decision. / She has a lot of .... in the fashion world.

E Add one letter to one of the words.
1 When do we have to had in the essay?
2 They're planning a merge with a bigger college.
3 I was pushed round a bit at school.
4 What ran did he reach in the army?
5 We need to sock up on stuff for the party.
6 Would you like a ray for your drinks?

Score ___/25

Wait a couple of weeks and try the quiz again. Compare your scores.

VOCABULARY Birthdays

bunch	cosy	fancy-dress	pretending
theme	get-together	spree	

I adore my girlfriend but we have very different ideas about birthdays. My ideal celebration is something really low-key like a [1] .... with a [2] .... of friends in a [3] .... local restaurant. But she can't resist making a big fuss. She always goes on a shopping [4] .... and buys me loads of presents. And I have to celebrate in a big way. Last year we had a [5] .... party. She made me dress up as a Roman emperor and she went as Cleopatra. I spent the whole evening [6] .... it wasn't happening. I'm 40 soon and she's already talking about a [7] .... party, maybe a Hawaiian night or something based on 'Pirates of the Caribbean'. I can't wait!

GRAMMAR The future perfect

A Complete the conversation with the correct form of the verbs in brackets.

A: Have you seen this feature in the magazine, *By the time I'm 30* … ? There are some pretty ambitious people out there. One guy says by the time he's 30, he [1] .... (make) his first million. And a 17-year-old girl says she [2] .... (become) a top fashion designer.

B: Wow, sounds a bit out of my league! By the time I'm 30, the odds are I [3] .... (get) my master's and I hope I [4] .... (find) a decent job.

A: Do you think you and Elena [5] .... (get) married by then?

B: I don't really know. It's hard to say. What about you? Do you think you [6] .... (meet) Mr Right by then?

A: Oh, you know me, I'm so unlucky in love, so I [7] .... (not set) up home with anyone, I don't think. But work is going well, so I think [8] .... (should / be) promoted a couple times.

B: Yes, you're bound to do well and I'm sure Mr Right will turn up soon.

B Complete the sentences with your own ideas.

1 In a month's time, I ....
....

2 By the end of this course, we ....
....

3 By the end of the year, our local football team ....
....

4 By this time next year, my family and I ....
....

5 In five years' time, I ....
....

6 By the end of this decade, my country ....
....

7 In 20 years' time, I ....
....

8 By the time I've retired, I think ....
....

DEVELOPING CONVERSATIONS
Arranging to meet

Complete B's replies with an alternative suggestion from box A and an explanation from box B.

1 A: Shall we meet at 12.30?
  B: ....

2 A: Would it be OK to meet at the factory?
  B: ....

3 A: Would Thursday 19th be good for a get-together?
  B: ....

4 A: Do you fancy eating at The Old Mill?
  B: ....

5 A: How about a game of squash after work?
  B: ....

A	Can we make it somewhere a bit cheaper?
	Could we make it somewhere nearer the office?
	Any chance we can make it the following week?
	Could we make it something a bit less strenuous?
	Can we make it after lunch?

B	My wrist is still hurting after that accident.
	I'm a bit short of cash just now.
	We won't have got back from holiday.
	I haven't got the car with me today.
	I'm in a meeting until midday.

DEVELOPING WRITING A webpage – do's and don'ts

Hi, Kim. You've put weight on since we last met!

A Read the introduction. Who is the information for?
a British business people
b people who don't socialise much
c visitors to the UK

SUCCESSFUL SOCIALISING

People are socialising more and more in a range of different contexts and with people from different cultures. British society has become less formal in recent years but there are still a few golden rules if you want to avoid making a social gaffe.

B Choose the correct words.

MEET AND GREET

✓ **DO** [1] *shake / hold* hands when meeting for the first time. [2] *Giving / Making* eye contact is important too, but not for too long or you might make the other person [3] *uncomfortable / unwelcome*. It's usual to move to using first names quite quickly.

✗ **DON'T** kiss someone on the cheek as a greeting [4] *in case / unless* you know them well. Also respect their personal [5] *place / space* and don't stand too close.

THE ART OF CONVERSATION

✓ **DO** be prepared to [6] *initial / initiate* conversation, as a prolonged silence can feel [7] *awkward / difficulty*. Keep any questions you ask fairly neutral at first.

✗ **DON'T** dominate the conversation but be prepared to take [8] *roles / turns*. Both genders and people of a range of ages often chat together.

OUT AND ABOUT

✓ **DO** check the dress [9] *code / rule* of the event you are invited to. Modern [10] *norms / normals* of dress are often quite casual but you don't want to turn up to a five-star hotel in jeans. In a pub, it's usual to pay for a [11] *circle / round* of drinks for everyone in your group.

✗ **DON'T** leave your mobile on in more intimate venues like restaurants and cinemas.

THE HOME FRONT

✓ **DO** [12] *be / arrive* punctual if invited to someone's home for dinner or a party. It's usual to take a gift, either flowers, chocolates or wine.

✗ **DON'T** [13] *assume / agree* it's OK to smoke. Ask if your hosts [14] *matter / mind* and offer to go outside if you want a cigarette.

C Read these do's and don'ts. Which section of the guide in exercise B could they go in?
1 Do wait your turn. Nothing irritates the locals more than people pushing in at the bar or in queues.
2 Don't outstay your welcome. You might be a night owl, but your hosts may not, so leave at a reasonable time.
3 Do keep the volume low. Talking and laughing loudly or gesturing wildly might attract negative attention.
4 Don't stretch across the table for the wine, salt or bread. Ask another guest to pass you what you want.
5 Do smile to help break the ice. First meetings are difficult for everyone so a friendly face is always welcome.
6 Don't invite yourself along to a night out. Wait to be included in the group even if this means a few nights alone.

D Cross out the phrases that don't collocate.
1 Avoid *too much alcohol / personal questions / telling jokes / smoke* if invited to a person's house.
2 Don't expect *people to be on time / that you will chat during the meal / your guests to pay for their meal / small portions of food.*
3 It's considered polite *not to open gifts immediately / to serve women first / taking a gift / for children to keep quiet.*
4 Don't forget *to bow / using your chopsticks correctly / to send a thank-you card / a gift for your hosts.*
5 Let *to take off your shoes / your host pay / others serve themselves first / children join in.*
6 Never *swear in front of others / don't drink too much / hug members of the opposite sex in public / use the wrong hand for eating.*

E Write a set of do's and don'ts (150–190 words) for socialising in your country. Use the ideas in exercises B and C, and your own ideas.

VOCABULARY Making mistakes

A Complete the conversations with the phrases in the box.

sending a private email	copying in everyone
organising a surprise party	

1 A: Why on earth did you send that message to Kati about her birthday? You knew I was
   [1] .... for her.
   B: Sorry. I thought I was [2] .... but I ended up [3] .... by mistake.

put your foot in it	burst out crying	hadn't realised

2 A: What's up with Carrie?
   B: I asked her how her Mum was and she
   [1] .... I [2] .... that she'd been ill.
   A: You're hopeless! How do you always manage to
   [3] .... ?

dressed casually	turned up	top politician

3 A: Did you see that [1] .... looking totally out of place?
   B: No, what happened?
   A: He [2] .... in a suit and tie to talk to a group of school kids. Of course, everyone else was
   [3] ....

is due	made a stupid joke	isn't actually pregnant

4 A: I could've died of embarrassment. I've just asked Sue from Sales when her baby [1] ....
   but she [2] ....
   B: Oh, you didn't! She's just put a bit of weight on.
   A: I know that now. And to make things worse, I
   [3] .... about not having to go through the birth.

didn't have a clue	live on air	
didn't see the funny side	meant to be a joke	

5 A: Did you hear Radio Rebel this morning? The DJ was talking to a record producer and he was criticising the bands on his label, not realising he was
   [1] .... He [2] ....
   thousands of people could hear him.
   B: That sounds a bit mean.
   A: It was [3] .... but he
   [4] .... of it when he realised what had happened.

READING

A Read the article opposite quickly. From whose point of view is it written?
mainly:
a the family
b the journalist
c the police

B Read the article again. Are these statements true or false?
1 About 500 teenagers gatecrashed Maddie's party.
2 Maddie's mother had made no plans to deal with gatecrashers.
3 Maddie was allowed to invite as many guests as she liked.
4 Maddie's dad was unaware she'd posted details of the party on *Facebook*.
5 Most of the damage to the property was external.
6 When the police were called, the last gatecrasher had already arrived.
7 The police officer had some sympathy for the family.
8 Maddie feels guilty about what happened.

C Who in the article might have said these things?
1 What were you thinking of, putting the details on the site in the first place?
   ....
2 "Call for back-up. It's like a riot, with kids all over the place."
   ....
3 "That's the last party you'll have under this roof!"
   ....
4 "What can I do to make it up to you?"
   ....
5 "If you're still up for it, get over here now. You don't want to miss the fun."
   ....
6 "What on earth is going on over the road? It sounds like a rock festival."
   ....
7 "It's not my fault! I've never even met half of them."
   ....
8 "We're attending more of this type of thing. The technology can get the information out there incredibly quickly."
   ....

PARTY ANIMALS

Police stopped an 18th-birthday party after it was invaded by HUNDREDS of *Facebook* gatecrashers.

By Adrian Lee

A long-awaited coming of age party turned into a nightmare when hundreds of teenagers descended on a family home in the suburbs of the city. Invitations had gone out to about 50 friends to a fancy-dress party at Maddie Clarke's four-storey house in a residential area of the city, but ten times that number turned up when the party was advertised on the social networking site *Facebook*.

Maddie's mother, Janet Clarke, described the droves of teenagers who seemed to arrive out of nowhere, 'It was horrendous. By midnight the house and garden were packed with people. We'd asked two or three friends to act as bouncers for us, because we thought there might be some gatecrashers, but we didn't have a clue that hundreds would turn up. We couldn't do anything to stop them.'

'We thought we had everything under control,' added Mike Clarke, Maddie's father. 'Maddie had been given a strict limit of numbers. She'd designed the invitations herself and sent them via email, so we thought we knew exactly who was on the list. Then, without any warning, she posted the details on her *Facebook* page the day before the party. So, the information just spread. Within hours, half the city knew about it.'

The family had just finished decorating their property and landscaping the garden but now complain of extensive damage. 'By the time we'd got rid of everyone, the place looked more like a crime scene than a family home,' Mrs Clarke said. 'There was mud trodden right through the house, broken windows and cigarette burns on the furniture, and plants uprooted around the

garden. I'd never seen anything like it. And the number of empty bottles was incredible. I found out later that the gatecrashers had been stopping off at the local supermarket to buy vodka and cider.'

A neighbour called the police at about 11.30 to complain about the noise and number of teenagers hanging around near the property. A police officer who attended the scene said, 'When we arrived there were teenagers still turning up and passing on the address. It took us over an hour to clear the house. I feel really sorry for the family. They tried to do the right thing, but things got out of their control. But they're not the only victims – this cyber-gatecrashing is a growing phenomenon across the world.'

No arrests were made but the family have been very shaken up by their experience. Maddie burst out crying when she realised her party was turning into a disaster. 'I just

couldn't believe all these strangers were invading my party and creating havoc. I still feel really bad about the whole thing,' she said. 'I can't stop saying sorry to mum and dad. I just wish I'd never had a party. I didn't think putting the information on *Facebook* would have such a knock-on effect. I don't think I'll be bothering with social networking sites again.'

Glossary

coming of age: the age at which someone is legally considered an adult
gatecrasher: a person who goes to a party / event without an invitation
bouncer: a person employed by a club or at a party to prevent troublemakers entering or force them to leave

GRAMMAR Question tags

A Add the missing question tag.

1 I've upset you, ... ?
2 The post should be here soon, ... ?
3 I'm right about the dates, ... ?
4 You're going to meet the deadline, ... ?
5 They got the 3.30 train, ... ?
6 The new guy in Marketing thinks a lot of himself, ... ?
7 She's bound to get the job, ... ?
8 You haven't been waiting long, ... ?

B Write a statement and question tag for these situations. Use the words in brackets.

1 The weather is really good. (lovely day)
   It's a lovely day, isn't it?
2 You thought the new CD was a rip-off. (wasn't worth)
3 You suggest meeting at 12.30. (shall)
4 Your team haven't scored yet. (haven't been playing)
5 The food you're eating isn't very nice. (tasty)
6 You want the person next to you on a train to close the window. (couldn't)
7 You didn't enjoy a concert very much. (didn't play)
8 You want your sister to turn the light on. (will)

C Make these question tags sound more formal.

1 She's just got promoted, right?
2 You can still lend me the car, yeah?
3 You're up for coming to the gig, no?
4 She hasn't replied yet, right?
5 It's been a really long week, yeah?
6 They weren't very helpful, no?

VOCABULARY Talking about parties

A Choose the correct words.

I went to the party from hell and ...

1 *dragged / pulled* some friends along. Then no-one spoke to me and I felt *let / left* out.
2 hardly anyone else turned *up / in*. I spent all night talking to the *guest / host* about trains!
3 this guy started to *talk / chat* me up and wouldn't get *away / lost* whatever I did.
4 my girlfriend and the DJ fancied *each other / themselves*. I left so I don't know if they got *off / through* with each other.

B Complete the conversation with the correct form of the verbs form in box A and the phrases in box B.

A	get	spend	throw	break	go	set up	burst

B	to waste	a bit out of hand	into tears	a marquee
	a fortune	a surprise party	it up	

A: It's Lucy's 30th soon. I'm thinking of [1] .... for her. What do you think?

B: Nice idea, but make sure you get accurate numbers of guests. I went to one last year and it was a bit of a disaster. They [2] .... on all the preparations – you know, hiring a band, [3] ...., ordering loads of food. It all looked beautiful but not many people came and most of the food [4] .... But a few of the guys there were drinking quite a lot and they got argumentative. Then it [5] .... and two of them started fighting. My boyfriend had to [6] .... and calm everyone down. Then his cousin, whose party it was, [7] .... The poor girl looked so sad and shocked.

A: Sounds awful. I think I might take Lucy away somewhere and then just have a small get-together with friends.

C Match the sentences (1–8) with the correct type of party / celebration (a–h).

1 We ended up spending a fortune, as she wanted a theme party. You've no idea how much it costs to decorate the house with Disney characters.
2 It was fun but the place was in a real mess afterwards. I'm glad we hadn't decorated the sitting room before we invited everyone round.
3 It was just great. He had no idea that the whole family was coming. You should have seen his face when he walked in.
4 The whole department turned up. The MD gave a really good speech and she burst into tears. Everyone is really going to miss her but she's got a great new job.
5 I cooked far too much food and most of it went to waste. Milly wanted just a few friends at the local pizza place but her dad and I wanted to celebrate properly. It's a real achievement after all.
6 It was quite a small get together, just the couple, and close family and friends. Quite refreshing that it was more about the vows than showing off with a huge reception.
7 We all had a great time. He'd worked for the company for years and so was really looking forward to having time to do new things.
8 It was a civilised dinner in a nice restaurant and no-one got out of hand. Lucy and the bridesmaids wanted to look their best on the big day so they went home by 11 pm.

a leaving party
b housewarming
c hen party
d wedding
e surprise party
f retirement party
g children's party
h graduation party

LISTENING

Language note *do*

In informal English, *do* can be used as a noun to mean a party or other social event:
Are you going to Joe's **leaving do**?
He's having his **stag do** in Germany.

The plural is *dos* /duːz/ (sometimes written *dos*).
Have you been to any good **dos** lately?

A 🔊 **10.1 You are going to hear two colleagues talking about parties. Listen and circle the five events that Emma talks about.**

21st birthday party	graduation party
hen do	retirement party
children's party	leaving party
housewarming	wedding

B **Listen again and number Emma's opinions in the order she gives them.**
a   There's no point throwing a party for a shy person. ....
b   I'd like to have a less busy social life. ....
c   Graduation celebrations used to be quite simple. ....
d   I spent more than I wanted to. ....
e   Children's parties have become much more elaborate. ....
f   People buy gifts for no special reason. ....

PRONUNCIATION Linking vowel to vowel

A **Listen to the sentences.**
                    /w/
I know that some parents do go over the top.
      /j/
Why organise a big party for someone who won't even enjoy it?

B **Listen and mark the links /w/ or /j/. Then practise saying the sentences in exercises A and B.**
1   She is, and I don't mean to sound horrible.
2   Modern mums like to organise an event or a function.
3   It means the parents have to go along too.
4   Tell me about it!
5   She's insisting on a fancy dress do and the whole family has to be there.
6   Now you're just winding me up. transport and travel

Vocabulary Builder Quiz 10 (*OVB* pp38–40)

Try the *OVB* quiz for Unit 10. Write your answers in your notebook. Then check them and record your score.

A   **Which adjective from *OVB* Unit 10 goes with the sets of nouns.**
1   a .... room / chat / little café
2   a .... remark / conversation / glance
3   a .... mood / speech / film
4   a .... meal / flower / woman
5   a .... room / atmosphere / environment

B   **Replace the underlined words with an expression from *OVB* Unit 10.**
1   He's told the boss he is going to leave.
2   The interviewer tried to make me feel relaxed.
3   He told a dirty joke without realising he was broadcasting.
4   She was saying some very rude things.
5   They're playing very well at the moment.
6   The situation became hard to control.

C   **Complete the sentences with a word ending in *-ity*.**
1   The scandal attracted a lot of negative .... in the press.
2   The bank had to improve .... after the robbery.
3   I want promotion because I'm ready for more ....
4   Spicy fish and rice is a local ....
5   Singapore has high .... levels all year round.
6   The only way to lose weight is to increase physical ....

D   **Which word is missing from each the sentence?**
1   I'm not much into fancy-............ parties.
2   Let's have an office ....-together.
3   I'll check the booking, just to be on the .... side.
4   You can't be in the .... eye and expect privacy.
5   When she saw the baby, she .... out crying.
6   It was a shame they .... up after being together for so long.
7   I wasn't sure about him but he turned .... to be a really nice guy.
8   It was a .... of time queuing as they'd already sold out.

Score ___/25

Wait a couple of weeks and try the quiz again. Compare your scores.

VOCABULARY Problems with vehicles

Complete the tips with the correct words in the boxes.

Better safe than sorry –
tips for happy motoring

engine	flat	bald	overheat	tyres	spare

Before you get in

🚗 CHECK ALL [1] ...*tyres*... regularly including the
[2] .... If you drive over a nail and get a [3] .... ,
you'll need it. [4] .... tyres are potentially lethal, especially
in wet conditions.

🚗 CHECK UNDER THE BONNET, including the levels of oil
and coolant. The last thing you need is for your [5] .... to
[6] ....

fill	wing mirrors	front	brakes	windscreens	tank

Before you get going

🚗 CHECK VISIBILITY. Clear your [7] .... and rear
[8] .... of any ice or dirt. Check the position of your rear-
view and [9] .... , especially if someone else has just
driven your car.

🚗 CHECK YOUR FUEL LEVELS. Before a long journey,
[10] .... the [11] .... with petrol or diesel,
remembering to use the right one!

🚗 CHECK YOUR [12] .... by driving just a short
distance. Remember is takes longer to stop in wet weather. Any
problems or weird noises, don't drive.

battery	dents	flat	scratches

When you stop

🚗 CHECK THE BODYWORK for any damage and deal with
it quickly. Light [13] .... can be polished away but deep
[14] .... need specialist attention.

🚗 CHECK YOU HAVE TURNED EVERYTHING OFF. Leave
your lights on and your [15] .... will end up as
[10] .... as a pancake!

DEVELOPING CONVERSATIONS
Expressing shock

**Complete the conversations. Repeat the information
that surprises you and add a question or comment.**

1 A: It should take us about six hours to reach the
    hotel by road.
   B: *Six hours? Isn't there a quicker route?* ....

2 A: The only available flight lands at 2.30 in the
    morning.
   B: ....

3 A: They have no record of our booking. The next
    available room isn't for six weeks.
   B: ....

4 A: The car-hire firm have made a mistake. We need
    to pay them an extra €150.
   B: ....

5 A: Dan was caught on camera doing 160kph.
   B: ....

6 A: We've broken down but the recovery guy can't get
    here for an hour and a half.
   B: ....

DEVELOPING WRITING
A story – using the last line

**A Read the story opposite quickly. How many problems
did the writer have? Which one was his own fault?**

Language note inversion

Inversion is a way of adding emphasis in your writing.
You change the normal position of the subject and verb
or use the question form of the verb:
No sooner had I *got up than the problems started.*
(no sooner + past perfect)
Not only did they *cancel the flight, they also
lost our luggage.*

**B Read the story again. Underline examples of the
following uses of language.**

1 past continuous
2 past simple
3 future in the past
4 past perfect
5 inversion

When I set off I had no idea how difficult this simple trip would become. My best friend had asked me to be the best man and of course I'd said yes. I decided to hire a car to get to the wedding, as I wanted to be there nice and early.

After checking I had my suit, the rings and my speech, I picked up the car. The journey through town was fine, but no sooner had I reached the motorway than things started to go wrong.

Suddenly the car felt very bumpy. I pulled off the motorway and realised I'd got a flat tyre. Fitting the spare was a nightmare and took over an hour. I also got filthy but had no time to stop and change.

While I was trying to make up time, I suddenly realised I needed fuel. I stopped, filled up the tank, set off again but a few metres up the road the engine just stopped. I had put petrol in a diesel car. I couldn't believe how stupid I'd been.

I finally hitched a lift with a lorry driver and got to the wedding in dirty jeans and a T-shirt. I can safely say it was the worst journey I've ever had.

C Rewrite the sentences using inversion and the words provided.

1 The fog lifted and we realised we were in the middle of nowhere.
   Only when the fog lifted did we realise we were in the middle of nowhere

2 We caught the wrong train and left our bags on the platform.
   Not only ....

3 They never explained that we had to return the car by midday.
   At no time ....

4 We had only just set off when we ran out of petrol.
   Hardly ....

5 We didn't know how rough the crossing would be.
   Little ....

6 I got to the check-in and then realised I'd left my passport at home.
   No sooner ....

D Match the verbs in the box with the words and expressions.

cancel	turn up	damage	lose	get	miss

1 .... ripped off / on and off the plane / stuck in a queue / left behind

2 .... your passport / luggage / tickets / room key

3 .... a hire car / your suitcase / your camera / the equipment

4 .... the flight / the correct stop / the train / the connection

5 .... at the last minute / a reservation / a crossing / a flight

6 .... late / at the wrong terminal / without your luggage / three days later

E Write a story (150–190 words) based on the title below.

> **You have decided to enter a short story competition in an English-language magazine. The story must end with the words:**
>
> *I can safely say it was the worst journey I've ever had.*

GRAMMAR Uncountable nouns

A Complete the sentences with a quantifier from box A and a noun from box B.

A	plenty of	enough	great deal of
	less	more	hardly any

B	experience	information	work
	furniture	traffic	money

1 It's a nice flat but really packed with stuff. It would look better with a lot ....
2 I can't decide which course to go on. I think I need .... from the tutors.
3 She's the ideal candidate. She's got a .... in Human Resources.
4 We made really good time. There was .... on the motorway.
5 Could you lend me a few euros? I haven't got .... to pay for the drinks.
6 You should find a summer job easily. There's .... about in restaurants and bars.

B Rewrite the sentences with the words in brackets and a suitable uncountable noun.

1 You haven't got many bags. (hardly any)
....
2 There won't be many cheap rooms left by now. (not much)
....
3 Have you had an update on the flight delays? (any)
....
4 The agent gave us plenty of travel tips before we left. (loads)
....
5 There haven't been many improvements up to now. (not much)
....
6 We had a few problems finding our way here. (a bit)
....

Language note *a … of …*

You don't usually use *a / an* with uncountable nouns but we often use the pattern *a … of … ,* = e.g. *a piece of advice / information / news, a loaf of bread, a grain of rice,* etc. Make a note of these combinations and add to them as you go along.

READING

A Read the webpage opposite quickly. Under which headings might it appear?

technology	sport	transport
environment	money	finance

B Read the webpage again. Choose the correct answers to these questions.

1 Service on trains in Japan
    a relies on technology.
    b needs to be more welcoming.
    c is already good.
2 The scanning equipment
    a was devised by the train company.
    b give staff a range of feedback.
    c checks workers' performance throughout the day.
3 Most users of the scanners
    a don't seem to mind it.
    b like dealing with customers.
    c will have more contact with the public.
4 What's the writer's general opinion of the 'smile scan'?
    a positive
    b negative
    c more or less neutral

C Read the *Over to you* responses. Write the correct names?
Who …
1 is concerned about a wider issue?
2 suggests the company has too much power over its staff?
3 is the most enthusiastic about 'smile scan'?
4 doesn't think it would be adopted in their country?
5 is a little sarcastic?
6 is critical of transport staff in their country?

D Choose the correct words.
1 The worst thing about working in the city is the daily *commuter / commute*.
2 People always need to travel so the train companies don't care about *keeping / giving* us happy.
3 It's important to look smart and come *through / across* as positive when dealing with customers.
4 The taxi driver I had this morning was so *grumpy / welcoming*. He bit my head off when I asked to go to the city centre in rush hour.
5 We welcome customer *comeback / feedback* whether it's positive or negative.
6 Travelling long distances would be a lot more *bearable / supportable* if everything ran on time.

| Home | News | Lifestyle | Finance | Culture | Sport | Technology | Travel | Food | Contact |
| World | Regional | Celebrity | Fashion | Science | Politics | Health | Videos | Topics | Blogs |

HOME ➤ NEWS ➤ WORLD NEWS

It's service with a smile on Japanese trains

It's hard for commuters to feel positive about the daily grind to and from work on public transport. But the Japanese think they have come up with a technological solution to keeping people happy.

The Keihin Electric Express Railway has introduced a 'smile scan' system in its busier stations in Tokyo. Over 500 employees will face daily checks on the quality of their smile to make sure they look happy and welcoming to passengers. Japan is well known for its attention to detail and customer service. It's common to see uniformed train conductors bowing to travellers as they get on and off the train. So perhaps monitoring employees' smiles is the next logical step.

The 'smile scan' system has been developed by Japanese electronics company Omron.

The 'smile scan' system has been developed by Japanese electronics company Omron. The software works by analysing the movement of the lips and eyes when smiling, and other changes to the face like the appearance of wrinkles. Before starting work each day, employees sit in front of a laptop computer equipped with a webcam and simply smile. The machine then gives a score between 0 and 100 depending on the quality of their expression. Feedback is also provided on the screen with comments like 'You still look too serious,' or 'Your smile is getting better.' The employee also gets a print-out with an image of their best smile to use as a reference during the rest of the working day.

Although workers in some countries may see the tests as an imposition, the railway company maintains that it is simply a way to improve their service to customers. Taichi Takahashi, a public relations employee at the train company, says that it gives employees an opportunity to check how they come across before they have contact with the public. Users of the system seem to agree, 'Using the "smile scan" system is especially useful for everyday customer interactions. It really helped me develop a natural smile,' says Asami Takahashi, a 28-year-old employee.

Would the smile-scanner be a useful tool in improving your commute to work? Or what other sour-faced staff might benefit from a daily diagnosis?

OVER TO YOU

➤ The bosses of the railway company sound a bit like control freaks! You can't force people to be, or even look, happy.
Zoltan, Budapest

➤ Sounds fine by me – anything that makes my journey into work more bearable is welcome. Can't imagine it working in Manhattan, though.
Richie, NYC

➤ You have to congratulate the Japanese on their ingenuity, but it would never work in the UK. I reckon we have the grumpiest workforce in Europe. You couldn't get a worker on the Tube to smile even if you scanned them all day!
Val, London

➤ This is a fun story but there's a serious side to it too. We are all monitored by cameras 24/7 and I think it's scary. Some bosses want to have cameras at people's workstations so they can watch what they do all day.
Nico, Paris

Glossary

daily grind: something that is hard work, boring and tiring
wrinkles: lines of your skin
sour-faced: looking unfriendly or in a bad mood

VOCABULARY Driving

A Complete the conversation with the verbs in box A and phrases in box B.

A	overtake doing drive slam look

B	in your mirror and indicate a hundred and fifty
	the car in front on your brakes
	in the middle lane

A: Have you seen this survey about what irritates motorway drivers most?

B: No, but I bet it's a long list. People are so impatient nowadays. They feel they have to [1] .... like they're in a race. And the speed. I was driving home the other day and a guy went past me. He must have been [2] .... at least. So, is speeding at the top of the survey list?

A: It isn't actually. What people hate most is when another car drives up very close behind them.

B: I can understand that. I think it's quite dangerous. What happens if you suddenly [3] .... and they have only a short distance to stop.

A: Apparently, it is the cause of quite a lot of accidents.

B: I can imagine. So what gets you about motorway driving?

A: People who [4] .... They don't understand they should be in the left if they don't want to overtake. And the other thing is not signalling. The golden rule is [5] ' .... ' or how are other drivers going to know where you're going?

B: I know exactly what you mean.

B Match the sentence halves.

1 I can't see a thing! That guy just flashed
2 Be careful. We're on a hill so make sure you put
3 It's only a small dent so I won't make
4 It could've been very nasty if I hadn't swerved
5 He's such a speed freak. He's bound to get

a your handbrake on securely.
b points on his licence soon.
c to avoid the other vehicle.
d his lights right in my rear-view mirror.
e a claim on my insurance.

GRAMMAR Emphatic structures

A Find and correct a mistake in each sentence.

1 What's good is fact that people are using the trains more.
2 That really makes me annoyed is people speeding in residential areas.
3 The thing that irritates me is the lacking of staff on the stations.
4 It's harmful to the environment fly everywhere.
5 What gets me is the amount empty buses you see on the roads.
6 The thing bothers me about flying is the amount of hanging around.
7 Its dangerous when people do follow the rules of the road.
8 What I hate is that people not moving their stuff off the seat on a train.

B Rewrite the sentences with the words provided.

1 People using their horn for no reason really irritates me.
   It ....
   ....

2 Driving at night is much more tiring.
   It's ....
   ....

3 I love the freedom of travelling around by train.
   What ....
   ....

4 The number of people changing to public transport is encouraging.
   What's ....
   ....

5 The fact that the airline gave us a refund was totally unexpected.
   What ....
   ....

6 I was really annoyed that they didn't explain the delay.
   The thing ....
   ....

LISTENING

🔊 **11.1 You are going to hear five speakers talking about funny episodes related to travelling. Match the speakers (1–5) to the letters (a–f). There is one letter that you don't need.**

Speaker 1 ☐
Speaker 2 ☐
Speaker 3 ☐
Speaker 4 ☐
Speaker 5 ☐

a Someone didn't do their job very well.
b Someone relied too much on technology
c Someone overtook a police car by mistake.
d Someone was on the wrong type of road.
e Someone couldn't get somewhere by road.
f Someone built something the wrong size.

PRONUNCIATION
Same sound or different?

A Are the letters in bold the same sound (S) or different (D)?

1 He must have taken the wrong **tu**rning? / What made it w**o**rse was having to circle in the skies. ☐
2 The air traffic contr**o**ller had fallen asleep. / The usual boy racers were **o**vertaking. ☐
3 The pil**o**t kept calling the control tower. / He ended up on the m**o**torway by mistake. ☐
4 People are asking to book river cr**ui**ses. / The tunnel they b**ui**lt was too small for the trains. ☐
5 The navig**a**tion is only as good as the map. / The sat nav had said 'go str**ai**ght on'. ☐
6 He's got a h**u**ge old tower. / The guys building the t**u**nnel didn't communicate very well. ☐

B 🔊 11.2 Listen and check. Practise saying the sentences.

Learner tip

Don't forget you can use the recordings more than once. Go back to a unit and listen again to see what you can pick up and keep trying the pronunciation activities to see if you're improving.

Vocabulary Builder Quiz 11 (*OVB* pp42–44)

Try the *OVB* quiz for Unit 11. Write your answers in your notebook. Then check them and record your score.

A Which is the odd one out in each set?
1 boot brake windscreen fare
2 bump fuel lane pavement
3 vast desolate claustrophobic crossing
4 indicate appeal swerve overtake

B Match 1–5 and a–e.
1 They charge for parking a by heart.
2 I know all the words b by the rules.
3 He won't change. He's shy c by the hour.
4 Don't cheat. Always play d by sight.
5 I don't know him well, just e by nature.

C Choose the correct words.
1 Someone *scarred / dented* my new car.
2 The village is too *remote / untouched* if you don't have a car.
3 My insurance *covers / takes out* other drivers.
4 Check regularly that your tyres haven't *worn / bald*.
5 Why did he just *flash / slam* me?
6 There was no warning of the petrol *spill / spillage* on the road.
7 I have complete faith *for / in* you.

D Which words do you need to complete the sentences in each set?
1 I give you my .... / Take my .... for it. / It's his .... against yours.
2 Now is the .... period. / It's risen to an all-time .... / He's at his .... now.
3 What did they .... about? / They had a blazing .... / There was a huge .... between the family.

E What form of the words in brackets do you need to complete the sentences?
1 It's (infuriate) when people break the speed limit.
2 Modern life lacks a (spirit) dimension.
3 The view was absolutely (breath).
4 The house was in a state of total (repair).
5 She's a (remark) confident person.
6 It wasn't a very (worth) experience.

Score ___ /25

Wait a couple of weeks and try the quiz again. Compare your scores.

VOCABULARY Health problems

A **Complete the spidergram with the verbs in the box.**

remove	have	use	be	suffer from

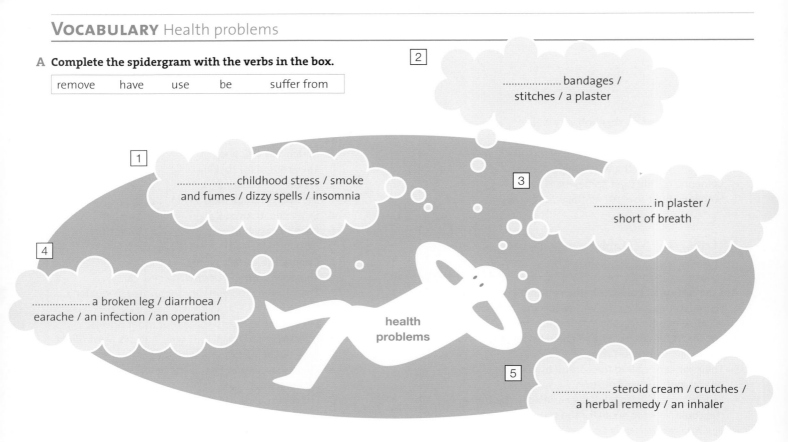

1 .... childhood stress / smoke and fumes / dizzy spells / insomnia

2 .... bandages / stitches / a plaster

3 .... in plaster / short of breath

4 .... a broken leg / diarrhoea / earache / an infection / an operation

5 .... steroid cream / crutches / a herbal remedy / an inhaler

health problems

B **Circle the word or expression in each set that doesn't relate to the illness.**

1	**eczema**	rash	scratch
		itchy	faint
2	**a cold**	bump	runny nose
		sore throat	cough
3	**asthma**	short of breath	pin
		inhaler	tight chest
4	**upset stomach**	a bug	settle
		high blood pressure	throw up
5	**an allergy**	swell up	bruises
		sneeze	nuts
6	**flu**	scratches	fever
		sore throat	stiff

DEVELOPING CONVERSATIONS
Passing on messages

A **Choose the correct words.**

1 *Tell / Give* him our *wishes / regards* and wish him luck in his new place.

2 *Give / Send* her a hug from me and *tell / tell to* her not to be nervous about her finals.

3 Give them my *apologises / apologies* for not coming and *say / tell* I hope the do goes well.

4 *Say / Send* them my *hug / love* and hope they have good weather on their special day.

5 *Give / Pass* them my *apologies / congratulations* and tell them we can't wait to see the new arrival.

6 *Tell / Tell her* there's no need to apologise and to *take / make* it easy until she's ready to come back.

7 *Say / Tell* hi from all of us and tell them *we're thinking / we think* of them at this very sad time.

B Match the messages in exercise A to the situations (a–g).

a having a baby
b taking important exams
c missing a party
d being off work
e getting married
f suffering a bereavement
g moving house

GRAMMAR
Supposed to be -ing and should

A Find and correct a mistake in each sentence.

1 I supposed to be having a check-up tomorrow but I've got too much work.
2 My knee hurts a bit now but it shouldn't be OK in a few days.
3 I shouldn't to need to be in hospital for very long.
4 She's supposed to walking with crutches but she just refuses.
5 I'm afraid the side effects of the drugs should last a few days.
6 They've supposed to be launching a new flu treatment but it's been delayed.

B Complete the conversations with the correct form of the pairs of verbs in the box.

should / be	supposed / play
supposed / go	should / feel
should / take	supposed / visit
should / clear up	supposed / give

1 A: Look at the time! I .... mum in hospital in 15 minutes but I'm running late.
   B: I'll go if you like. I've got my car so it .... me long to get there.
2 A: It's nothing serious. Just stay off school for a couple of days and you .... fine.
   B: A couple of days? I .... in a football match tomorrow.
3 A: Use this cream and the rash .... in a week or so.
   B: A week? We .... on holiday tomorrow.
4 A: My friend .... blood later but she's got a bit of a headache.
   B: There .... a problem but check with the nurse first.

LISTENING

A ⏺ 12.1 You are going to hear a couple preparing for a barbecue. Listen and match three adjectives to Sam and three to Kate. There are two adjectives you don't need.

stressed	confident
cautious	a control freak
unhelpful	good fun
easy-going	very poorly

B Who said the equivalent of these things? Listen again and write the correct name, Sam or Kate.

1 I've never hurt myself before.
2 Don't forget about hygiene.
3 I don't feel too well.
4 I've got some medicine that could help you.
5 There's nothing wrong with me.
6 Let's have a drink.
7 I'd forgotten about that.
8 It's not my problem if you get ill.
9 I'm glad the guests are here.

PRONUNCIATION Intonation on question tags

A Listen and mark the intonation of the question tags:
 or ⟶.

1 We've had hundreds of barbecues and I've never burnt myself, have I?

2 You will wash your hands, won't you?

3 You'll be OK for the party, won't you?

4 Sam, you're not getting a cold, are you?

5 You're not going to drink too much tonight, are you?

6 Yeah, you haven't forgotten, have you?

7 You're not going to eat it, are you?

8 Well, it won't kill me, will it?

B Practise saying the sentences.

VOCABULARY Parts of the body and illnesses

A Write the missing vowels in the parts of the body. Then read the clues and circle the correct answer.

Test your body knowledge

Clues	Answers
1 The largest organ in the human body.	l _ ng sk _ n
2 The bones of this part of the body are not joined at birth.	sk _ ll h _ p
3 A yellowing of the skin indicates a problem with this.	br _ _ n l _ v _ r
4 They are quite fragile and could be broken by sneezing.	r _ bs wr _ sts
5 These each have two bones.	big t _ _ s f _ ng _ rs
6 A bone called the femur connects to this.	_ lb _ w kn _ _
7 You need at least one of these to live.	k _ dn _ ys _ nkl _ s

B Choose the correct words.
1 My *arthritis / athlete's foot* is improving. My joints are much less stiff than they were.
2 I don't need insulin. I manage my *hepatitis / diabetes* with diet.
3 Being a bit forgetful doesn't necessarily lead to *Alzheimer's / Parkinson's*.
4 It was only a very mild *stress / stroke*. Her speech and movement are fine.
5 Before the introduction of antibiotics, *tuberculosis / AIDS* used to be a major health problem.

Language note silent letters

Remember to keep a note of words with silent letters. Quite a few of them are parts of the body, e.g. *knee, wrist, thumb*. Find more examples and add to this list.

READING

A Read the article on page 73 quickly. Match the headings to the main paragraphs.
a What if you don't get any?
b How can you get more?
c What actually happens?
d How much is enough?

B Read the article again. Which of these statements are true, according to the writer?
1 You should sleep between five and nine hours a night.
2 Movement of the eyes in a sleeping person indicates dreaming.
3 We experience physical changes in pre-sleep and slow wave sleep.
4 We typically get one stage of REM sleep and one of non-REM sleep a night.
5 You are more likely to have a nightmare close to the time of getting up.
6 There's no fixed right amount of sleep for each individual.
7 Older people tend to have problems getting to sleep.
8 There's no point staying in bed if you can't sleep.

C Complete the quotations about sleep with the words in the box.

nap	snore	awake	amount of sleep
insomnia	night's sleep	like a baby	lying

1 ❛The best bridge between despair and hope is a good ....❜

2 ❛People who .... always fall asleep first.❜

3 ❛No day is so bad it can't be fixed with a ....❜

4 ❛Nothing cures .... like the realisation that it's time to get up .❜

5 ❛If you can't sleep, then get up and do something instead of .... there worrying. It's the worry that gets you, not the lack of sleep.❜

6 ❛People who say they sleep .... usually don't have one.❜

7 ❛I'm not asleep ... but that doesn't mean I'm ....❜

8 ❛The .... required by the average person is five hours.❜

The guide to a good night's sleep ᶻ ᶻ ᶻ ᶻ ᶻ ᶻ ᶻ

Some of us can get away with four or five hours a night and others claim they can't function with less than nine. The one thing we have in common is that we all need to sleep in every 24-hour period.

1 ......

Researchers distinguish two main types of sleep:

REM (Rapid Eye Movement) sleep

During this stage, the body is totally relaxed but the brain is active. The closed eyes move from side to side very rapidly and this is the period when dreaming occurs.

Non-REM sleep

Four key stages have been identified in this type of sleep:

> **pre-sleep** during which there is a lowering of the body temperature, the heart starts to beat more slowly and the muscles relax.
>
> **light sleep** when you could easily be woken up by something but not feel disorientated.
>
> **slow wave sleep** which is characterised by a fall in blood pressure. This is the stage when some people talk in their sleep or sleep walk.
>
> **deep slow wave sleep** when it is difficult to wake the sleeper. If a person is woken up during this stage, they often feel disoriented or confused.

We typically change between the two main types of sleep about five times a night, with phases of dreaming being more common towards the morning. We also experience short periods of being awake – up to one or two minutes about every two hours. You may not remember these periods unless you were woken by a person snoring or other disturbance.

2 ......

The amount of sleep you need will of course depend on your age, but there are also very wide individual variations. Babies get the longest period, sleeping on average 17 hours a day – hence the expression 'sleep like a baby' – with older children dropping to nine or ten hours a night. The average night's sleep for an adult of any age is eight hours but older people tend to have only one period of deep sleep after which they wake more easily.

3 ......

We all have the odd sleepless night but what if you are troubled by more prolonged insomnia? This can lead to feeling sleepy all the time, wanting to have a nap during the day, difficulties in concentrating and making decisions, and irritability. An extreme lack of sleep can even lead to depression. Everyday tasks such as driving or using machinery become difficult or even dangerous.

4 ......

Check practical things like being too hot or cold or having a lumpy mattress aren't stopping you from dropping off. Avoid caffeine, alcohol and big meals just before bedtime. Create a sleep routine by getting up and going to bed at more or less the same time. Don't be tempted to catch up on lost sleep by having a lie-in at the weekend. And most importantly don't just lie awake counting sheep. Get up and read, listen to gentle music or watch TV for a while and then try again.

> **Glossary**
>
> **snore:** breathe in a noisy way when you are asleep
> **mattress:** the part of a bed that makes it comfortable to lie on
> **count sheep:** to imagine sheep and count them as a way of getting to sleep

GRAMMAR Determiners

A Cross out one word in each set that isn't possible.

1 Can you pass me *those / another / some / my* painkillers?
2 *Every / Each / No / Half* employee has reported symptoms of swine flu.
3 *This / Many / Other / A few* doctors mix conventional medicine with holistic therapies.
4 *Both / All / Neither* of my parents have diabetes.
5 I don't have *many / the / much / any* time to take regular exercise.
6 If you need to see a dentist, I'll phone *mine / one / a.*

B Choose the correct words.

1 A: I need *few / some* antibiotics for my cold.
   B: They won't work. There *is / isn't* no cure for the common cold.
2 A: Did *some / that* cream I gave you help your eczema?
   B: I'm afraid not. *None / None of* the things I've tried have worked.
3 A: I can't take aspirin. Have you got any *others / other* painkillers?
   B: No, but I'll get you *some / some of* when I'm in town.
4 A: Have you had *another / other* check-up recently?
   B: Yes, they did several tests but *neither / none* of them have given a clear result.
5 A: Have you taken out *a / any* insurance?
   B: Yes, *all / both* medical and dental care is covered in the policy.

DEVELOPING WRITING
A letter – showing sympathy

A Read the letter quickly. What do think is the relationship between Erik and Melanie?
a employee and boss
b good friends
c husband and wife

B Read the letter again. Number the content in order.
Melanie
makes a promise   ....
asks about future treatment   ....
offers help   ....
expresses sympathy   ....
passes on a message   ....
makes a joke   ....
asks how Erik is now   ....
tells Erik about a gift   ....

C Match the sentence beginnings (1–5) with two endings (a–j).
1 If there's anything you need,
2 I know it's hard but try
3 I'm free most afternoons if you
4 When you are feeling a bit better, I'll
5 Everyone here says

a to keep smiling.
b take it easy and get better soon.
c pop round for a chat.
d fancy some company.
e you only have to ask.
f take you out for a drive.
g hi and look after yourself.
h need me to run any errands.
i not to worry too much.
j just let me know.

D Write a letter to a friend (150–190 words) to show sympathy about an accident or illness. Use the ideas in exercise B and the language in this section to help you.

Dear Erik,

I wanted to drop you a line to say how sorry I was to hear about your accident. I couldn't believe it when Sasha told me that you'd fallen down the stairs and broken both legs. It must have been an awful shock.

How are you feeling now? Sasha said that you were in plasters from ankle to knee and that you were having problems getting around on crutches. I know that it's difficult at first but it should become easier. If you get an itch under your plaster you can always use the crutch to scratch it!

When are they supposed to be removing the plaster? I hope it's soon and that you can start to get back to normal. I expect they'll organise some physiotherapy for you at the hospital but if not let me know. My sister knows the name of a good therapist.

I'm really sorry we haven't been to see you but things have been really hectic. I'll definitely drive over in the next couple of weeks. In the meantime, I've sent you a few novels and DVDs to help pass the time.

Get better soon and send my love to all the family.

Love,
Melanie

Learner tip

Don't forget to do as much writing as possible outside the classroom. There's nothing to stop you sending 'real' letters, notes and emails to English-speaking friends.

Vocabulary Builder Quiz 12 (*OVB* pp46–48)

Try the *OVB* quiz for Unit 12. Write your answers in your notebook. Then check them and record your score.

A Which words that are both verbs and nouns can complete these sentences?

1 Don't drop the apples. You'll .... them.
   The .... on my leg was blue and orange, and it took ages to fade.
2 I'd like to make a cash .... into my account.
   It's best to .... anything valuable in the hotel safe.
3 I never .... on horses or cards. I value money too much.
   Having an outdoor party in winter is always a ....
4 He's on the waiting list for a heart .... operation.
   They're going to .... the kidney from an anonymous donor.
5 Don't be a show-off and .... about your own success.
   He said he was the best but it was just an empty ....

B Complete the sentences with nouns ending in -ence.

1 They closed the restaurant early but no-one apologised for the ....
2 The .... was so complete I could hear my own heart beat.
3 When did the country gain .... from France?
4 The company failed to protect their staff and were found guilty of ....
5 I never watch films with scenes of fighting or street ....

C Complete the verbs that begin with *re*.

1 I broke one of your glasses but I'll re............. it.
2 There are tough rules in place to re............. the food industry.
3 They're going to re............. me to a consultant.
4 It took a few weeks to re............. after the operation.
5 Take some aspirin to re............. the pain.

D ~~Cross out~~ *out* in the sentences where it is not needed.

1 They had to postpone out her operation.
2 Don't let this problem detract out from your success.
3 It was so hot I nearly passed out in front of everyone.
4 They think the fire broke out in the basement of the property.
5 Don't stick your head out of the car window.
6 There's a nasty bug going round out at my kids' school.

E What object / treatment do these people need?

1 'My asthma is really bad today. I can hardly breathe.'
2 'I've sprained my ankle and it's a bit swollen.'
3 'I broke my leg in two places. It's really hard to walk.'
4 'It's quite a deep cut. It needs more than a plaster.'

Score ___ /25

Wait a couple of weeks and try the quiz again.
Compare your scores.

13 LIFE EVENTS

VOCABULARY Life events

A Write the expressions in the correct categories.
- family life
- education and work
- results of bad decisions
- the end of life

changing careers	getting killed
dropping out of college	being sacked
getting a degree / Masters / PhD	moving house
a couple getting together / splitting up	passing away
being sent to jail	giving birth

B Read the sentences. Which event in exercise A are they talking about?

1 'I'm really pleased they've finally started going out. They seem to be getting on very well.'

2 'We were quite surprised when she told us. I always thought she'd be in nursing for life but she sounds very enthusiastic about the new training.'

3 'They say it's almost as traumatic as getting divorced but ours went pretty smoothly and it's wonderful to have more space.'

4 'He'd had a long and fulfilling life and he wouldn't want people to feel sad about him now.'

5 'He said he would take them to a tribunal but I doubt he would win. They found out he'd be fiddling his expenses.'

6 'He got three years for credit card fraud, but he'll probably be out in about 18 months.'

7 'She's very modest but it is an amazing achievement at her age. She was by far the youngest at the graduation ceremony.'

8 'I reckon he'll regret it in the future. He was in his final year and it's so hard to get a job these days without good qualifications.'

C Choose the correct words.

1 They warned us that the cancer might continue to *move* / *spread* but it seems to be responding to treatment.

2 I went through a *hard* / *rough* patch with my career but things have looked up since I *retrained* / *reformed* as a counsellor.

3 They found out he'd taken *fines* / *bribes* and so he didn't *have* / *get* offered the job.

4 Mother and baby are doing fine but Ana was in *labour* / *birth* for hours.

5 We've *been* / *played* on a terrible run but getting *knocked* / *beaten* out of the cup is too much for most fans.

6 If you like him so much, why don't you ask him *go out* / *out*?

7 I think they should *stop* / *call* it a day – they do nothing but argue.

GRAMMAR Past perfect simple and continuous

A Look at the information about key events in William's life. Write sentences using the verbs and time expressions in brackets.

2000	left school
2001	went travelling
2002	started uni, met Lucy
2004	gave up course, unemployed for 6 months
2004–2009	worked in catering
2010	set up own business, married Lucy

1 start university / be travelling for a year (when / already)
When William started university, he'd already been travelling for a year.

2 give up course / study for only two years (after)
....

3 be unemployed for six months / start working in catering (before)
....

4 set up business / work in catering for five years (by the time)
....

5 know each other for eight years / marry Lucy (already / by the time)
....

6 set up own business / leave school (ten years after)
....

B **Complete the conversations with the past perfect or past perfect continuous form of the verbs.**

1 A: Well, it was good to catch up with Ian. We
   [1] .... (not see) each other for ages. You
   know that he lost his job last month? Apparently,
   the company [2] .... (be) in trouble for
   months. And he split up from Kate a year ago.
   B: Mm, I heard from Kate's friend that they
   [3] .... (not get on) very well. Poor things.

2 A: It was such a relief to finally move in after we
   [4] .... (spend) so long looking for a place.
   B: I know what you mean. By the time we found
   our flat, I [5] .... (nearly / give up). We
   [6] .... (live) with my parents for over a year.

3 A: Sorry I missed the wedding. I [7] .... (not be)
   very well for a few days before and so didn't want
   to risk it.
   B: Don't worry. I wasn't really expecting you because
   Helen told me [8] you .... (come down with)
   a virus.

DEVELOPING CONVERSATIONS
Showing uncertainty

Choose the correct words.

A: Did you hear about Dr Clarke being kicked out of the
university?
B: No, really? How come?
A: As [1] *far / much* as I know, she'd been taking bribes to
hand out better grades.
B: You're kidding.
A: I'm not, and [2] according *to / of* my room mate she
wasn't really a PhD.
B: What?
A: [3] *Accordingly / Apparently*, she'd faked her CV to get
into the department in the first place. [4] *As / From* I
understand it, she graduated with just a lower class
degree.
B: So what's going to happen now?
A: Well, from [5] *that / what* I heard, she's been
suspended while they investigate, so they need a
new head of department.
B: I was [6] *told / said* they were looking for new staff but
I didn't know that was why. I can't quite believe it,
can you?

LISTENING

A 🔊 **13.1 Listen to James and Emily talking after an important event. What has just taken place?**
a   a funeral
b   a graduation
c   a wedding

B **Listen again and number the events in Helen's life in order. There is one event you don't need to use.**

Helen ...

was a teacher of French	....
ran an environmental campaign	....
organised a strike	....
did voluntary work in Africa	....
went to university	....*1*....
retired	....
got married	....
set up a writing group	....

PRONUNCIATION   Strong and weak forms

A 🔊 **13.2 Choose the correct symbol for the <u>underlined</u> sounds.**

1 /ə/   /æ/
   I wish th<u>a</u>t I'd seen her more often.
   No, what was th<u>a</u>t?

2 /ɒ/   /ə/
   I'm now wondering where all these people have come fr<u>o</u>m?
   Those ladies over there are fr<u>o</u>m her writing group.

3 /ə/   /uː/
   Nice to meet y<u>ou</u>.
   Did y<u>ou</u> know about the student strike?

4 /ə/   /ɜː/
   Education was very important to h<u>er</u>.
   But I knew h<u>er</u> from long before that.

5 /ɒ/   /ə/
   Helen was obviously very well thought <u>of</u>.
   She was head <u>of</u> French at my school.

B **Listen and check. Then practise saying the sentences.**

GRAMMAR

be always -ing / wish and *would*

A Complete the sentences with the correct form of the pairs of words in the box.

always / organise	wish / not be
wish / buy a round	always / leave
wish / be	wish / not have
constantly / get	constantly / borrow

1 He's a great guy but he's always broke. I .... he .... in the pub once in a while.
2 We get on OK but he .... his washing-up in the sink.
3 He used to be such a good kid but he .... into trouble this term.
4 I love being married but I .... she .... so interfering. We never get any time to ourselves.
5 He's amazing. He .... trips and things to say thanks to the team.
6 The new place is great but I .... they .... so many late-night parties next door.
7 You need to get a part-time job. You .... money from me for clothes and make-up.
8 He's very efficient when I have a check-up but I .... he .... a bit easier to talk to.

B Who are the people in exercise A talking about/to? Match 1–8 in exercise A above, to a–h.

a a schoolchild ....
b their neighbours ....
c their boss ....
d a friend ....
e their doctor ....
f their teenage daughter ....
g their flatmate ....
h their mother-in-law ....

READING

A Read the article opposite quickly. What is the writer's main purpose?
a to question recent research
b to give people advice on how to handle life events
c to compare two societies

B Which paragraphs (1–5) contain mainly facts or mainly opinions?

C Read the article again. Choose the correct answers to these questions.
1 What does the process of 'adaptation' allow people to do?
   a get over bad experiences
   b deal with both the positive and negative aspects of life
   c prepare for difficult life events
2 What did the research team find?
   a The people in the study got happier over the 20-year period of the research.
   b Most of the life events had no immediate effect on levels of happiness.
   c Only one life event affected levels of happiness over a longer period.
3 What does the writer say about money?
   a Having additional money starts to feel normal very quickly.
   b Lottery winners spend too much and then they are broke again.
   c Celebrities are too interested in money to find lasting happiness.
4 Why doesn't the writer think 'adaptation' applies to relationships?
   a Couples who have been married for a long time are less happy.
   b Children should be a source of happiness to their parents.
   c People feel differently about each other at different times.
5 What is the writer's main point about bereavement?
   a You never adapt to losing a loved one.
   b It takes a long time to heal the sadness.
   c He really misses his brother.

D Choose the correct words.
1 They've been married for 50 years and their love for each other hasn't *faded / adapted* at all.
2 Life has ups and downs. It's impossible to live in a *major / constant* state of happiness.
3 When I was made redundant, I just didn't know what to make *of / up* things for a while.
4 She used to be a bit arrogant but getting divorced has made her come back down to *ground / earth*.
5 She was widowed young but she *went / lived* on to marry again in her forties.
6 Their ideas of moving from place to place just don't seem to *suit / fit* with family life.

opinion : DO LIFE EVENTS LEAD TO HAPPINESS?

From **'We're having a child.'** to **'We're getting divorced.'** Just two of the major life events that an average couple may experience. Events like these are often described as life-changing, but recent research seems to suggest otherwise.

1 A team of psychologists and economists recently published a study that suggests both the positive and negative feelings that result from life events are relatively short-lived. So, the joy experienced when you are first married tends to fade over time due to a process called 'adaptation'. You simply get used to the new set of circumstances. Similarly, bad experiences like getting divorced or getting the sack don't seem to affect your long-term satisfaction with life. Put basically, your overall level of happiness remains more or less constant throughout your adult life.

2 The research team surveyed thousands of people in Germany over a period of 20 years. The study plotted their levels of happiness before and after one of six life events: getting married, having a child, getting divorced, becoming widowed, losing your job, and being laid off. While most of these events had a strong effect on happiness at the time they took place, the positive or negative feelings faded relatively quickly. Interestingly, only unemployment had a longer-term detrimental effect.

3 So what do we make of this idea of adaptation? When it comes to money, I can see it makes some sense. No matter how much money any one of us has, we quickly get used to the lifestyle that it provides. And we've all heard of lottery winners who, after the initial spending sprees, come back down to earth. Having extra money is nice but you only have to look at the problems experienced by some of today's celebrities to know it doesn't bring you lasting happiness.

4 It's when we think about relationships that I start to query the research. Sure, a couple that have been married for years aren't going to wake up each morning and feel the same joy as they did on their wedding day. But even if they have got used to being married, they could still go on to experience greater levels of happiness in the future. It's the same with children. Perhaps most of the people who were surveyed had children of school age, which is generally recognized as a difficult stage in family life. Once these children are grown up, they could become a source of renewed happiness to their parents.

5 The idea of adaptation seems to suggest that you can get used to more or less anything. For me, the area of life where it just doesn't fit is bereavement. I wouldn't say anyone really gets used to losing someone they love. I only have to look at my own life since my brother passed away. What I could never say is that I'm as happy now as I was before he died. Yes, time is a healer but some things you just never really adapt to.

Glossary

plotted: assessed
widowed: if someone is widowed, their husband or wife has died
detrimental: negative or damaging
bereavement: the situation you are in when someone close to you dies

VOCABULARY Birth, marriage and death

A Choose the correct words.

A: Eric was telling me you're ¹ *waiting / expecting* another baby. Congratulations.

B: Thanks.

A: When's it ² *due / born*?

B: Well, I've only just ³ *had / made* my first scan, so not till the summer.

A: A summer baby, how lovely!

B: To be honest I'm just hoping for a more ⁴ *straightforward / straightaway* birth this time round.

A: How come?

B: Well, last time I ⁵ *started / went* into labour in a supermarket of all places. The manager ⁶ *rushed / hurried* me to the hospital but Ellie wasn't born for hours afterwards. I was ⁷ *in / during* labour for about 18 hours!

A: 18! I bet you needed your maternity ⁸ *ward / leave* after that!

B: Actually, I went back to work after a couple of weeks at home.

B Complete the texts with the words in the box.

honeymoon	reception	best man
bride and groom	town hall	

It was a wonderful day. The ¹ .... both looked so happy. They had a civil ceremony in the ² ...., a lovely old building. The ³ .... was held in a hotel with a beautiful garden. The ⁴ .... was Leo's oldest friend from school. He told some very funny stories in his speech. Leo and Nina have just gone off on ⁵ .... to the Maldives for a couple of weeks.

grave	condolences	ashes
mourners	coffin	cemetery

My grandmother is buried in the local ⁶ .... I'll always remember her funeral. Hundreds of ⁷ .... came to the church and offered their ⁸ .... to the family. I was only little and I didn't realise that the ⁹ .... was going to be put into the ground. Mum explained that we could visit the ¹⁰ .... and put flowers there but I still found it a bit shocking. Although I don't like to think about it too much, I'll probably be cremated and have my ¹¹ .... scattered somewhere memorable, maybe along my favourite stretch of coast.

DEVELOPING WRITING
A description – using vivid language

A Read the description below quickly. Why is the event so memorable for the writer?

a Someone was nasty to her.

b Things were different from how she'd imagined.

c She felt very nervous before starting school.

B Read the description again. Replace the underlined words with the more vivid equivalents.

demanded	burst into tears	weary	deafening
beamed	enormous	endless	identical to
hurrying	chattered	gulped	incredibly

MY FIRST DAY AT SCHOOL

I remember it like it was yesterday. I woke up ¹ <u>very early</u> and ² <u>asked for</u> my favourite breakfast – boiled eggs, toast and milk. I was so excited about joining my big sister, Susie, at school. I ³ <u>talked</u> about what we were going to do that day. I ⁴ <u>drank</u> the milk between sentences while my ⁵ <u>tired</u> mother drank her tea.

The time before leaving for school seemed ⁶ <u>very long</u>. And then we were on our way. My sister, mum and I all ⁷ <u>walking</u> along the street hand in hand. I looked at my new uniform and school bag, and ⁸ <u>smiled</u> with pleasure.

Then we turned into the entrance to the school and the noise seemed ⁹ <u>very loud</u>. I had never seen so many children in one place. But why did they all look ¹⁰ <u>the same as</u> me? I had thought the uniform was just for us, for Susie and me.

And then an even bigger shock. Two ladies appeared, both seemed ¹¹ <u>very tall</u>. One took Susie by the hand. I went to follow but was stopped. 'No, darling,' said my mother, 'You're in a different class from Susie!' I looked straight at her and ¹² <u>started to cry</u>.

Language note describing feelings

You don't always have to use just adjectives to describe people feelings. You can vary your language by using expressions with nouns, e.g. *proud – full of pride, nervous – overcome with nerves*, etc.

C Change the underlined word to make it fit in the new sentence.
1 My parents were very <u>proud</u>. / My parents were bursting with ....
2 She looked <u>embarrassed</u>. / She nearly died of ....
3 He was <u>nervous</u>. / He felt sick with ....
4 I was <u>disappointed</u>. / I could have cried with ....
5 He felt <u>pleased</u>. / His face shone with ....
6 I was <u>confused</u>. / I couldn't hide my ....
7 She felt <u>sad</u>. / A feeling of .... came over her.
8 They <u>laughed</u>. / They burst out ....

Learner tip

When describing an event or an experience, what you write about doesn't have to be true! You can add or adapt details to make your description more interesting. Take time to plan your answer and think about what will make the reader want to read on. Remember to use as big a range of language as you can.

D Write a description (150–190 words) about an important event in your or someone else's life. Use one of these ideas or an idea of your own.
- the first day at school
- a wedding
- starting university
- a child being born

Vocabulary Builder Quiz 13 (*OVB* pp50–52)

Try the *OVB* quiz for Unit 13. Write your answers in your notebook. Then check them and record your score.

A Match the follow-up comments (a–e) to the sentences (1–5).
1 Excuse me a second.
2 I wish they'd stop making so much noise.
3 I'm not going to iron the sheets and towels.
4 They never come to my parties.
5 You needn't turn the music down.

a It doesn't bother me.
b Sorry to bother you.
c I didn't bother to invite them this year.
d I can't be bothered.
e It's really starting to bother me.

B Write the missing word in the correct place.
1 It's time to call a day and go home.
2 Don't let the children get own way all the time.
3 She'll be going on maternity quite soon.
4 He's so serious. I wish he would lighten a bit.
5 Why was he kicked of university after only one term?

C Choose the correct words.
1 It may take a while to *arrive / reach* a compromise.
2 It's better to be honest than worry about *missing / losing* face.
3 I think it's time we moved *on / up* to the next point on the agenda.
4 They decided to stay together *to / for* the sake of their children.
5 Their youngest son *has / does* terrible temper tantrums.
6 She's going to be *buried / burial* in the grounds of the church.
7 Please send the family my *condolences / mourners*.
8 I'd like to propose a *feast / toast* to the happy couple.

D What form of the words in brackets do you need to complete the text?
"A couple of years ago my wife and I went through a rough patch. I was working away all week, and being at home only at weekends was very [1] (disrupt) to our son's routine. If I made a suggestion about his [2] (bring), my wife would [3] (react) and think I was criticising her. Every weekend, there would be a [4] (fall) out about some aspect of family life. So we went to see a [5] (counsel), who helped us deal with the [6] (underlie) problems. I changed my job, so now I'm a daily [7] (commute) but I have much more time to share in looking after my son."

Score ___/25

Wait a couple of weeks and try the quiz again. Compare your scores.

VOCABULARY Banks and money

A Choose the correct words.

A: [1] *I'm / I've* a bit short of cash. I'm just going to the [2] *cash desk / cash point*. ... Oh, hell.

B: What's the matter?

A: It won't let me [3] *deposit / withdraw* any money from my [4] *accountant / account*.

B: Why? Has it run out [5] *from / of* money?

A: No, I've gone over my overdraft [6] *limit / level*.

B: But I thought you were making [7] *lots / good* money.

A: Well, I am but I've also [8] *got / spent* into some debt. I bought a lot of stuff on [9] *sales / credit*.

B: You must be mad. If you end up with a bad credit [10] *rating / number*, you'll never get another overdraft [11] *facility / loan*.

A: Don't worry. It's just a temporary [12] *money / cash* flow problem. I won't end up going to a [13] *loan / debt* shark or start *borrowing / laundering* money.

B Cross out the word or expression that doesn't fit.

1 *go into / pay in an / apply for an* overdraft
2 *be in a / apply for a / pay off my / a student* loan
3 *strengthen the / be good with / a stable* currency
4 *be in / write off / run up huge* debts
5 *be refused / offer / run up* credit

C Complete the sentences with the pairs of words in the box.

strengthen / the economy	make / good money
buy / on credit	get into / debt
run out of / money	withdraw / some money
apply for / a loan	pay off / my student loan

1 I'd rather have a rewarding job than work just to ....
2 I'd like to .... from my current account. How much is the daily limit?
3 He's got a huge overdraft. I don't know how anyone can .... like that.
4 I can't afford to replace my car so I'll need to ....
5 The government needs to take measures to .... and help us out of recession.
6 I'm in my first job but it's going to take me ages to ....
7 It's madness to .... stuff .... – the stores charge such huge interest rates.
8 Could you lend me some cash? I've .... and I don't get paid until Friday.

DEVELOPING CONVERSATIONS
Apologising and offering explanations

Choose the correct statement in each of A's lines. Then cross out the word that isn't needed in B's answers.

1 A: I've been sent the wrong credit card. / I've been waiting ages.
   B: I do apologise for. There must have been some kind of mix-up.
2 A: I'd like to pay in this cheque. / I only need a short-term loan.
   B: I'm very sorry. I'm afraid there's absolutely not nothing we can do.
3 A: I've been trying to get cash for 20 minutes. / This pen doesn't work.
   B: I'm have really sorry. I'm afraid the system is down at the moment.
4 A: I'm here to see the manager. / I was told I could withdraw all the money today.
   B: I do apologise. I'll have a word with my manager about and see what I can do.
5 A: I'm after some Australian dollars. / I'd like to extend my overdraft.
   B: I'm awfully sorry. I'm afraid I'm not authorised for to make that decision.
6 A: Why is each customer taking so long? / Is it possible to set up online banking?
   B: I'm terribly sorry about. The computers are being very slow today.
7 A: I need to give you my new address. / A thousand pounds has gone missing from my account.
   B: I do apologise. I'll take look into the matter at once.

GRAMMAR Passives

A Find and correct six errors in the sentences.

1 I was given a bad credit rating but the debts were run up from my girlfriend.
2 When I looked at my bank statement I couldn't believe what was happened.
3 Money from organised crime is currently laundering through online businesses.
4 I'll never forget to be refused credit in a shop. It was so embarrassing.
5 I don't know why my loan application turned down.
6 They think my card was cloned when I handed it over in the restaurant.
7 All customer signatures have to check before any cash is handed over.
8 The local cash point was removed because it was broken in to.

B Complete the questions with the correct passive form of the verb. Then choose the correct answers.

Money quiz

1 What .... paper money in Britain .... of? (make)
   a wood   b cotton and linen c plastic

2 Where .... the account details .... on modern credit cards? (store)
   a in the black   b in the logo   c in the hologram
   magnetic strip

3 What is the largest value bank note that can currently .... ? (spend)
   a 1,000 US   b 10,000 Hong   c 500 euros
   dollars   Kong dollars

4 When .... fully printed bank notes .... in the UK? (first / see)
   a 1755   b 1855   c 1955

5 Which two of these things .... as money at some time? (use)
   a shells   b fish   c leather

6 In which country .... a common system of payments via mobile phone .... ? (recently / introduce)
   a the USA   b South Korea   c Australia

7 In which year .... the first euro notes and coins .... ? (launch)
   a 1999   b 2000   c 2002

8 How long on average is a dollar bill in circulation before it .... ? (destroy)
   a 12 months   b 21 months   c 24 months

LISTENING

🔊 **14.1 Listen to five short recordings and choose the correct answers.**

1 Why didn't the woman buy what she wanted?
   a It took too long.
   b The cashier was rude.
   c The cashier couldn't accept cards or cheques.
2 What has Eric done recently?
   a paid off his overdraft with his own money
   b borrowed money from his mum and dad
   c taken out a mortgage
3 What is Rachel trying to do?
   a publicise a day of action
   b raise money for a campaign
   c criticise shoppers
4 How much did Millie win on the lottery?
   a £5 million
   b £10
   c nothing
5 What happened to Richard?
   a His card was used to commit fraud.
   b The bank closed his account.
   c He went on a spending spree.

PRONUNCIATION Silent letters

A **Underline** the silent letters in these extracts from the listening exercise above.

1 I've been trying to pay for over half an hour.
2 Did Eric tell you he'd applied for a mortgage?
3 He's already up to his eyes in debt.
4 They paid the whole lot off.
5 Come on, support our campaign.
6 I was about to go out and buy some champagne.
7 I was looking at the wrong ticket.
8 I went straight to the bank to sort it out.

B **Listen and check. Practise saying the sentences.**

Language note silent letters

Some silent letters form patterns, e.g. silent *g* before *n* in words like *sign, foreign, campaign*; silent *k* before *n* in words like *knee, knowledge, knife*. Others are 'one-offs', e.g. silent *s* in *island* and *isle*.

GRAMMAR *wish*

A Match the sentence halves.

1 I'm so overdrawn. I wish
2 Jo is always broke. I wish
3 I'd love to get my own place. I wish
4 I'm sorry I can't help you out. I wish
5 Mike is always talking about money. I wish
6 It was such a beautiful ring. I wish
7 I've lost a fortune buying shares. I wish
8 It took me an hour to pay in a cheque. I wish

a I could get a mortgage.
b he wouldn't show off so much.
c I hadn't spent so much on holiday.
d I'd kept the money in the bank.
e I hadn't gone to the bank at lunchtime.
f I could lend you the money.
g he would sort out his finances.
h I could have afforded it.

B Write a sentence for each situation. Use *wish* and the words in brackets.

1 My brother is hopeless with money. (start saving)
   I wish he would start saving.

2 The interest on the loan is enormous. (never take it out)
   ....
   ....

3 It's taking ages to pay off my student loan. (have a better job)
   ....
   ....

4 I going to see my bank manager about my overdraft. (not have to go)
   ....
   ....

5 We lost some money on the house sale. (sold it two months earlier)
   ....
   ....

6 Our flat is tiny. (can afford something bigger)
   ....
   ....

7 My parents are always criticising my spending. (be a bit more understanding)
   ....
   ....

8 My flatmate has run up a big phone bill. (she not chat for so long)
   ....
   ....

READING

A Read the article opposite quickly. Match the questions to the answers. There is one question that you do not need.

a What happens in everyday shopping?
b Isn't it just a publicity stunt?
c And you're not breaking the law by using it?
d How does having your own currency benefit the town?
e Who designed the banknotes?
f So, what's the thinking behind the Lewes Pound?
g What about security?

B Read the article again. Are these statements true or false?

1 The Lewes Pound isn't the only initiative the town has signed up to.
2 The people of Lewes aren't allowed to shop outside the town.
3 The Lewes Pound functions in a similar way to other currencies.
4 You can't buy as much with a Lewes Pound as with a pound sterling.
5 Lewes is the first city to have its own currency.
6 The pound sterling will always be in circulation in the town.

C Complete the text with the words in the box. Look back at the article if you need to.

counterfeiting	worth	voucher
economic	stable	bank notes
currency		

I was in the town of Lewes a while ago. I'd popped into a café to get a sandwich and the owner asked if I minded having my change in the local [1] .... I expected something like a simple [2] .... and couldn't believe it when she gave me real [3] .... They even had all the usual features to protect against [4] .... The lady then explained that the local pounds were [5] .... the same as sterling and that the scheme was bringing [6] .... benefits to the town. It was good to see a community trying to create a [7] .... local economy.

1 **one** lewes pound
29108
Transition Town LEWES
'We have it in our power to build the world anew' Thomas Paine
Lewes resident 1768-1774

Creative currency

We're all aware we're living in a global economy. It seems one minute a currency is strong and stable, and the next it's about to collapse. So how do small business owners deal with these high and lows? One solution is to print your own currency. We talk to Sara Nicholls, a trader in the East Sussex town of Lewes, where the Lewes Pound has been in circulation since September 2008.

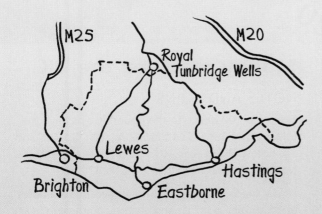

1 Q ...

A Well, the currency is part of a bigger project called Transition Town Lewes. This aims to help make the town less dependent on oil, a resource that is under threat, to lessen the harmful effects of climate change, and also to encourage greater independence in the local economy.

2 Q ...

A Basically, it keeps money and growth circulating within Lewes instead of disappearing into the big black hole of the global economy. It also builds a sense of community. Seeing the high street full of thriving small businesses encourages people to use local traders rather than out-of-town suppliers that give nothing back to Lewes.

3 Q ...

A It's very much like everywhere else. You can use the Lewes Pound in any of the participating outlets in the town – everything from food shops to the jeweller's. And it isn't just for buying goods. Lots of local specialists have signed up to the scheme – decorators, IT professionals, even yoga teachers. There are over 130 traders currently taking part, but we're always looking for new people.

4 Q ...

A No, it's completely legal when used as a voucher. It is worth exactly the same as a pound sterling but it isn't actually legal tender. That means businesses in Lewes are not obliged to accept it and it is only valid when used in participating outlets. There are four places in the town where you can get the pounds themselves.

5 Q ...

A As with any currency, we've had to be careful about counterfeiting. The pounds are printed on high-quality paper, similar to that used for national bank notes, and they have the usual features such as serial numbers and watermarks. Lewes isn't the only town to have its own currency so we were able to follow the example of places like Totnes in Devon, who launched before us.

6 Q ...

A No, I really don't think so. Lewes did in fact have its own currency before, from 1789 to 1895. We're still in the early stages of the new scheme but the economic benefits are growing. The campaign is not only raising awareness of broader issues but also showing people the advantages of supporting their own town. In the longer-term, we hope create a sustainable community with lower unemployment and a stable economy. Of course, the Lewes Pound isn't going to replace sterling. That was never the idea.

Glossary

legal tender: coins or banknotes that must be accepted if offered in payment
counterfeiting: making an exact imitation of something valuable with the intention to deceive
watermark: a mark on a bank note which can only be seen if it is held against the light

VOCABULARY Metaphor

Complete the pairs of sentences with the correct form of the same word. Then mark each sentence L (literal) or M (metaphorical).

1   Anyone who smokes g.................. with their health.
    There is a growing problem of people becoming addicted to online g.................. .
2   What's the minimum s.................. that they accept in the casino?
    We must win that contract. The future of the company is at s.................. .
3   Finding a good school in this area is a bit of a l.................. .
    He'd never done the l.................. before but he won £1 million for a one-pound ticket.
4   Have a great time. You've e.................. a nice holiday after all your hard work.
    I e.................. more money in my old job but working as a counsellor is much more rewarding.
5   My shoes fell apart in less that a month. They were a total w.................. of money.
    Don't w.................. your breath asking her for help. She's really uncooperative.
6   She worked against all the o.................. to get a place at a top university.
    He put £50 on the favourite at o.................. of 2 to 1.
7   It's surprising how many j.................. winners regret coming into so much money.
    She really hit the j.................. when she found that flat. It's in a great location.
8   She loves horseracing but she never b.................. more than £5 on each race.
    I b.................. it was wonderful to finally pay off your mortgage.

DEVELOPING WRITING An online guide – giving information and advice

A **Read the first part of the guide. Six parts have been removed. Write the correct letter (a–f) in the gaps.**

a   but these may not be readily accepted in the rest of the UK.
b   differ from branch to branch
c   provided you have a four-digit PIN
d   for things like bus fares, vending machines
e   give change in sterling
f   commission is charged

Money matters: the UK

NOTES AND COINS

There are 100 pence to the pound. Coins have the following value: £2, £1, 50p, 20p, 10p, 5p, 2p, and 1p; notes: £50, £20, £10, and £5. Scotland and Northern Ireland have their own banknotes [1] …

A few shops, services, and hotels accept euro notes or US dollars, but [2] … and charge commission. It's a good idea to carry small change [3] … , etc.

BANKS / CHANGING MONEY

General banking hours are 9.30–4.30 Monday to Friday, though this can [4] …. There is a huge network of ATMs for withdrawing cash [5] … with your credit/ debit card.

Foreign currency is easily exchanged at banks, post offices, some hotels, and bureau de change kiosks. Exchange rates vary and [6] … on most exchange transactions.

B **Match the sentence halves.**

1   You have to enter a four-digit
2   Dollars and travellers' cheques are
3   If you change currency, commission
4   Remember to carry small
5   It's a good idea to check banking
6   Shop around as exchange rates differ

a   readily accepted in shops and hotels.
b   hours in the area where you are staying.
c   change for buying from street vendors.
d   from place to place.
e   PIN to withdraw cash.
f   is charged at the relevant rate.

C Correct the <u>underlined</u> mistakes in the rest of the guide.

TIPPING

It isn't usual to tip bar staff in pubs or hotels. In restaurants service [1] <u>often includes</u>, so make sure you check your bill. Where it is not [2] <u>comprised</u>, a tip of 10–15% of the bill is appropriate. In taxis, about 10–15% of the [3] <u>fee</u> is customary. It's really up [4] <u>for</u> you whether to tip for other services like porters, room service, and hairdressers.

HAGGLING

Although it isn't the custom [5] <u>for haggling</u> in the UK, you can sometimes ask the seller to [6] <u>pay</u> you a deal in a market or when the item is already second-hand, e.g. buying two items for [7] <u>fewer</u> than the combined cost, asking for a [8] <u>lowest</u> price on a piece of jewellery / antique.

D Write an online guide (150–190 words) for using money in your country. Use the headings in exercises A and B, and/or some of the following ideas.
- Tax-free shopping
- Price guide for everyday items
- Using credit cards
- Keeping money safe
- Making phone calls

Learner tip

If you have access to a computer, why not 'publish' some of your writing on the Internet. Uploading pieces of writing like guides and do's and don'ts is a great way of giving useful information to visitors to your country.

Vocabulary Builder Quiz 14 (*OVB* pp54–56)

Try the *OVB* quiz for Unit 14. Write your answers in your notebook. Then check them and record your score.

A Which is the odd one out in each set?

1	rope	courtyard	mansion	stable
2	withdraw	launder	authorise	subsidise
3	proof	cash flow	commission	credit rating
4	stake	jackpot	bet	mortgage

B Complete the sentences with a verb ending in *-en*.
1 The curtains are too short. Can you .... them?
2 A poor diet can .... your immune system.
3 What should the government do to .... the economy during a recession?
4 This part of the road is very narrow but it will be very expensive to .... it.
5 It's too easy to commit credit card fraud. They need to .... the law.

C Complete the sentences with an adjective from *OVB* Unit 14.
1 There's only ever a very .... chance of winning the lottery.
2 He's a .... gambler. I don't think he'll ever give it up.
3 He spent all his fortune and died completely ....
4 I was in such debt I had to stop spending and adopt a more .... lifestyle.
5 My granddad has such a .... voice that no-one ever disobeyed him.
6 I was .... to borrow more money because of the recession.

D Add one letter to one of the words.
1 We need to cut down some of the overhanging ranches.
2 The water flows very fat along this stretch of the river.
3 We could see the lights of the village listening in the distance.
4 I think to amble is a complete waste of money.
5 What are the odd of ever getting our money back?

E Add the missing half of the words to complete the sentences.
1 A lot of companies go bankrupt because of cash .... problems.
2 Don't bother inviting them. They're both a bit anti-............ .
3 The banks .... played the extent of the credit crisis.
4 I'm always broke days before I get my pay ....
5 We put forward a strong case but they had a number of counter ....

Score ____/25

**Wait a couple of weeks and try the quiz again.
Compare your scores.**

15 ENTERTAINMENT

VOCABULARY Food and cooking

A Which is the odd one out in each set?

1 clams   cod   octopus   fennel
2 pumpkin   rosemary   cumin   chilli
3 broccoli   cabbage   basil   sweet potato
4 cherry   radish   blackberry fig
5 lentils   raisins   kidney beans chickpeas
6 beetroot   spring onion celery   eel

B Who would eat what? Match the food in the box with the statements. There are a different number of items for each person. Then add two more examples of what each person might eat.

almonds	chocolate	courgette
peaches	parsley	chickpeas
coconut	trout	grapefruit

1 'I can't afford to buy meat very often, so beans and pulses are a good source of protein for me.'
....

2 'I'm a fruitarian. People think it's odd but I feel fine on my diet of fruit, nuts and seeds.'
....

3 'I'm not much of a meat-eater but I love fish.'
....

4 'Being a veggie is no problem as I love my greens and salads.'
....

5 'I have such a sweet tooth. I could live on the stuff.'
....

C Choose the correct words.

1 If you *fry / steam* the fish, you don't need any oil.
2 For breakfast I usually just *squeeze / blend* some fruit with yoghurt.
3 *Remove / Sprinkle* some chopped nuts onto the mixture and then bake.
4 There's no need to *peel / slice* fruit and vegetables if you wash them well.
5 Be careful with the meringues. It's really easy to *melt / crush* them.
6 *Soak / Boil* the dried mushrooms in cold water for an hour or so.
7 *Stir / Chop* the onions quite finely so that they cook quickly.

DEVELOPING CONVERSATIONS
Vague language

Add the words / forms in brackets in the correct place.

1 A: What's that smell? It's sweet and spicy at the same time. (kind of)
   B: It's mulled wine. It should be ready in 10 minutes. (or so)
2 A: I'm not that hungry so just a small portion for me, please. (-ish)
   B: Sure. It's a light stew anyway so it shouldn't be that filling. (sort of)
3 A: I love Thai cooking. All those hot and citrus flavours. (-y)
   B: Mm. It's OK if it's mild but I can't stand too much chilli. (-ish)
4 A: What's 'mizuna'? Is it like spinach? (sort of)
   B: Not really. It's a Japanese vegetable with a mild mustard flavour. (-y)
5 A: I saw this big fruit in the market just now. I think it was called a 'pomelo'. (-ish)
   B: Oh, I know. It's a grapefruit but with much thicker skin. (like)
6 A: How much sugar do I need to add?
   B: The fruit is sharp so I'd say double the amount of berries. (roughly)
7 A: How's your salad?
   B: Very soggy. They must have used a litre of dressing on it. (about)

GRAMMAR Linking words

A Correct the underlined linking words.

1 <u>Although</u> receiving great reviews in the press, the restaurant didn't stay open long.
2 You need to beat the eggs <u>unless</u> they're light and fluffy.
3 <u>Afterwards</u>, you've tried this dead easy recipe, you'll be cooking it every week.
4 I've bought a mousse from the supermarket <u>provided</u> my soufflé doesn't come out well.
5 Season the beans really well. <u>Afterwards</u>, they can be a bit bland.
6 <u>Unless</u> you keep all kitchen surfaces clean, you won't have any food hygiene problems.

B Complete the review with the linking words in the box.

although	however	then	for	once
unless	so	during	as	if

reviewspot.com

Fig

19 Middle Row

★ ★ ★ ★ ☆

Fig is a welcome addition to the area, ¹ .... you've managed to get a table. It's in a great location just opposite the theatre, ² .... it's packed most evenings. But ³ .... you book a table in advance, ⁴ .... you won't be disappointed. We were given a warm welcome at the door and only had to wait ⁵ .... a few seconds before being given a table. There were some amazing dishes on the menu, which is changed on a daily basis. ⁶ .... , there wasn't a huge choice for vegetarians, so ⁷ .... you eat meat or fish, I would perhaps give Fig a miss. We didn't order starters, ⁸ .... the main courses looked pretty big. Our Greek lamb and fish soup were both beautifully cooked and full of flavour. The service ⁹ .... the meal was just right, and there was a comprehensive wine list, ¹⁰ .... I thought the house wine was a bit pricey.

LISTENING

Language note food pairings

There are a number of 'natural' pairings of foods that usually have a fixed word order, e.g. *bread and butter* (not *butter and bread*). Other examples include *strawberries and cream, burger and fries, oil and vinegar, salt and pepper*.

A 🔊 15.1 Listen to people talking about food. Do they call these things food heaven (✓) or food hell (✗)?
salads
tofu
fish
burger and fries
tea
garlic
curry and rice
meatballs and spaghetti

B Listen again. Tick the opinions / statements that are given in the interviews.
1 Not all meat-free food is nice.
2 Seeing fish with a head on puts me off.
3 Drinking a lot of tea isn't good for you.
4 You shouldn't eat summer fruits all year round.
5 I like garlic but only in small amounts.
6 My wife and I have very different tastes.
7 I like most foods.
8 I never eat vegetables of any type.

PRONUNCIATION Connected speech

A Underline the main stresses and mark the linking in the sentences.
1 What's your idea of food heaven and food hell?
2 So I'd have to say the good old American burger and fries.
3 My children just think I'm old-fashioned, but it's not for me.
4 I got the taste for spicy food when I was in the army.
5 My favourite thing is meatballs and spaghetti in tomato sauce.
6 That's it from me and the people here in Brighton.

B 🔊 15.2 Listen and check. Practise saying the sentences.

VOCABULARY Prefixes

A Complete the texts with the prefixes in the box.

pre	super	re	ex

Our neighbour is an ¹ ....chef and so he's
² ....-talented when it comes to preparing food.
If there's the slightest thing wrong with a dish, he'll
³ ....do it from scratch. It makes him a difficult
dinner guest, though, because he always brings
something he's ⁴ ....-cooked in case he doesn't
like the food.

over	out	pro	multi

I live in a ⁵ ....-ethnic area, which is great for
trying different food. I think the Asian eating places now
⁶ ....number the old cafés. It's made me a bit
more ⁷ ....-vegetarian because a lot of them don't
serve meat or fish. The only problem is that the food is so
tasty that I tend to ⁸ ....eat.

mis	non	semi	dis

My first attempt at making a cake was pretty
⁹ ....heartening. I ¹⁰ ....understood the
recipe and so it was ¹¹ ....-cooked in the middle.
I also forgot to use a ¹² ....-stick tin and it was all
burnt on the bottom.

B Which prefix can complete each pair of sentences?

1 The beef was really tough. I think I'd ....cooked
   it.
   Mum made far too much food but she always tends to
   ....cater.
2 It's gone a bit cold. Shall I ....heat it in the
   microwave?
   Your glass is empty. Can I get you a ....fill?
3 All restaurants nowadays are ....-smoking.
   I'm driving so do you have any ....-alcoholic
   drinks?
4 I ....understood the instructions and my cake
   turned out like a biscuit.
   The menu hadn't been translated very well and it was
   full of ....spellings.
5 Be careful. That chilli sauce is ....-hot.
   I never eat pre-cooked food. It's always
   ....-salty.
6 It was a really appetising dish, full of
   ....-coloured vegetables.
   They have so many visitors from around the world
   that the waiting staff are ....-lingual.

READING

A Match the food items in the photos to the captions. Then read the article opposite quickly and check.

the most dangerous	the most valuable
the hottest	the least accessible
the least appetizing	

B Read the article again. Match the statements (1–8) to the correct food description (A–E) in the article.

1 It may help your love life.
2 People sometimes supply fake versions of it.
3 Its flavour relies on the intervention of a mammal.
4 It needs to be prepared by an expert.
5 You can't grow it on a farm.
6 It has been tested against other similar foods.
7 It can't be collected by machine.
8 It might have anti-crime uses.

C Complete the sentences with the correct form of the words in brackets.

1 Don't harvest mushrooms unless you are sure they aren't
   .... (poison).
2 Fresh bread always smells so .... (appetite).
3 Spices are the most .... (value) ingredients in anyone's
   kitchen.
4 It had a lovely hint of .... (spicy) without being too hot.
5 The .... (scarce) of water made the harvest very poor.
6 Growing asparagus is quite a .... (special) process.

LIFE*style*

Food superlatives

We all have memories of the best and worst food we've ever eaten, but here are some other food superlatives that you may or may not want to try.

A The **hot**test

If you like your curries hot, then a sauce made from the Bhut Jolokia chilli presents the ultimate challenge. It has officially been accepted as the hottest chilli by the Guinness Book of Records. The name translates as 'ghost chilli' and it measures more than one million SHU, Scoville Heat Units, the scale used to determine spiciness. This is 200 times hotter than the average jalapeño. And it isn't just a weapon in the kitchen. Indian security have trialled the use of the Bhut Jolokia in hand grenades.

B The most **dangerous**

Fugu is one of the most expensive Japanese fish dishes, served at feasts and celebrations by specially licensed chefs. But it isn't just the price that might put you off. The meat used in the dishes is from the pufferfish (sometimes called blowfish), parts of which are deadly poisonous. A toxin called tetrodoxin, which currently has no known antidote, is stored in the fish's organs. If wrongly prepared, the unfortunate diner could end up with nausea and vomiting, and in some cases muscle paralysis and asphyxiation.

C The least **accessible**

For gourmets around the world, the ultimate prize is the elusive white truffle. Found underground on the roots of certain tree species in areas of Italy, Croatia and Slovenia, the white truffle has stubbornly resisted attempts to be cultivated commercially. With the aid of pigs or dogs, truffle-hunters seek out the precious fungi in an annual autumn harvest. Their searches can often prove fruitless as the truffles require a special set of conditions to develop. Changes in climate and overdevelopment have added to their scarcity. This elusiveness and the truffle's reputation as an aphrodisiac have made it one of the most coveted foods in the world.

D The most **valuable**

There have been times when saffron has been literally worth its weight in gold. It is still considered the world's most valuable spice. Extracted from the saffron crocus, it commands a high price because of the need for specialised growing conditions and labour-intensive harvesting by hand. To produce a kilo of saffron, it's estimated that 150,000 flowers are needed. This highly-prized ingredient has almost inevitably been subject to fraud and adulteration during its 3,000-year history. Unwary buyers may end up with dried marigolds or the cheaper turmeric passed off as the king of spices.

E The least **appetizing**

Kopi Luwak, one of the most expensive coffees in the world, is prized for its unique taste. Produced in small quantities mainly in Indonesia, its set apart from other coffees in the way it is processed before it is even harvested. Put bluntly, the coffee berries are eaten in the wild by small cat-like animals called Asian palm civets. The animals don't digest the actual coffee beans and these are then excreted in the animals' droppings. Apparently, their stomach acids create a process that gives the beans a unique and complex flavour.

Glossary

antidote: a medicine that counteracts a poison
asphyxiation: being unable to breathe, usually resulting in death
marigolds: plants with yellow or orange flowers

VOCABULARY Food in the news

A Replace the underlined words in the headlines with the phrases in the box.

| food shortages | food production | food poisoning |
| food waste | fast food advertising | |

1
Council bans promotion of junk food

2
Lack of food due to increase

3
Vomiting hits local schools

4
UK tops list of throwing away food

5
Factory halts processing

B Match the headlines (1–5) to the phrases (a–e).

a
US soya called 'Frankenstein food'

b
UK turns from potatoes to pasta

c
Rise in food intolerances in the under-5s

d
Strike leads to empty shelves across city

e
Restaurant shut down after inspection

a food allergies
b food hygiene
c food supplies
d GM foods
e staple foods

GRAMMAR Reporting verbs

A Choose the correct words.

1 We asked the waiter for some salt and pepper but he refused *to give / give* it to us.
2 We have to warn *all our friends / to all our friends* not to give our son nuts.
3 We tried to encourage the kids *to get / getting* involved in cooking.
4 They rang to confirm *that our booking / our booking*.
5 I was a bit offended as she insisted *to add / on adding* chilli sauce to everything I cooked.
6 All my friends recommended *trying / to try* the new restaurant but I didn't think it was up to much.
7 Farmers have blamed the shortage of fresh fruit *on / to* the poor weather.
8 It was a pricey place so we all agreed *dividing / to divide* the bill four ways.

B Choose the correct verb in brackets and report the sentences.

1 'It's your fault that the burgers were burnt.' (deny / blame)
Jane ....
2 'Why don't you send it back if it's overcooked?' (advise / complain)
Mum ....
3 'Let's order the set menu to be delivered.' (urge / suggest)
Ellie ....
4 'Don't worry. I won't forget to take it out of the oven.' (promise / persuade)
Dad ....
5 'We don't use any products that have been genetically altered in any of our products.' (deny / refuse)
The managing director ....
6 'Don't forget to ask Meena about her secret ingredient.' (admit / remind)
Mark ....
7 'I'm sorry we didn't make it on Saturday.' (apologise for / invite)
Lili ....
8 'All the affected premises have been closed.' (threaten / declare)
The health minister ....

C Match the sentences in exercise B (1–8) to the situations (a–h).

a cases of food poisoning
b a problem in a restaurant
c having a takeaway meal
d asking for help with a recipe
e cooking on a barbecue
f a scandal about GM foods
g missing a party
h baking a cake

DEVELOPING WRITING
An anecdote – a food experience

A Read the anecdote. Choose the correct words.

I'll never forget ¹ *to try / trying* sushi for the first time. It was in Tokyo and I loved seeing the chefs ² *prepare / to prepare* the beautiful little parcels of rice, seaweed and fish. As we watched the plates on the conveyer belt move round in front of the customers, I couldn't wait to get started. We sat at the bar, ordered a beer, and I chose my first plate. The sushi was quite small, so I ³ *put / ate* the whole thing in my mouth. It was then the flavour of the wasabi ⁴ *hit / strike* me. There must have been an awful lot of it, as it ⁵ *made / brought* tears to my eyes. Combined with the slippery texture of the fish, I found it impossible to ⁶ *bite / chew*. I could feel the sushi just resting in my mouth. I started to ⁷ *cold / cough* but didn't want to offend anyone by ⁸ *throwing / spitting* it out. I ⁹ *got / took* a sip of beer and that seemed to help. The taste of the wasabi started to ¹⁰ *fail / fade* and was replaced by the freshest of fish. By the end of the evening, I'd become a sushi fan but it was a difficult introduction.

B Complete the sentences with the words in the box. Was each experience positive or negative?

wrong	undercooked	crave	sinking
smothered	mouthful	succulent	smeared

1 The memory of .... my teeth into that perfect peach will stay with me forever.
2 Cutting into the .... chicken made me lose my appetite immediately.
3 The smell of freshly-baked bread .... with butter is so comforting.
4 I was about to take a sip when I noticed the glass was .... with lipstick.
5 I took one .... and then spotted a hair floating in the sauce.
6 It had the perfect contrast of a crisp pastry and a .... filling.
7 The memory of that meal always makes me .... barbecued pork.
8 A piece of the meat went down the .... way and I nearly choked.

C Write an anecdote (150–190 words) about a good or bad food experience. Use this opening sentence and some of the language from this section.

I'll never forget trying ... for the first time.

Vocabulary Builder Quiz 15 (*OVB* pp58–60)

Try the *OVB* quiz for Unit 15. Write your answers in your notebook. Then check them and record your score.

A Match the cooking verbs 1–5 with the sets of nouns a–e.
1 soak   a the garlic / almonds / biscuits
2 slice   b the potatoes / apples / onions
3 crush   c the bread / tomatoes / courgettes
4 steam   d the beans / chickpeas / dried mushrooms
5 peel   e the fish / vegetables / spinach

B Complete the sentences with verbs ending in -*ise*.
1 She employed a PR agency to .... her new career.
2 At the end of your talk, ... the main points.
3 The head of Finance has to .... any expenses claim.
4 After her general training, she's going to .... in childhood diseases.
5 I can't .... strongly enough the need for tight security.

C Correct one letter in the underlined words.
1 Where's the <u>hid</u> of the jam jar?
2 Add <u>toughly</u> 300g of pasta to the soup.
3 I'm vegetarian and so don't eat anything made with meat <u>stick</u>.
4 The price was so low it must have been <u>bake</u> caviar.
5 Stop <u>buttering</u>, I can't heard what you're saying.
6 The <u>tire</u> of public opinion turned against us.

D Which word do you need to complete the sentences in each set?
1 .... some juice over the fish. / Can I .... past? / It will be a bit of a .... with five of us in the car.
2 It was a lot of .... about nothing. / Please don't make a .... / What was all the .... about last night?
3 They launched a takeover .... / The prisoners made a .... for freedom. / The politician toured the country in a .... to win support.
4 She was .... influenced by her mother's politics. / He has serious health problems because he drinks so .... / .... armed rebels have surrounded the city.

E Choose the correct words.
1 If I eat dairy products, my stomach problem flares *up / out*.
2 It's *informed / alleged* that they were trading without a licence.
3 There was a serious *outbreak / break out* of food poisoning.
4 Our family *originated / allocated* from Holland.
5 Good levels of *hygienic / hygiene* are essential in a kitchen.

Score ___ /25

Wait a couple of weeks and try the quiz again. Compare your scores.

VOCABULARY Reasons for phoning

Complete the sentences with the pairs of words in the box.

check / stock levels	chase up / payment	pass on / thanks
remind / appointment	arrange / time	

I'm just phoning to ...
1 .... a suitable .... for the next conference call.
2 .... current .... at the printer's.
3 .... my .... to you and your colleagues.
4 .... you that you have an .... with Sr Lopez.
5 .... an overdue .... from last month.

confirm / booking	apologise / losing	let / make
enquire / options	see / taking	

I'm just calling to ...
6 .... you know I won't be able to .... Jan's leaving do.
7 .... whether you're .... on any work experience candidates at the moment.
8 .... a .... for the conference room next week.
9 .... for .... my temper in the meeting.
10 .... about the buffet lunch .... on your menu.

DEVELOPING CONVERSATIONS
Using *would* to be polite

Replace the underlined words to make the sentences more polite. Use *would* and the words in brackets.
1 If it's OK with you, I'll give it a miss. (mind / rather)
   ....
2 Please spell your surname. (mind)
   ....
3 Can you make 3.30 tomorrow? (at all)
   ....
4 Have you got the figures with you? (happen)
   ....
5 Do you want to come to dinner? (wondering / like)
   ....
6 Any time is good for me. (suit)
   ....
7 Email me directions to your office. (possible)
   ....

GRAMMAR The future continuous

A **Complete the sentences with the pairs of verbs in the box.**

'll be finishing / 'll deal
going to be taking / 'll send
won't make / 'll be working
won't manage / 'll be finalising
'll be travelling / won't be

1 I .... the meeting on Friday because I .... from home.
2 I .... up to the conference tomorrow so I .... available until the evening.
3 We .... the session in about 10 minutes and I .... with any questions then.
4 They aren't .... on any new staff but I .... them my CV anyway.
5 We .... to join you for dinner because we .... the presentation.

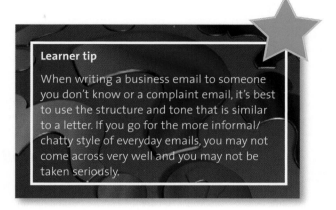

B **Put the verb in brackets into the future continuous. Then match 1–6 and a–f.**

1 .... (you / see) the new recruits later?
2 If you .... (pop) down to the canteen later
3 As you .... (not / come) to the dinner,
4 When .... (you / leave) for the conference?
5 If you .... (not / use) the pool car today,
6 .... (you / do) any photocopying later?

a Could you run off three sets of these proofs?
b should I invite someone else from the team?
c do you mind If I take it?
d I need to give them a copy of their contract.
e could you bring me a sandwich back?
f The head of sales needs this CD for her presentation.

DEVELOPING WRITING
An email – chasing an order

A **Read the email and choose the correct words.**

To: giftline.customerservice.co.uk
From: ml@citymail.com
Subject: Order number: D61290X

Dear Head of Customer Services

I am writing to enquire about an order I ¹ *placed / put* online on 14/9/09. The order number is as shown above and the item ² *in / of* question is a watch priced £69.99. In addition to this amount, I paid £12.00 for special delivery ³ *for / in order* to receive the watch the following day.

When there was no delivery on the ⁴ *due / bound* date, I contacted your customer helpline and the operator assured ⁵ *me / to me* that the package had been ⁶ *returned / despatched* and would be with me within 48 hours.
⁷ *In spite / Despite* repeated calls to the helpline to chase up the order, I have still not received the watch and delivery is now ⁸ *over / over than* a week late.

I have checked my current account and can confirm that it has been ⁹ *credited / debited* to the sum of £81.99. As both the price of the item and the delivery charges have been paid ¹⁰ *in / to* full, I am very disappointed not have received my order. I ¹¹ *would / will* be grateful if you could look into the delay and make sure the watch is delivered to me within 48 hours. Please acknowledge ¹² *receive / receipt* of this message. I can be contacted at the above email address.

Yours
Marcus Linnemann

Learner tip

When writing a business email to someone you don't know or a complaint email, it's best to use the structure and tone that is similar to a letter. If you go for the more informal/chatty style of everyday emails, you may not come across very well and you may not be taken seriously.

B **Underline in the text the more polite ways of saying these things.**

1 Where the hell is my order?
2 That woman said it was coming.
3 I must have phoned a hundred times.
4 You've already had your money.
5 Sort it out quickly.
6 Get back to me.

C **Read the checklist and find examples of each point in the email in exercise A.**

When chasing up an order, remember to:

State the date of your order and any reference numbers. ☐

Include your full name. ☐

Say where you can be contacted. ☐

State what you ordered and the price.

Say clearly when the order was meant to be delivered. ☐

Confirm that you have paid for the order. ☐

State what action you want to be taken. ☐

D **Write an email (150–190 words) to an Internet company to chase up an order. Use the checklist and the language in this section to help you.**

VOCABULARY Building up a business

A Complete the text with the pairs of words in the box. You may need to change the order.

capital / raise	break / even
floated / stock	having / turnover
set up / company	competition / face
takeover / subject	business / plough
loss / run	making / profit

Business rules, **big** or *small*

The news is full of stories of business highs and lows – companies that have been [1] .... on the .... exchange and others that have been the [2] .... of a hostile .... bid. This may seem a million miles from the world of small enterprises but the same advice applies:

• Think carefully about why you want to [3] .... your own .... Don't do it for the wrong reasons.

• [4] .... any .... you need at the lowest possible interest rates.

• Don't be content just to survive in the early years. Businesses that
[5] .... at a .... or just [6] .... usually have a shaky future.

• Think profit. [7] .... an annual .... of a million pounds, but not making much profit, isn't really business.

• When you are [8] .... a healthy .... ,
[9] .... as much as possible back into the ....

• Most companies [10] .... stiff .... so know your rivals and keep ahead of the game.

READING

A Read the profile opposite quickly. Choose the most appropriate title.
a Musician becomes chef
b A recipe for success
c New products at carnival

B Read the profile again. Are these statements true or false?
1 Levi's grandmother invented the secret recipe for the sauce.
2 He found the transition from the Caribbean to the UK difficult.
3 His first customers were people from his local area.
4 He didn't try to ask for a business loan until he went on Dragons' Den.
5 He used a range of skills and techniques to promote his products.
6 He had to agree to hand over half his business in return for the dragons' backing.
7 After the deal, he didn't have to wait long before his sauces were produced on a big scale.
8 He has remained tied in to working with just one outlet.

C Who in the article might say / have said these things?
1 'Remember not to tell a soul about the secret ingredient.'
2 'I can't believe people finally know about it outside Brixton.'
3 'What are your projected sales in year 1?'
4 'Sorry, we've just sold the last. Come back next week or check me out at Notting Hill.'
5 'We've run out I'm afraid but we should have some more stock in soon.'
6 'Are you the boy who cooks like a dream? My sister told me about your jerk chicken.'

D Read the update about Levi. Choose the correct words.
After his successful [1] *pitch / bid* on Dragons' Den, Levi's [2] *stock / brand* has gone from strength to strength. Not only is he a successful [3] *entrepreneur / commercial* but also an [4] *enterprise / inspiration* to other [5] *budding / breaking* businesses. He has [6] *raised / struck* a deal for a TV series about Caribbean cooking, in addition to publishing two recipe books. His personality and [7] *passion / passionate* for food and music continue to be his best [8] *competition / marketing* tools. To use his own words, 'Put some music in your food'.

Name: Levi Roots

Born: Clarendon, Jamaica, 1959

Product: Reggae Reggae Sauce

Background: The history of Reggae Reggae Sauce begins in Jamaica, where Levi learned to cook with the help and inspiration of his grandmother. She held the key to a secret recipe of herbs and spices that had been passed from one generation to another. It was here that Levi's passion for Caribbean was born and nurtured by his grandmother. The young Levi learned to combine flavours, working with home-grown plants, herbs and spices. This love of cooking was matched only by a passion for Jamaican music. It was these two loves that would lead Levi to a successful career as a reggae musician and entrepreneur.

When Levi moved to the UK, he so missed the sounds and flavours of the island that the only way to cure his homesickness was to cook his favourite food. Slowly but surely, he developed his grandmother's secret recipe for jerk chicken until he had the perfect formula.

Early days: Word spread and before long Levi had a loyal group of fans. He and his family would prepare batches in his kitchen in Brixton and sell the sauce at the local market and at the Notting Hill Carnival. The large local black community in Brixton took Levi and his sauces to their heart, and soon he couldn't keep up with the demand.

Despite several unsuccessful attempts to get financial backing and launch the sauce into a bigger commercial market, Levi never gave up. The annual Notting Hill Carnival proved to be the ideal outlet for the combined talents of this musician and chef, who played reggae to the crowds and also had a stall selling his unique sauces and dishes.

Business break: In 2006, Levi appeared at the World Food Market. His unusual marketing method of singing about his Reggae Reggae Sauce caught the attention of a BBC researcher. Levi was invited to appear on the BBC's Dragons' Den, in which budding entrepreneurs pitch their ideas to a group of venture capitalists. These 'dragons' are notoriously difficult to please and, despite misgivings from his family, Levi agreed. In January 2007, he played the guitar and sang about his sauces in a musical pitch to the dragons. He won them over and two of them offered him the full £50,000 investment he needed in return for a 40% stake in the business.

As soon as the programme went to air, interest in Levi and his brand spread across the country. An exclusive deal was struck with the supermarket chain Sainsbury's. Levi's dream was turning into a reality, but he had to turn from a one-man operation in his kitchen to a commercial producer almost overnight. Within six weeks stock appeared on the supermarket shelves and then sold out almost immediately. Invitations for Levi to do interviews, TV appearances and gigs came thick and fast.

Levi has extended the range and his products are now stocked by every major supermarket in the UK. It's estimated that nearly 10 million bottles have made their way into UK homes and restaurants.

Glossary

jerk chicken: a dish cooked by covering meat in spices and baking it
Brixton: an area of south London with a large black/Caribbean community
Notting Hill Carnival: an annual street carnival in west London involving people from the black / Caribbean community
venture capitalists: providers of finance for companies that may be considered risky

GRAMMAR Expressing necessity and ability

A Correct one mistake in each sentence.

1 I can't talk now so I'll must call you back later.
2 It will be great not have to commute to work every day.
3 When do you think you'll able to finish the report?
4 This new software will able us to protect the system from viruses.
5 It's unfair to force people take reduced hours at short notice.
6 Why won't my password let access the file?
7 What do you need to enable you for finish the project on time?
8 Sadly we've been force to make some redundancies.

B Complete the conversation with the correct form of the pairs of verbs.

not let / get	make / wonder
not be able / offer	force / look for
be able / keep	not be able / park
be able / keep	have to / buy in
not allow / bring	

A: So, how come things have started to go wrong with the business?

B: Well first off, my main supplier went bust and so I ¹ .... new stock at short notice. That means I ² .... the same choice as before. Plus there's been a drop in customers as the council now ³ .... people .... their cars into the centre. It's surprising how ⁴ .... puts people off. To cap it all, they've put the rents up, so I ⁵ .... new premises soon anyway. The whole thing ⁶ .... me .... why I bothered opening a shop in the first place.

A: ⁷ .... it .... you down. I'm sure you ⁸ .... going.

VOCABULARY Business collocations

A Complete the director's speech with the correct prepositions. You sometimes need two words.

❝Since we set ¹ .... the company sales have shot ² .... and we've added ³ .... our sales team. Last year customers complained about items being ⁴ .... stock or having to chase ⁵ .... orders. This year we've kept most lines ⁶ .... stock. And when we've been flooded ⁷ .... new orders and we've kept ⁸ .... much better.

Building ⁹ .... the business has been satisfying but we can't be complacent. Hundreds of small companies are being taken ¹⁰ .... or put ¹¹ .... business. Our long-term goal is still to break ¹² .... the American market and then branch ¹³ .... other areas but for now I'd like to say well done. ❞

B Match the sentence halves.

1 It's a niche market so I wouldn't advise
2 She went from area manager
3 The mobile phone market is saturated so
4 The product is aimed at teenagers as
5 Sales have plunged,
6 Launching in just a few target markets

a is potentially a risky business.
b the youth market is still worth billions.
c it isn't a growth area.
d which is a huge area of concern.
e getting into such a specialist area.
f to head of the company in a short time.

C Complete the list with the verbs in the box.

have	fulfil	boost	do	develop
expand	launch	market	improve	exploit

THINK YOU CAN BE THE NEXT BILL GATES?

There are a few key steps on the way to making your millions:

1 .... a lot of market research
2 .... a gap in the market
3 .... a product line
4 .... and then 5 .... the products
6 .... orders
7 .... sales and marketing
8 .... sales
9 .... the business
10 .... a controlling stake in the company

LISTENING

🔊 **16.1 You are going to hear five speakers talking about why they are in business. Match the speakers (1–5) to the letters (a–f). There is one letter that you don't need.**

Speaker 1 ....
Speaker 2 ....
Speaker 3 ....
Speaker 4 ....
Speaker 5 ....

a I felt a sense of duty to the family business.
b I saw a gap in the market.
c I saw a way of making a lot of money.
d I had a talent that someone spotted.
e I improved an existing service.
f I missed doing what I was good at.

PRONUNCIATION
Sounds that aren't pronounced

A **How many syllables are there in the underlined words when said in context?**
1 Why not set up a Spanish food <u>business</u> online?
2 We've just redesigned our first fairly <u>rudimentary</u> website.
3 I spent more time <u>travelling</u> on planes.
4 I'd done about 50 <u>different</u> designs.
5 My older brother and sister took an avid <u>interest</u> in the animals.
6 After I graduated in <u>medicine</u>, I chose to work as a GP.
7 <u>Eventually</u> I took early retirement.
8 I ended up doing nine-to-five or just <u>temporary</u> work.
9 We worked late in the <u>evening</u> when she'd finished.

B 🔊 **16.2 Listen and check. Then practise saying the sentences.**

Vocabulary Builder Quiz 16 (*OVB* pp62–64)

Try the *OVB* quiz for Unit 16. Write your answers in your notebook. Then check them and record your score.

A Add the missing preposition.
1 We still haven't received the payment, so you need to chase them ....
2 If you're seeing Jo later, can you pass .... a message to him?
3 The company is planning to branch .... into other areas of business.
4 The bank is planning to take .... two of its smaller rivals.
5 We won't make any profit or a loss, but breaking .... is acceptable in our first year.

B Complete the sentences with a verb noun ending in -y.
1 There was a delay in the .... of the goods.
2 They're launching a public .... into the accident.
3 I hope she makes a speedy .... from her operation.
4 The .... of oil in the area has doubled the population.
5 It can take years to achieve .... of a musical instrument.

C Add the missing half of the words to complete the sentences.
1 They're designing a new .... ship store in Beijing.
2 All the goods in the .... house were damaged by fire.
3 You need to always be on the look .... for new business ideas.
4 Their accounts show a .... over of just under one million pounds.
5 The pay gap between blue- and white- .... workers needs to be addressed.

D Choose the correct words.
1 They're planning to *plough / float* on the stock exchange.
2 Can we do a *deal / venture* on the price of the car?
3 It's essential to *network / pitch* across a broad range of people to make new contacts.
4 They will invest but only for a 25% *niche / stake* in the company.
5 Please refer carefully to the notes *at / on* the foot of the page.

D What form of the words in brackets do you need to complete the text?
'My brother first showed [1] (entrepreneur) skills when he set up a bike repair service as a teenager. He was very [2] (strategy) in his approach and by the time he was 18, he had a workshop and five employees. After [3] (negotiate) with a local company, he sold the business, and got into buying and selling properties. Despite the recent [4] (unstable) of the market, he's continued to be successful and he's considering further [5] (expand).'

Score ____/25

Wait a couple of weeks and try the quiz again. Compare your scores.

🔊 1.1

1

M = Man, W = Woman

M: What did you think of it?

W: It was OK but it wasn't as good as I'd expected.

M: Really? I thought it was the best film I've seen in ages. I couldn't take my eyes off the screen for a second.

W: Yeah, it *was* gripping, but they'd missed out loads of details. You see, I've read the book several times – it's one of my favourites – but they just didn't stick to the plot. Some of the most important parts of the story were just jumped over. I wish they wouldn't do that. And they even made the main character less complicated than she was in the book. I just think that they should be true to the original story.

2

There's so much more variety nowadays. When I was younger, people used to go out to have fun – to the cinema, theatre or to a concert. Now technology has changed everything, so it's all at your fingertips at home. People can listen to music, watch a DVD, even watch the cup final live, all in the comfort of their own home. It's convenient but people don't socialise like they used to. I think that's a great shame. Even people in the same family don't share or enjoy entertainment together.

3

W = Woman, M = Man

W: You used to be a really keen theatre-goer, didn't you. Do you still go a lot?

M: Not as much as I'd like to.

W: I suppose it's quite expensive nowadays.

M: It's not so much that. In fact you can get some really good deals if you book online. And there are often discounted tickets during the week. The thing is I spend every spare moment on my course. It's really hard working full-time and studying for my masters. At times, life gets pretty dull and I think about giving it up but it's the last year now so I ought to keep going. I'm just looking forward to when I can get my life back.

4

I suppose it's not bad here, considering it's only quite a small town. We've got the usual things – a multi-screen cinema, a couple of clubs, pubs and restaurants, and a small local museum. But if you want to see a top band, opera, or even a play you need to go into one of the bigger cities nearby. It's the teenagers I feel sorry for. I mean, there really isn't much for them to do. And then when they get to 18, it's hardly surprising they spend the whole weekend in the pub.

5

M = Mum, S = Son

M: Richard, will you turn that TV off, please?

S: Sure. This films nearly finished anyway.

M: No, Richard. I'm not asking you, I'm telling you. Turn it off, *now*.

S: Why are you getting on my case? I must be the only kid in my class without a TV in his room. It's just not fair. If you

bought me my own TV, I could watch it when I wanted.

M: That's the whole point. I don't want you to watch any *more* TV. You already watch *far* too much. You hardly ever do anything else. You never touch the guitar we bought you and that cost a fortune.

6

It really annoys me when people complain about the local art scene. Just last month, our town put on an exhibition and sale of local artists and craftspeople. Lots of people put forward their work – painters, photographers, weavers and furniture makers – and it was well promoted in the local paper and online. And what happened? There were hardly any visitors. It was awful. We had two or three people an hour. It was just such a disappointment. What was the point of all those artists being there?

🔊 1.2

1

I wish they wouldn't do that.

I just think that they should be true to the original story.

2

People used to go out to have fun.

People don't socialise like they used to.

3

You used to be a really keen theatre-goer.

Not as much as I'd like to.

4

It's the teenagers I feel sorry for.

I mean, there really isn't much for them to do.

5

I'm not asking you, I'm telling you.

I don't want you to watch any more TV.

🔊 2.1

J = Jodie, R = Raúl

J: I can't believe it's our last day already. So, what do you feel like doing?

R: Well, we mustn't miss the annual parade tonight. It's supposed to be amazing. Everyone dresses up and they play traditional music and songs. It starts in the town square and then goes all the way through the main streets.

J: Sounds like fun. So, that's this evening organised. Just the rest of the day to plan. According to the guidebook, the City Museum has one of the best collections of modern and abstract art in the country.

R: Hmm, to be honest, I'm not that keen on modern art. It's all a bit too weird for me.

J: No problem. We can give that a miss. The book also recommends a tour of the temple ruins. Apparently, you can get some great views of the city from up there.

R: How long does it take to get there?

J: About an hour and a half by bus. ... Mmm three hours there and back is quite a long time out of our day and, unfortunately, it's not the kind of place you can see in just a short time.

R: OK, so let's stay nearer to the centre. There must be something interesting we can do.

J: Just a second. A friend of mine recommended the street market here. She said it's packed with amazing local crafts and stalls with souvenirs and stuff.

R: Street market ... here it is in the guidebook. 'Take a trip into the past and soak up the atmosphere at the street market, where stallholders wear traditional costume and demonstrate local crafts. The aromas of sweetly-scented oils mix gently with herbs and spices,' etc, etc. Sounds good but it closes at one o'clock, so we'd need to go there first.

J: Fine by me. So, we spend the morning at the market and we end up at the parade.

R: How about going back to the old town after lunch?

J: Mmm, I think we've seen everything there, haven't we? I took loads of photos of the buildings. The architecture was stunning.

R: Mm, it was pretty amazing. But, you're right, we ought to see something different.

J: Have another look at what's round the main square. We need to be up there for the parade anyway.

R: Good thinking. ... Hmmm ... There's The Old Merchant's House 'a private house dating back to the 18th century now open to the public. The collection of art and objects collected by the owner and his family provides a delightful insight into history in an informal setting.' Open today until seven.

J: Ideal. We can have a drink in the square before the parade starts.

R: Sure, but we'd better get going. The market has already started.

🔊 2.2

1

It starts in the town square and then goes all the way through the main streets.

2

The city museum has one of the best collections of modern and abstract art in the country.

3

It's not the kind of place you can see in just a short time.

4

Take a trip into the past and soak up the atmosphere at the street market.

5

So, we spend the morning at the market and we end up at the parade.

6

We need to be up there for the parade anyway.

🔊 3.1

Speaker 1

A lot of people confuse what they *need* with what they *want*. They think they really must have that bigger house, the latest mobile phone, a designer top, or some luxury food. To me, the difference between wants and needs is clear. We all only really need somewhere to live, food and water, basic health and hygiene products, and clothes for different situations. All the other stuff is really just what we want – things that make us feel better for a time. My advice is just to ask 'Do I really need this?' and if the answer's 'yes', then of course I'll go ahead and buy it. But most of the time, the answer is 'no'. It may sound a bit dull to people who love shopping, but it means I don't have any credit card debts to pay and my apartment isn't full of useless stuff.

Speaker 2

I used to be a complete shopaholic. All my spare time was taken up with trips to shopping malls, buying and selling on eBay and browsing my favourite internet sites. I remember in one weekend I bought six pairs of trousers, eight shirts, around 20 CDs and a new mobile phone. In fact, in one year I changed my mobile *eight* times. Every time I saw my friends, they said, 'Go on then, show us your new phone.' Anyway, by the time I was twenty I had debts of around £20,000 – a thousand pounds for every year of my life. Then losing my job was the reality check I needed. I couldn't pay any of the bills. It was so scary. Now I realise I didn't really need all that stuff and I'm slowly paying off what I owe. And I've had the same mobile phone for years.

Speaker 3

I don't really plan my spending, even when I go food shopping. I just look around and spot what's on special offer. I always go for the 'buy one, get one free' and 'three for two' deals in the supermarket. I sometimes end up with loads of bottles of shampoo, but I guess it's always useful. The high street is full of great value shops nowadays. I usually pop in to one or two of them on my way home from work. They are full of cheap clothes and accessories and they always have a sale rail of cut-price stuff. I'll usually pick up one or two things each week. In fact, just yesterday I bought a bag, a pair of sandals, a pair of jeans and two white shirts. When I got home, I realised I already had six white shirts but I can always put one or two in the charity shop.

Speaker 4

I used to be a dream customer. If I saw something I liked, I would always buy it. It didn't matter if it was in a shop window, in a magazine or catalogue, on a website, or even in an auction. 'See it, want it, buy it' used to be my motto. I have a good salary and so money has never been a problem, and I've never been very much in debt. A couple of years ago, I decided I needed a bigger flat because I was running out of space for all my stuff. Then I saw a TV programme on impulse buyers like me and they came across really badly – just like spoilt children. I decided there and then that I had to stop being so self-indulgent. I took bags and bags of things to the charity shop and stayed in my old flat. I still enjoy shopping but I don't have to buy something every time.

Speaker 5

I love all shopping opportunities. Not because I'm a shopaholic but because I earn a living by getting people to buy things. It's my job to make people aware of the benefits of different brands so that they sell well. Nowadays, there's a lot of talk about people being addicted to shopping and buying stuff they don't need. But what would happen if we only bought the basics in life? Our economy would suffer, workers in the developing world would lose their jobs, and life would be very dull. I'm not saying that people should get into serious debt, but to have the car, the phone, or the food that you want makes life fun. We all work very hard in this country and not to have a few luxuries on the way would be very hard. It's all a question of balance but we also have to be realistic. Shopping is one of the most popular leisure activities in the western world, and that's not necessarily a bad thing.

🔊 3.2

1

They think they really must have that bigger house, latest mobile phone, designer top, or luxury food.

2

We all only really need somewhere to live, food and water, basic health and hygiene products, and clothes for different situations.

3

I remember in one weekend I bought six pairs of trousers, eight shirts, around 20 CDs and a new mobile phone.

4

In fact, just yesterday I bought a bag, a pair of sandals, a pair of jeans and two white shirts.

5

It didn't matter if it was in a shop window, in a magazine or catalogue, on a website, or even in an auction.

6

Our economy would suffer, workers in the developing world would lose their jobs, and life would be very dull.

🔊 4.1

N = Nat, A = Adam

N: Have you got today's paper, Adam? I want to catch up on the news.

A: Sorry, I haven't. I've given up on buying a paper. I just can't be bothered reading it any more.

N: So, how do you find out what's going on?

A: I usually check online for any update on the most important stories or I listen to the headlines on the radio. To be honest, I find the news so depressing just now. Everywhere you turn, the only thing you hear about is the recession and people

going bankrupt. And it's the same at work. I walked into the office the other day, said 'Good morning,' and my colleague replied, 'What's good about it?'

N: Why was he in such a bad mood?

A: He'd just been reading the paper. He told me what was going on and then I felt fed up, too.

N: Sounds like you need cheering up. You should check out that website that covers only good news. What's it called again? The Good News Network, or something like that.

A: What's that? I've never heard of it.

N: I just came across it one day when I was online. It's an American site set up by a woman who used to work in TV news. And she just wanted to give people access to some more positive stories.

A: Erm, I'm not sure I'm interested in stories about cats and flowers.

N: It's not like that! They deal with serious issues like the economy, crime, and the environment but they select only news stories that have a more positive content. When I first saw the website, they had headlines on signs of economic growth in the US economy and a drop in crime in the States, too, despite the recession.

A: So, it's all about the USA? No good news in any other part of the world?

N: Of course not. They cover international news, too. There were stories from Europe, China and South America when I looked.

A: But if it's all good, is it really news? They must have quite a lot of cute stories about animals and stuff.

N: Sure, they do have those 'feel-good' stories about family life and pets, but you don't have to read them if you don't want to. For me, it just gave a bit of balance. In TV news and newspapers, the biggest stories all tend to be the negative ones.

A: Tell me about it, Natalie! *I'm* the one who's given up on newspapers, don't forget!

🔊 4.2

1

I've given up on buying a paper.
It just gave a bit of balance.

2

They deal with serious issues like the economy.
I just can't be bothered reading it.

3

The only thing you hear about is the recession.
You should check out that website.

4

They had headlines on signs of economic growth.
How do you find out what's going on?

5

I listen to the headlines on the radio.
My colleague replied, 'What's good about it?'

6

They cover international news.
They must have quite a lot of cute stories.

🎧 **5.1**

P = Presenter, A = Angie, S = Simon

P: Welcome back to *Sports Talk*. We'll be catching up on all the sporting headlines in just a while but first one of our regular features on less common sports that are played around the country. Today it's the turn of touch rugby and in the studio we have two keen players, Angie Mitchell and Simon Parker.
Angie, let's start with you and ... if you don't mind me saying, you're a woman and you play on the same team as the guys?

A: Yes, Nick, that's right. Touch rugby is for pretty much everyone. You can play in men's, women's and mixed teams. It's a sport that's growing in popularity around the world because it appeals to lovers of traditional rugby and people who have never played it.

P: OK, so how did it all start and how similar is it to the original game of rugby?

A: Touch rugby started in Australia in the 1960's as a warm-up game for players of the traditional sport. What's great about it is the simplicity – all you need is a rugby ball, a space to play and a group of friends. The object of the game is for each team to score touchdowns and to prevent the opposition from scoring. So, in terms of how you play, it's similar to rugby but without the tackling, scrumming, you know, all the really physical stuff.

P: So, Simon, it's quite a soft game, then?

S: *No*, not at all! It's very fast and exciting! There's a *lot* of running involved so people find that their fitness levels improve really quickly. It's a great way to get your heart pumping and burn off those excess kilos. And people develop stamina, ball skills and hand-eye coordination, like in a *lot* of team sports.

P: Mmm, sounds quite demanding.

A: Yes, it can be, but to be honest, we get people of all shapes, sizes, and ages. You can play at your own level. It's so simple that after two to three games, you get the basic skills. Then it's up to you to keep playing and develop your game. And as with everything, the more you play, the better you become.

P: So what brought you two into the game? Simon?

S: I'd got really out of shape due to my job. I used to travel a lot for work and so couldn't find the time to exercise. I'm not really one for working out at the gym or jogging. Then I changed my job and a lot of my colleagues played touch rugby and they invited me along.

P: And you, Angie?

A: I was looking for something my husband and I could do together, I suppose. I've tried a lot of sports in my time – everything from aerobics to windsurfing – and he's really sporty too, but we never did any of these activities together. So, we both joined up at our local club and we've been enjoying the game for the last eighteen months or so.

P: Very interesting to hear about that, thanks to you both.

Check out our website for more information on touch rugby. Sounds like a fun thing to do. Now over to Jilly for ...

🎧 **5.2**

1

You can play in men's, women's and mixed teams.

2

It's similar to rugby but without the tackling ...

3

We get people of all shapes, sizes, and ages.

4

It's so simple that after two to three games you get the basic skills.

5

It's up to you to keep playing and develop your game.

🎧 **6.1**

1

L = Lisa, P = Phil, M = Man

L: Phil, where on earth are we?

P: Don't worry. I'm sure it's just over there. I remember seeing that group of trees. ... Yes, this is it ...

M: What are you doing? We're trying to sleep!

P: Oops, sorry!

L: We're lost, aren't we? And I'm so tired. I need my sleeping bag.

P: I know, Lisa. I need mine too, but everything looks the same at this time of night.

L: I can't stand this anymore. I'm covered in mud. I'm going to sleep in the car.

P: No need!

L: Shhh!

P: Sorry, no need. It's over there. I can see my shorts hanging on the rope.

L: Oh, thank heavens for that.

2

P = Presenter, E = Eddie, C = Claire

P: Right, Claire, Eddie. After three, open your eyes. One, two, three. Surprise! We've given this boring old cottage a bright new makeover. ... OK starting in here, we've had the original fireplace taken out and a new gas fire put in. And we've had new lighting installed, so it's much more modern.

E / C: What? Why?

P: And our very own Leonardo da Vinci, decorator Mike, has painted a lovely mural on the wall. Look, it shows the view out of your kitchen window.

E: Why do we need to have the view *in*side the house?

P: Oh, it's just a design feature.

C: And what have you done with our lovely wooden floors? They're all different colours.

P: Well spotted! Yes, the floor of each room has been painted so we have green, blue, red ...

C: Stop, stop, I can't stand it. You've ruined our home. Eddie, we're going to have to change it all back.

P: So, a few small changes maybe needed here for Eddie and Claire. That's it from 'Home is where the heart is'. Join us again next week when we'll be …

3

H = Helen, M = Magda

H: Hi Magda, have you just finished your shift?

M: Oh, hi, Helen. No, not yet. It's been really hard work today. It's taken me an hour and a half to do just one room.

H: Sorry to hear that. Had the guests left the rooms in a bit of a mess?

M: You could say that. It looked like the couple in room 129 had had a huge party. There were bottles and glasses everywhere. And half-eaten food from room service. Half of it was trodden into the carpet.

H: Oh what a nightmare. Considering that this is a five-star hotel, we get some very demanding guests.

M: Well, money doesn't buy you good manners, I suppose.

H: You're right there, Madga! Listen, go and have a break now. I'll ask Gita to come and help you with the rest of your rooms.

M: Thanks, Helen. That's great.

⬤ 6.2

/eɪ/

/ɪə/

/aɪ/

/ɔɪ/

⬤ 6.3

1 boy, nowadays, spoilt, employment
2 site, fixed, quite, height
3 liar, weird, idea, beer
4 leader, self-catering, breakdown, training

⬤ 7.1

E = Eddie, J = Jan

E: Hey, Jan, did you hear about that guy who thinks he's found a new type of cloud?

J: A new type of what?

E: Cloud. You know, those things that are up in the sky. They're usually black and full of rain in this country.

J: OK, no need to be sarcastic.

E: Sorry. I just thought it was really interesting. Apparently, this guy – can't remember his name now – was sent photos from around the world showing these clouds in really weird shapes. They're not like anything people had really seen before.

J: Eddie, are you winding me up? It's not April Fools' Day, is it?

E: No, look, I'll show you on my laptop. Here it is, Gavin Pretor-Pinney – that's him. He set up the Cloud Appreciation Society.

J: No way! You're kidding. … Let me see that. Wow! You're right. Those photos are amazing. They look like they've been created on a computer. In this one, it looks like there's a huge storm about to break. Look at all those dark shapes.

E: Apparently, they aren't necessarily storm clouds. Sometimes they just break up without actually turning into a storm.

J: Really? Look, this one's a bit like the surface of the sea when it's really rough and choppy.

E: I know. In fact, that cloud guy is suggesting they call the new formation 'asperatus', which is Latin for 'rough'.

J: Wow, you've really got in to this, haven't you? So, who is this cloud guy? Click on that link to his society. I've never heard of it before.

E: OK, 'Cloud Appreciation Society' … hmmm … Seems like he's set it up just because he enjoys looking at clouds. He just loves the beauty and the variety.

J: Well, as hobbies go, it's quite unusual but people must be interested if he's set up a society. So, what happens now with this new cloud?

E: I'm not sure. Let's have a look … erm … well, apparently the Royal Meteorological Society is collecting evidence of the weather patterns that produce asperatus clouds.

J: Right. *Who would've thought a cloud could create so much interest?* It's incredible.

E: I know, really amazing. You were a bit sceptical at first but I'm glad you've found it interesting. I showed the pictures to my family but it left them cold.

J: Ah, well. You can't please everyone.

⬤ 7.2

1

A new type of what?

2

Eddie, are you winding me up? It's not April Fools' Day, is it?

3

No way! You're kidding. … Let me see that.

4

Wow! You're right. Those photos are amazing.

5

Wow, you've really got in to this, haven't you?

6

Who would've thought a cloud could create so much interest?

⬤ 8.1

M = Marcus, V = Victoria

Part 1

M: Good afternoon and welcome to Bookmark, our weekly look at the world of books and literature. Today we have a special feature on that perennial favourite of many of our listeners – crime fiction. The genre has moved from quite humble beginnings to a multi-million pound industry. Gone are the days when to write about crime was to be a second-class author and reading crime fiction was seen as something less than challenging. Our special guest is Victoria Marshall, director of Black Orchid Publishers, who specialise in crime fiction. Victoria, welcome.

Part 2

V: Thank you, Marcus. Great to be here.

M: So, Victoria, just how popular is crime fiction today?

V: Well the latest figures show that crime books and thrillers represent 59% of the general fiction market – that's a staggering 22 million books.

M: Wow! That's a lot more than I would've guessed. Is that why you decided to set up a publishing house just for the crime genre?

V: Well, in fact, we didn't. Initially, we were a general fiction publisher who did a bit of everything really – you know romance, science fiction, even horror and ghost stories. But it was clear in the first few years that the crime writers were by far the most successful. So, slowly but surely we started to focus on just crime and detective stories. And it's paid off. Two of our authors, Leo Hunt and Belinda Warraner, have won the coveted 'Page-turner of the Year' award, so that has helped to put us on the publishing map.

M: It sounds like it was a good move. But what actually is it about crime fiction that we love so much? Why do people continue to buy books year in, year out?

V: Of course some people enjoy being scared, in a kind of 'safe' way. But the one thing all readers *love* is a good plot. It's the aspect of having a puzzle to solve that gets people coming back time and time again. Even if a reader has a favourite detective like Hercule Poirot or Inspector Rebus, a plot that is full of twists and turns will keep them turning the pages and picking up the next novel in the series.

M: So, crime fans are among the most dedicated, then?

V: Yes, I would say so. Another important thing, of course, is the sheer variety of characters, settings and plots. I had a quick look at some of the newly-published titles and they are literally set in countries all over the world – from green and leafy cities like Oxford and Edinburgh, to the sultry and gritty streets of Havana, even rural parts of Scandinavia. The genre is also very diverse in terms of timing of the plots – we're all familiar with Agatha Christie's portrayal of England in the 1920s, but crime novels can take you much further back in time – to Renaissance Italy, 11th-century Japan, Ancient Rome, even Ancient Egypt.

M: Amazing. But would you say there's a gender split in the readership? I mean do more men read – or write – crime fiction?

V: Mmm, well I don't have any up-to-date figures on the readership but I'd say that the genre has something for everyone. There was a time when it was thought of as more of a male area of interest, but there are plenty of female writers, *and* readers of course.

M: And is the debate still on as to who makes better crime writers, men or women?

V: Oh, that one will never go away. As a publisher, it's our job to encourage talent wherever it comes from, so I don't tend to worry too much about the gender side of things. A good story is a good story, after all.

M: Very diplomatically put! ... Well, thanks, Victoria, great to see you. And you can go to our website for a list of Victoria's all-time top 10. See if you agree with her choice and let us know about ...

🔊 8.2

/eɪ/

/əʊ/

/eə/

/ʊə/

🔊 8.3

1 know, crown, thousand, surround
2 although, promote, court, throat
3 plural, tour, cure, sour
4 dreadful, wear, millionaire, prayer

🔊 9.1

A = Alice, M = Martine, G = Greg, W = Wendy

A: Hello and welcome to Education Matters. A look at the packed schoolbag of the average teenager will tell you that the national curriculum is crammed with different subjects. There is often talk of streamlining the number of subjects, so let's get some opinions from those who attend school every day ... but we're not asking the students, this time it's the teachers' turn. So, Martine, Greg and Wendy, all teachers at a local secondary school, which two subjects would you cut? Martine, let's start with you.

M: I think PE and RE.

A: So that's physical education and religious education.

M: Sorry, yes. I think sport is best done in after-school clubs – the sporty students can choose what they like best and become good at it. And I think religious education is best left to the family. It shouldn't have anything to do with state education, like the system we have in France.

G: I agree about cutting RE but not PE. A lot of our kids are already pretty unfit. For some of them, an hour's PE is the only exercise they get. And it teaches them about winning and losing. I think it can also help with behaviour problems – you know, doing something active gets rid of excess energy and just breaks up the day.

A: So, Greg, which subjects would get your vote?

G: As I said, I agree with Martine about RE – if students want to find out about a religion, they can do so outside school. Erm, my other choice would be ICT, that's Information and Communications Technology.

A: Wow! That's a mouthful – basically computer studies, yeah?

G: More or less, yes. My feeling is that there's no need to teach it as a separate subject. In a well-equipped school, ICT should be part of every lesson. And most kids have computers at home and are pretty proficient at using them anyway.

W: Can I come in here?

A: Wendy, you've been waiting patiently ...

W: Yeah, I have to say I'm not with Greg on ICT. There's more to computers than just playing games or chatting on MSN and that's what kids use their home computers for. Wide-ranging computer skills are essential for our future economy.

G: I'm not saying that we shouldn't teach computer skills, I mean we should integrate them across other subjects.

W: I just don't see it that way. It's too important not to cover properly in the syllabus.

A: So, Wendy, what *would* you lose from the current list of subjects?

W: Personal, Social and Health Education, PSHE for short, and – sorry Martine – modern foreign languages

M: But learning a language is …

A: Just a second, Martine. Let Wendy have her say and we'll come back to you.

W: I just think that a lot of time is dedicated to foreign languages and quite a lot of students still struggle to come up with one or two sentences. I'm not saying get rid of languages altogether, but just make them optional so that the kids who have aptitude are the ones who take them up.

M: I agree with Wendy up to a point – my job would be much easier if all my students were good at French – that's obvious, but even weaker students can make progress if they have help. And it is not just about the words. Learning a language gives students the opportunity to find out about other cultures and societies – and that's so important in today's global economy.

A: OK, we're running out of time, so your other subject, Wendy?

W: I would do away with PSHE. A lot of it can be integrated into other subjects, like covering drug and alcohol education in science lessons.

M: I'm with you on that, Wendy, It's not an essential subject in its own right.

G: Yes, I'd also agree with that. A lot of the kids think PSHE is a bit of a waste of time. We might as well cut it.

A: So, some consensus here at last. Thanks to Martine, Greg and Wendy for their opinions and …

9.2

1 I think PE and RE.
2 I'm not with Greg on ICT.
3 I would do away with PSHE.

9.3

BBC
UCLA
ATM
VAT
UN
FBI
IMF
PC
SMS
ISP

10.1

E = Emma, M = Mikel

E: Oh, what's this now? I was about to go for lunch. … Oh it's from my friend Abigail. … Let's have a look. … Oh, she's having a party. Not *another* one.

M: Don't sound so enthusiastic, Emma! I thought she was a good friend of yours.

E: She is and I don't mean to sound horrible, but there have been *so* many parties and get-togethers recently. I had my cousin's hen do last month. Well, it was more of a hen weekend, not just a few drinks out with the girls the night before the wedding. She'd booked a spa weekend in Portugal. She paid for the hotel but we had to cover our flights and all the treatments. It cost a fortune, much more than I hoped. Then we had the wedding itself, of course. And this month, I've been to six kids' parties already. *Six*!

M: Well, all kids have birthday parties.

E: Yes, I know, but it's not like the old days. You know, when you turned up, dropped the kids off and picked them up a few hours later. Modern mums like to organise an event or a function – swimming pool parties, haunted house parties – and these places are so big, it means the parents have to go along too. So you have to dress up in your party gear, make polite conversation for hours, *and* help to clear up. It's exhausting.

M: I know that some parents do go over the top!

E: Tell me about it! My sister's the same. Her husband retired so I was expecting a nice family meal in the local pub, just for the adults. But no! She booked the four-star place down by the river and invited 75 people – I didn't know they *knew* 75 people! And I wouldn't mind but my brother-in-law, Keith, hates being the centre of attention. Why organise a big party for someone who won't even enjoy it?

M: That does sound a bit silly.

E: And the next thing is my niece finishing university. Gone are the days when students celebrated down the pub when they'd got their degree. She's insisting on a fancy dress do and the whole family has to be there. And she's actually posted a list of graduation presents on her *Facebook* thing. It's getting out of hand. Soon we'll be buying people presents for getting up in the morning and turning up at work or school!

M: Now you're just being silly! Some people would love to have a busy social life like yours.

E: I know. I'm sorry. I must sound really mean. I just wish things would calm down a bit.

M: OK, let's go for lunch and get some fresh air. I can tell you about my plans for my 40th …

E: Now you're just winding me up. Please don't …

10.2

I know that some parents do go over the top.
Why organise a big party for someone who won't even enjoy it?

🔊 10.3

1

She is and I don't mean to sound horrible.

2

Modern mums like to organise an event or a function

3

It means the parents have to go along too.

4

Tell me about it!

5

She's insisting on a fancy dress do and the whole family has to be there.

6

Now you're just winding me up.

🔊 11.1

Speaker 1

I couldn't believe my eyes. I was driving along quite happily and the usual boy racers were overtaking and speeding past when I looked over to the left and saw this old man in a mobility scooter crawling along the hard shoulder. Goodness knows how he got there. I guess he must have taken a wrong turning and he ended up on the motorway by mistake. Anyway, I turned on the traffic news and they said there was a lot of congestion in the area and that the police were on the scene. The next day, I checked online and luckily there hadn't been an accident or anything. The police had managed to get to the man and pick him up before anything went wrong. He seemed really confused, apparently ... the poor guy. What really surprised me was the top speed of his scooter – only 8 miles an hour!... when everyone else was doing 70!

Speaker 2

The landing is always the worst bit of the flight for me but what made it worse was having to circle in the skies above the airport for more than half an hour. The weather was fine so we couldn't work out what the problem was. The crew tried to keep everyone calm and we eventually touched down about 45 minutes late. We asked the ground staff what had happened but we couldn't get an answer. It wasn't until we got home that we found out what the problem was. It turned out that the air traffic controller had fallen asleep! The pilot kept calling the control tower but couldn't get an answer. Can you believe it? Actually falling asleep while a pilot is trying to land a plane? Apparently, the controller was suspended from his job for not being alert during working hours.

Speaker 3

I was at home killing time and just surfing the net when I came across a funny story. I'm a bit of a train fan so it caught my eye. It was about this group of engineers who have been left with a lot of explaining to do because the tunnel they built was too small for the trains. Can you imagine the inspectors turning up and measuring the roof only to find it was too low to let any trains through!? It was in eastern Europe somewhere – can't remember exactly where – but it was in a big city. Apparently, the team that was laying the new track and the guys that were building the tunnel didn't communicate very well. The ground under the tracks had been raised and so the distance between tracks and the roof was shortened. It's bound to cost a fortune to put it all right.

Speaker 4

You hear a lot of disaster stories about people buying houses and then finding loads of problems with them, but a friend was telling me about a guy who bought a property you can only reach by helicopter! Apparently, he was a first-time buyer and he bought this old tower at auction to convert into a house. The thing he didn't realise was that the land around the house is private and there's no access - you can't drive or even walk to it from the main road. His only access is by air! What a nightmare! It seems that the house was a bit of a bargain, but the guy didn't check the legal position before he paid for it. So, now he's got a huge old tower that he can't do anything with unless he gets his own helicopter and pilot. The silly thing is the house only cost about £30,000 in the first place.

Speaker 5

I drive a lot for work so I rely on my sat nav to help me get around. I think they're brilliant gadgets. Mine has saved me from getting stuck in the middle of nowhere on more than one occasion, but the navigation is only as good as the map, so you have to update pretty regularly. And you have to have a bit of common sense. I heard about this taxi driver who followed the sat nav's instructions so fully that he ended up in a river! He had to ring his boss and ask for help and they found him still in the taxi, right in the middle of the water. Apparently, the sat nav had said 'go straight on' and so he did. It's unbelievable what some people will do. I heard that people are now calling the taxi company and asking to book river cruises!

🔊 11.2

1

He must have taken a wrong turning.
What made it worse was having to circle in the skies.

2

The air traffic controller had fallen asleep.
The usual boy racers were overtaking.

3

The pilot kept calling the control tower.
He ended up on the motorway by mistake.

4

People are asking to book river cruises.
The tunnel they built was too small for the trains.

5

The navigation is only as good as the map.
The sat nav had said 'go straight on'.

6

He's got a huge old tower.
The guys building the tunnel didn't communicate very well.

🔊 **12.1**

S = Sam, K = Kate

S: Here we go. The barbecue is getting going now.
K: Be careful, Sam, it looks like it's getting very hot.
S: Don't worry, it's fine! We've had hundreds of barbecues and I've never burnt myself, have I?
K: No, I know. It just makes me a bit nervous.
S: Kate, relax, it's all under control. I'm going to head in and finish preparing the food.
K: You will wash your hands, won't you? We don't want anyone getting an upset stomach.
S: Yes, of course, I will. Why don't you go and get changed and leave the food to me?
K: OK, I think I'll just take a painkiller. I'm getting a bit of a headache.
S: Oh, dear. You'll be OK for the party, won't you?
K Yes, I should be fine.
S: A-choo!
K: Sam, you're not getting a cold, are you? I've got a new herbal remedy you can try. Let me go and …
S: Don't worry, I'm fine. It's just this pepper I'm using – it went up my nose.
K: Oh, OK. But you look a bit hot. Are you sure you feel OK?
S: I've just been standing over the barbecue, that's all. I feel fine. People will be here soon, so why don't you open some wine? You can pour me a glass if you like.
K: You're not going to drink too much tonight, are you?
S: No, of course not! I've got loads of food to barbecue and my new boss is coming tonight.
K: Your boss …??!
S: Yeah, you haven't forgotten, have you?
K: Erm, well, it did slip my mind! I wish you'd reminded me, Sam. I'd have given the house a really good clean.
S: Kate, our house is spotless. No bacteria could survive anywhere in our place. … Ooops! … Chuck me that piece of cheese, Kate. Waste not, want not.
K: You're not going to eat it, are you!? It's been on the floor.
S: Well, it won't kill me, will it? A few germs never hurt anyone.
K: Well, don't complain to me if you start throwing up later. … Oh, the guests are arriving. I'll go and let them in.
S: Thanks, darling. … Thank goodness for that.

🔊 **12.2**

1

We've had hundreds of barbecues and I've never burnt myself, have I?

2

You will wash your hands, won't you?

3

You'll be OK for the party, won't you?

4

Sam, you're not getting a cold, are you?

5

You're not going to drink too much tonight, are you?

6

Yeah, you haven't forgotten, have you?

7

You're not going to eat it, are you?

8

Well, it won't kill me, will it?

🔊 **13.1**

J = James, E = Emily

J: Er, hello. I don't think we've met. I'm James Burford.
E: Emily Walker. Nice to meet you.
J: Yes, you too. … I thought it was a lovely service, didn't you? And wonderful to see all these people here.
E: Yes, Helen was obviously very well thought of.
J: Yes, everyone loved her here in the village. She was such a character. Did you know her well?
E: Actually, she was my great aunt but I hadn't been in touch for years. I can't say we were very close but I wanted to pay my respects. I'm now wondering where all these people have come from. She never married or had children so it's a bit of a surprise.
J: Well, those ladies over there are from her writing group. She set it up last year. But I knew her from long before that, when she taught me French.
E: Aunt Helen spoke French?
J: Yes, she was head of French at my school. She joined the school when she came back from Africa.
E: Er, what was she doing in Africa?
J: As far as I know, she was volunteering in Senegal. After she graduated, she wanted to travel and she ended up there. She set up a teaching programme with local teachers.
E: This is amazing. Why didn't anyone ever tell me?
J: … So I guess you don't know about Helen's environmental campaign either?
E: No! What was that?
J: Now, let me get this right. … She retired from my old school about five years ago and found herself at a loose end and so she started touring the area on her old bike. She was disgusted at the amount of damage to the local environment and so she set about putting it right. I was told she won an award from the local council.
E: This is such a revelation. I'd imagined Helen as an elderly lady living out her retirement in a quiet English village.
J: Oh, no, not Helen. Apparently, she's always 'done things different', so to speak. Did you know about the student strike she led at university?

E: I knew she was the first female in her family to go to university and that education was very important to her. But what's this about a strike?

J: Well, she decided that the tuition that the female students were getting wasn't as good as the males, and so she and hundreds of other girls went on strike. Unsurprisingly, things got better quite quickly.

E: I had no idea she'd had such an interesting life. She sounds amazing. But I'm a bit sad now. I wish that I'd seen her more often. There are lots of questions I'd like to ask.

J: Well, it's difficult to stay in touch sometimes. But you'll be glad to hear that she's written her life story. It isn't published yet but she's left that with me to organise.

E: Really? That's fantastic. I'm sure it'll be a fascinating read.

🔊 13.2

1

I wish that I'd seen her more often.
No, what was that?

2

I'm now wondering where all these people have come from?
Those ladies over there are from her writing group.

3

Nice to meet you.
Did you know about the student strike?

4

There are lots of questions I'd like to ask.
She ended up there.

5

Education was very important to her.
But I knew her from long before that.

6

Helen was obviously very well thought of.
She was head of French at my school.

🔊 14.1

1

C1 = Customer, C2 = Cashier

C1: Why are things taking so long? I've been trying to pay for over half an hour.

C2: So sorry to have kept you waiting. We're having problems with the computers.

C1: Does that mean I can't pay by credit card?

C2: I'm afraid so. It's cash only at the moment.

C1: What about a cheque?

C2: I'm afraid we don't take cheques anymore.

C1: Well, that's great! I haven't got any cash on me, so I'll have to leave it.

2

K = Kelly, M = Marcus

K: Did Eric tell you he'd applied for a mortgage?

M: You're joking! He's already up to his eyes in debt.

K: Not any more. His parents found his bank statement and went through the roof.

M: What do you mean?

K: They saw how big his overdraft was and so they paid the whole lot off.

M: Oh, it's OK for some. You and I have to pay our own way.

K: No, no, it's only a loan. Eric will have to pay them every penny back.

M: Oh, well, I suppose it makes sense not to have to pay interest to the bank.

3

Join us on November 28th for Buy Nothing Day. Anyone planning to go shopping then, do yourself a favour and have a day off from the things you really *don't* need. All those clothes that will hang in your closet for months unworn. Why not enjoy a whole 24 hours of freedom from shops? Come on, support our campaign and say no to consumerism and the effects of globalisation. Buy nothing for just one day on November 28th.

4

M = Millie, F = Frank

M: You should have seen me on Saturday night, Frank, I was on the edge of my seat.

F: Why, what happened?

M: I was checking the lottery tickets and I thought I'd got the big one. I was about to go out and buy some champagne.

F: So ... did you win?

M: No, I was looking at the wrong ticket.

F: What, not even a small prize?

M: Not even a tenner. And the jackpot was over five million. Just imagine.

F: Oh.

5

What a nightmare! I checked my account online and found loads of purchases I hadn't made. Someone must have got hold of my card details and bought tons of stuff. I went straight to the bank to sort it out and they made me feel a bit like a criminal, like I was the one who'd been on a spending spree. Of course, I'm hugely overdrawn now and on top of that there are £50 worth of bank charges. It makes me feel like closing my account altogether.

🔊 14.2

1

I've been trying to pay for over half an hour.

2

Did Eric tell you he'd applied for a mortgage?

3

He's already up to his eyes in debt.

4

They paid the whole lot off.

5

Come on, support our campaign.

6

I was looking at the wrong ticket.

7

I went straight to the bank to sort it out.

🔊 **15.1**

P = Presenter, G = Gina, A = Amy, L = Lisa, B = Brian, B2 = Bella, F = Frank, D = Darren

P: And now for our regular feature 'Food heaven, food hell'. Today our roving reporter, Gina Eriksson, is on the streets of Brighton to ask people what gets their tastebuds tingling, and what attacks their appetite. Over to Gina …

G: Yes, I'm here in The Lanes, Brighton's famous shopping and eating area. So let's see what the locals have to say … Excuse me, can I just ask – What's your idea of food heaven and food hell?

A: My food heaven is anything veggie – salads, stir fries, anything without meat, really. But food hell has to be tofu. Although people think it's great for vegetarians, I think it's soggy and bland.

G: And what about you?

L: Er, for me, food heaven is a really gooey chocolate cake – my mum has a brilliant recipe. And food hell is fish. I just can't stand to see a whole fish with its head on looking up at me. Yuck!

G: OK, thanks, ladies. And you, sir? Food heaven and hell – any thoughts?

B: Well, as you can probably hear, I'm from the US, so I'd have to say the good old American burger and fries are my food heaven. And food hell, sorry to say this, is English tea. How come you guys drink so much of the stuff?

G: It's a great British tradition. You can't beat a cup of tea. Thank you and enjoy your stay in the UK. … Now, there's a group of people sitting at a street café. Ladies and gents, do you mind if I ask about your food heaven and hell? This lady here, what would you say?

B2: Food heaven, let me think … oh, there's nothing better than English strawberries and cream, but only in season. I don't understand people who buy summer fruits at Christmas.

G: I'd agree with you there, and your food hell?

B2: Garlic. I just can't get on with it. No matter how little people put in, I can taste it. My children just think I'm old-fashioned, but it's not for me.

G: That's fair enough. And you, sir?

F: Well, I'm just the opposite of my wife here. I love a good curry and rice. The hotter, the better. I got the taste for spicy food when I was in the army. A group of old mates and I meet up for curry about once a month. And I don't really have a food hell. I'll eat pretty much anything.

G: Wonderful that you can agree to differ on your tastes. … And a group of schoolkids here. Let's have a chat with them. … Excuse me, what's your name?

D: Darren.

G: Hi, Darren. Can you tell us about your ideas of food heaven and hell?

D: Well, my favourite thing is meatballs and spaghetti in tomato sauce. I cook it every week. But the one thing I *hate* is cauliflower. I like lots of other vegetables but my mum keeps trying to get me to eat cauliflower. It's disgusting.

G: Sounds like we have a budding chef here in Darren. Let's hope he keeps it up. That's it from me and the people here in Brighton. Thanks to all of them for their ideas on food heaven and hell.

🔊 **15.2**

1

What's your idea of food heaven and food hell?

2

So I'd have to say the good old American burger and fries

3

My children just think I'm old-fashioned, but it's not for me.

4

I got the taste for spicy food when I was in the army

5

My favourite thing is meatballs and spaghetti in tomato sauce.

6

That's it from me and the people here in Brighton.

🔊 **16.1**

Speaker 1

Most people think that you go into business to make a fortune but for us it just wasn't like that. Don't get me wrong, it's good to make money but that wasn't our main motivation. It all started fifteen years ago when I came back to the UK with my Spanish husband after living in Seville for a few years. I found that I really missed all the wonderful food – of course I missed the people too – but getting Spanish ingredients was surprisingly hard, especially outside London. After networking online with Spanish people living in the UK, I did some market research on the availability of Spanish food over here. I found that apart from in a few specialist shops, you couldn't get stuff like good chorizo, saffron, or proper paella rice for love nor money. So, I thought 'why not set up a Spanish food business online?' and that's just what we've done. We've just redesigned our first fairly rudimentary website, and things are going from strength to strength.

Speaker 2

Some people thought I was mad when I left my job. I'd worked my way up from junior designer to creative director in a well-known advertising company and I suppose you could say I'd been very successful. But the higher I moved up the company, the more stressful it became. I spent more time travelling on planes than I did with my kids. Then while I was catching up on paperwork on a flight, I started thinking about the creative side of the job. I picked up a pen and started doodling on my paper napkin. Before I knew it, I'd done about 50 different designs and I suddenly realised that I didn't want to be a director any more but a designer. So, after persuading my wife this was the right thing to do, I resigned from my job and set up my own design agency – just me and two other talented youngsters. Sure, I don't earn half as much as I used to but I really enjoy working for myself.

Speaker 3
I had always sworn that I would never do it. I come from a long line of farmers but I was completely adamant about working in a different sector. My great-grandparents bought and developed the land in the 1920s and it's been passed down across the generations. While my older brother and sister took an avid interest in the animals and farm work, I ran off to college as soon as I could. After I graduated in medicine, I chose to work as a GP at an inner-city surgery as I wanted to keep as far away from the farm as I could. Then things started to get very tough for farmers. I saw my parents age from the work and responsibility and I felt bad about leaving all the admin to my brother and sister. So, eventually I took early retirement, moved back to the old farmhouse and I've taken on some of the behind-the-scenes work. I'll never be a country girl at heart but, you know what they say, blood's thicker than water.

Speaker 4
I suppose you could say I fell into business. I didn't do particularly well at school and so ended up doing nine-to-five or just temporary work. It wasn't very stimulating but I didn't mind too much because I never had to work late or give up my weekends. I'd always been interested in fashion and was pretty good at designing and making my own clothes. Then my friends starting asking me to make things for them. I did this as a favour or gave them away as presents. Then one day a group of friends and I were out in town, wearing some of my designs. I couldn't believe it when this guy walked up and asked where we'd bought them. I explained that they were all hand designed and the next thing I knew he was offering to help me set up a small business. It turned out he ran an enterprise scheme for young clothes designers. He helped me find a workshop, get funding for equipment and materials, and now the orders are rolling in.

Speaker 5
I never expected to have a career in business, let alone be running my own company. It all started when I was teaching English as a foreign language in Berlin. A friend of a friend asked me to do some one-to-one classes with a businesswoman who wanted help with presentation skills. She had such a busy schedule that we met at very odd hours of the day – 5.30 in the morning before she went to work, or late in the evening when she'd finished. I ended up getting quite a can-do attitude because I was willing to give classes anytime and anywhere, within reason. Most of the other language schools and tutors weren't available much outside general working hours, which wasn't much use to people with a packed schedule. Word spread and then a few colleagues and

I went freelance and set up a network of tutors. Five years later here I am with an agency of language teachers in 20 different cities, all of whom cater their timetable and tuition to the exact needs of the client.

🎧 **16.2**
1
Why not set up a Spanish food business online?

2
We've just redesigned our first fairly rudimentary website.

3
I spent more time travelling on planes.

4
I'd done about 50 different designs.

5
My older brother and sister took an avid interest in the animals.

6
After I graduated in medicine, I chose to work as a GP.

7
Eventually I took early retirement.

8
I ended up doing nine-to-five or just temporary work.

9
We worked late in the evening when she'd finished.

ANSWER KEY

UNIT 1

GRAMMAR Habits

A
1 e   2 f   3 a   4 b   5 d   6 c

B
1 As **a** rule, I go out once a week, usually on Saturday evenings.
2 I don't read for pleasure as much as I **would** like to.
3 I tend **to** see my family just on birthdays and at Christmas.
4 We used **to** go to the cinema about once a week before they put the prices up.
5 Why **are** you always sitting in front of that computer? Go outside and get some fresh air.
6 She must be really busy. She **hardly** ever comes to the badminton club anymore.
7 I enjoy going to the theatre but we only go once **in** a while.
8 We used to go walking every weekend. We **would** get up early and be out on the hills to see the sunrise.

VOCABULARY Describing films, music and books

A
1 uplifting   2 gripping
3 awful   4 over-the-top
5 commercial

B
1 hilarious   2 dull
3 disturbing   4 weird
5 catchy

DEVELOPING CONVERSATIONS Disagreeing politely

2 Really? It didn't do anything for me, I'm afraid.
3 Er, I'm not that keen on jazz.
4 Thanks, but I'm not very keen on musicals. I prefer something a bit more serious, more realistic.
5 To be honest, I'm not really interested in fiction.
6 Really? I'm not that fond of action movies.

LISTENING

1 b   2 c   3 a   4 c   5 b   6 b

PRONUNCIATION Strong and weak forms

A
1
I wish they wouldn't do th__a__t! /æ/
I just think th__a__t they should be true to the original story. /ə/
2
People used t__o__ go out to have fun. /ə/
People don't socialise like they used t__o__. /uː/
3
You used t__o__ be a really keen theatre-goer. /ə/
Not as much as I'd like t__o__. /uː/
4
It's the teenagers I feel sorry f__or__. /ɔː/
I mean, there really isn't much f__or__ them to do. /ə/
5
I'm not asking you, I'm telling y__ou__! /uː/
I don't want y__ou__ to watch any more TV. /ə/

B
When the function word is at the end of the sentence the pronunciation is usually strong.
When the function word is at the beginning of the sentence the pronunciation is usually weak.

VOCABULARY Talking about pictures

A
1 interpretation   2 atmospheric
3 dramatic   4 dated
5 ambiguous

B
1 abstract   2 life-like
3 sombre   4 intimate
5 pretty

C
1 d   2 g   3 c   4 f   5 b   6 h
7 a   8 e

GRAMMAR Adjectives and adverbs

A
1 correct
2 She said it was an absolute**ly** dreadful film.
3 If you arrive late~~ly~~ for work again, you'll be in real trouble.
4 Don't forget to check your work really careful**ly**.
5 She looks very sad~~ly~~. Do you think she's been crying?
6 Funn**ily** enough, I was thinking exactly the same thing.
7 correct
8 It's important to read the instructions **carefully**.

B
1 badly injured   2 completely rebuilt
3 terribly sad   4 absolutely amazing
5 wrongly arrested   6 unusually chilly

DEVELOPING WRITING
A review – making recommendations

A
Quest – the next big thing? / Triumphant return of Quest

B
Quest – the next big thing?

C
1 expertise   2 singing along
3 worth   4 downside
5 following   6 encores

D
1 b   2 d   3 a   4 f   5 e   6 c

E
Student's own answers.

READING

A
c

B
1 e   2 b   3 h   4 a   5 g   6 c   7 f

C

5 who benefits from Secret
4 the overall role of Secret
1 how Secret works
3 who made a good investment from Secret
2 who has taken part

D

1 heard
2 snap
3 viewing
4 captured
5 auction
6 raise

VOCABULARY BUILDER QUIZ 1

A

1 dull
2 sombre
3 ambiguous
4 disturbing
5 gripping
6 hilarious
7 initial

B

1 feature
2 disguise
3 revenge
4 despair

C

1 accidental
2 controversial
3 global
4 commercial
5 behavioural
6 exceptional
7 conventional

D

1 I can't **be** bothered to cook tonight.
2 The message in the poem is open **to** interpretation.
3 He **was** corrupted by mixing with older gang members.
4 The roles of hero and villain **have/had** been reversed.
5 The police accused **him** of burglary but he denied it.
6 Do you think they will get away **with** the robbery?
7 His reasons for leaving struck me **as** odd.

UNIT 2

VOCABULARY Buildings and areas

A

1 up-and-coming   trendy
2 historic   grand
3 rough   run-down
4 affluent   stunning
5 deprived   residential
6 high-rise   hideous

B

1 A: dominates
   B: dates back   has been renovated
2 A: to steer clear
   B: knocked down   have soared
3 B: were based
   A: have opened up

GRAMMAR Non-defining relative clauses

A

1 We'd walked round the same streets five times, at which point I decided it was time to buy a map.
2 The local people, who had at first appeared rather unfriendly, couldn't do enough for us.
3 Our hotel turned out to be in a pretty rundown part of town, which really spoilt the trip.
4 Most of the old town, where my parents had lived for many years, had been knocked down and completely rebuilt.

5 We booked several day trips to the surrounding areas, all of which were really good value for money.
6 The first day of the festival, when everyone dresses up in amazing costumes, is the one not to miss.

B

2 The tour didn't finish until 10 p.m., by which time we had missed dinner. B
3 We spent a week exploring the coastline, which was completely amazing. A
4 We couldn't have managed in Beijing without Nicola, who had done a course in Mandarin Chinese. C
5 My old boss gave us a lot of travel tips about Cape Town, where his family is from. D
6 We spent ages planning to visit different vineyards, none of which were open when we actually got there. F

DEVELOPING CONVERSATIONS
Agreeing, using synonyms

A

1 e   2 a   3 g   4 b   5 c   6 f
7 h   8 d

B

2 Yes, it's quite trendy.
3 I agree. It's awful.
4 I know. It's a really run-down area.
5 You're right. It's strange.
6 Yes, it's beautiful, isn't it?
7 Yes, they're wonderful old buildings.
8 Yes, it does look very wealthy.

LISTENING

A

the annual parade
the street market
old Merchant's House

B

1 the street market
2 old Merchant's House
3 the annual parade

PRONUNCIATION Connected speech

B

2 The city museum has_one_of the best collections_of modern_and_abstract_art_in the country.
3 It's not the kind_of place you can see in just_a short time.
4 Take_a trip_into the past_and soak_up the atmosphere_at the street market.
5 So, we spend the morning_at the market_and we end_up_at the parade.
6 We need to be up there for the parade_anyway.

VOCABULARY Festivals and carnivals

A

2 i   3 a and f   4 h   5 j

B

2 light
3 play
4 record
5 look
6 carry local
7 forbid
8 sit
9 get dressed
10 spray

Reading

A

1 f   2 b   3 e   4 a   5 d   6 c

B

2, 3, 6, 7

C

1 go   2 all
3 thing   4 odd
5 takes   6 treat

Grammar The future

A

2 do you do
3 bound to
4 We check out
5 do we meet
6 plans to start
7 hoping to
8 I take

B

1 You're bound to get the job.
2 When's your train due?
3 I might see you at the party.
4 We plan to take on / on taking on more staff next year.
5 I am dreading my next exam.
6 House prices are expected to fall in the next six months. / They expect house prices to fall in the next six months.

Developing writing An email – making a request

A

b

B

Hi Kati,
<u>How are things?</u> I hope all the family are doing <u>OK</u>.
I wanted to drop you a quick line to ask you a favour. As you know, <u>I'm finishing uni</u> at the end of this term and <u>I'm</u> going to do some travelling with a friend over the summer. We<u>'re</u> planning to visit Hungary and I was wondering if I could ask you for some local <u>info</u>. We <u>won't</u> have a huge amount of spending money so <u>can you recommend any bargain hotels and places to eat in Budapest?</u> Also, <u>when would be the best time to visit in terms of the weather and things to do?</u> Apart from the capital, <u>where would you recommend we go? A friend of mine suggested Lake Balaton. Do you think it's worth a visit?</u> Any advice you can give us on transport, sightseeing and local customs would be very welcome.
I'm really <u>looking forward</u> to the trip but I've got to <u>get through</u> my finals first! There's no rush for a reply as I know you're really busy, too. <u>Just get back to me when you can.</u>

1 Cheers
2 OK
3 drop you a quick line
4 There's no rush

C

1 put us up   2 picking me up
3 get around   4 book up
5 eat out   6 drop off
7 put on   8 hang out

D

Student's own answers.

Vocabulary builder Quiz 2

A

1 up-and-coming
2 upload
3 knocked down
4 leading up
5 upside down.
6 run-down.

B

1 glimpsed   2 hideous
3 showered with   4 race
5 dreading   6 steeply

C

a, c, d, f, h

D

1 e**r**ect   2 gran**d**
3 **t**ombs   4 bur**st**
5 **d**rought   6 spi**n**
7 stra**pp**ed   8 **t**ame.

UNIT 3

Vocabulary Useful things

A

2 needle and thread
3 bandage, plaster/band aid
4 dustpan and brush
5 ladder
6 charger
7 glue, sticky tape
8 cloth, mop and bucket

B

A pegs, washing powder
B iron, scissors, string
C an adapter
C hammer, nails.
A tin opener
D torch
A bowls
D screws
A file

Grammar so, if and to for describing purpose

A

2 I popped round to my neighbour's house to borrow her stepladder.
3 I need a plaster to cover this cut.
4 I went to the DIY store to get some paint.
5 I bought some files to organise all the papers from my course.
6 I'm looking for the dustpan and brush to sweep up this broken glass.

B

1 This cream is great **if** you need to treat a bite or sunburn.
2 I found some really nice paint **to** decorate the bedroom with.
3 Wipe up that wine quickly **so** it doesn't stain the table.
4 Here's the corkscrew **to** open the wine with.
5 The plasters are in the cupboard **if** your finger's bleeding.
6 Please turn off all appliances when leaving **in** order to conserve energy.

7 Keep the iron on low so that you don't **burn** your silk scarf.
8 Here's a needle and thread so you **can** repair the hole in your top.

DEVELOPING CONVERSATIONS Explaining and checking

A

1 A What
  A made, sort, thing
  B mean
2 A stuff, like
  B What, use
  B mean

B

1 Can't	2 something
3 do	4 enough
5 use	6 should
7 happen.	8 it'll

LISTENING

Speaker 1 e
Speaker 2 b
Speaker 3 f
Speaker 4 d
Speaker 5 c

PRONUNCIATION Intonation and lists

B

1 They think they really must have that bigger house, the latest mobile phone, a designer top, or some luxury food.

2 We all only really need somewhere to live, food and water, basic health and hygiene products, and clothes for different situations.

3 I remember in one weekend I bought six pairs of trousers, eight shirts, around 20 CDs and a new mobile phone.

4 In fact, just yesterday I bought a bag, a pair of sandals, a pair of jeans and two white shirts.

5 It didn't matter if it was in a shop window, in a magazine or catalogue, on a website, or even in an auction.

6 Our economy would suffer, workers in the developing world would lose their jobs, and life would be very dull.

VOCABULARY Word families

A

1 optimism	2 cautious
3 pessimistic	4 fears
5 criticise	6 economical
7 abilities	8 happiness

Student's own answers.

B

1 harmless	2 obsession
3 achievements	4 intentions
5 eviction	6 homeless
7 advertise	8 rainy
9 mysterious	

READING

A

c to highlight the amount of consumer choice

B

1 f   2 f   3 t   4 f   5 t   6 t
7 f   8 f

C

1 styles of jeans
2 flavours of jam
3 products
4 hits to an internet search
5 jams to choose from
6 time to pick a sofa in IKEA

D

1 popped	2 range
3 choose between	4 overwhelming
5 got round to	6 dissatisfied
7 choice	8 missed out on

GRAMMAR Indirect questions and statements

A

1 I was wondering if I could take some time off next week.
2 Do you think I could I speak to the chef?
3 Would you happen to know if this train stops at Middleton?
4 Do you know when you will get any more of these jeans in?
5 I was wondering if I could ask the pharmacist for some advice.
6 Do you have any idea whether all the planes from Paris land at this terminal?
7 Do you happen to know how long the film lasts?
8 Do you know which aisle the nails and screws are in?

B

1 I can't remember **if/whether** the shop open**s** on Sundays.
2 I don't understand what **you are** saying.
3 I don't know how long ~~does~~ the guarantee last**s**.
4 I wonder what he was so upset **about**.
5 I can't remember where **we are** supposed to meet.
6 I wonder where **they are** living now.

VOCABULARY Problems with things

A

1	funny	f
2	allergic	c
3	part	i
4	screen	a
5	ripped	b
6	outfit	g
7	scratched	d
8	flash	e
9	cracked	j
10	strap	h

DEVELOPING WRITING An anecdote – complaining

A

c to tell a story about something that went wrong

B

1 b   2 a   3 b

C

The anecdote:
contains direct speech.   t
is addressed to a specific person.   f
includes short sentences to keep the reader interested. t
uses a fairly formal style.   f
describes how different people felt.   t
uses full forms, rather than contractions.   f

D

1 customer	2 keep
3 refund	4 waste of
5 sort out	6 wrong
7 insist on	8 fall

E

Student's own answers.

VOCABULARY BUILDER QUIZ 3

A

1 hook	2 clip
3 vase	4 wire
5 bin	6 needle

B

1 scratched	2 stain
3 pin	4 rub
5 sample	6 optimistic
7 resigned	8 good

C

1 file	2 guarantee
3 hazard	4 funny

D

1 evictions	2 cautious
3 obsessed	4 consideration
5 expectations	6 sarcastically
7 Funnily	

UNIT 4

VOCABULARY The government, economics and society

A

1 made a difference
2 recession
3 booming
4 have gone bankrupt
5 make ends meet
6 too soft on

B

1 non-existent	e
2 shot	d
3 undermine	c
4 shortage	a
5 boost	b

GRAMMAR so and such

A

2 There were so many demonstrators that the police had to close the road.
3 This area has become so run-down that no-one wants to move there.
4 The economy is doing so badly that people are struggling to make ends meet.
5 Some students are in such serious debt that it will take years to pay it off.
6 The government have wasted so much money that no-one will vote for them again.

B

1 The factory closing caused **such** lasting damage to the local economy.
2 **So** few young people vote nowadays, they are thinking of making it compulsory.
3 correct
4 There are so **few** green spaces, it's hard to find somewhere to sit and relax.
5 The parade was such **a** great success that the city decided to hold one every year.
6 correct
7 correct
8 There are **such** a lot of positive things that he's done for the city.

DEVELOPING CONVERSATIONS
Responding to complaints

A

1 e   2 g   3 a   4 h   5 c   6 d

B

Student's own answers.

LISTENING

A

c

B

1 t   2 t   3 f   4 t   5 t   6 f   7 t
8 f

PRONUNCIATION Same sound or different?

A

1 D   2 S   3 D   4 S   5 D   6 S

VOCABULARY Social issues

A

1 school dropout rates
2 family breakdown
3 family size
4 racism
5 drug and alcohol abuse

B

1 c   2 e   3 a   4 b   5 d

READING

A

what society gets from learning about citizenship   3
what you might do in a citizenship class   4
a definition of citizenship   1
reasons for teaching citizenship   2

C

1 c   2 b   3 a   4 c   5 a

D

1 topical
2 behaviour
3 involvement
4 discussions
5 knowledge
6 politics

GRAMMAR *the ..., the ... + comparatives*

A

1 more, easier
2 simpler, successful
3 aggressive, confident
4 younger, faster
5 more, less
6 faster, more
7 more, less
8 better, popular

B

1 the sooner, the better
2 the more, the merrier
3 the faster, the better
4 the simpler, the better
5 the smaller, the better
6 the bigger, the better

DEVELOPING WRITING An essay – giving your opinion

A

The writer agrees with the statement.

B

1 this   2 not
3 who   4 Finally
5 as   6 Furthermore
7 for instance   8 In

C

1 take   2 consider
3 take part in   4 introduce
5 share   6 bring

D

Student's own answers.

VOCABULARY BUILDER QUIZ 4

A

1 e   2 f   3 a   4 b   5 c   6 d

B

1 non-ficiton
2 non-stick pan
3 non-stop flight
4 non-negotiable
5 non-profit making organisations

C

1 They're planning to cut **back** on investment in roads.
2 Why do you think their marriage broke **down**?
3 How long have the police been carrying **out** the investigation?
4 Even cooking meat goes **against** my vegetarian principles.
5 The price of oil shot **up** to $65 a barrel.

D

1 boost   2 abuse
3 claim   4 yield

E

1 is too soft   2 is stable
3 unjust   4 are aware of
5 bleak

UNIT 5

VOCABULARY Health and fitness

1 junk, healthy lifestyle
2 flexibility, strength
3 stamina, hand-eye coordination
4 demanding, sweat
5 shape, uncoordinated
6 breath, speed

DEVELOPING CONVERSATIONS Checking what you heard

2 They cost how much?
3 You didn't get home until when?
4 You'll be teaching pilates when?
5 Your parents are going where?
6 You've just heard from who?
7 It took your sister how long?
8 You ran how far?

READING

A

b

B

a Valeria
b Marcus
c Ricardo

C

1 M, R   2 M   3 M   4 V+H   5 R   6 R
7 R   8 M, V+H   9 R

D

1 a   2 b   3 a   4 a   5 b

VOCABULARY Football and life

A

1 thrashed   2 goalkeeper
3 fouled   4 off
5 dived   6 post
7 bar

B

1 promoted   2 substitute
3 disallowed   4 greedy
5 sack   6 close
7 fixed   8 tackle

GRAMMAR *shouldn't have, couldn't have, wouldn't have*

A

1 We should've scored in the first half.
2 I shouldn't have missed so many sessions.
3 They should've set off earlier.
4 I shouldn't have given up the gym.
5 We shouldn't have taken on so much work.
6 They should've apologised for swearing at the referee.

B

a 6   b 4   c 5   d 3   e 2   f 1

C

1 could've, could've
2 would've, should've
3 would've
4 wouldn't have
5 could've, could've
6 wouldn't have

DEVELOPING WRITING A report – evaluating proposals

A

passive forms
clear language and layout
headings
numbered points
fairly impersonal style

B

1 Actually	2 nor
3 purpose	4 benefit
5 allow	6 overall
7 bring	8 advantages
9 entertainment	10 attract
11 to	12 opportunities

C

1 The leisure centre will provide the city with more options
2 A state-of-the-art theatre would allow people to see a range of shows.
3 The sports centre will appeal to the majority of people.
4 A theme park is worth building.
5 Building a new library would be an improvement to the area.
6 Conferences can be held at the leisure centre.

D

Student's own answers.

GRAMMAR Present perfect continuous / simple

A

1 a   2 b   3 b   4 b   5 a   6 a

B

1 A: I didn't know you were keen on horse-riding. How long **have you been doing** that?
   B: **For** a year on and off. I'm not very good but I enjoy it. I've just **signed** up for classes at the Miller Stables.
   A: You're kidding! I've been working there part time since March.
2 A: You're into windsurfing, aren't you? I**'ve** never tried it in my life. What's it like?
   B: Amazing. I've already been ~~going~~ to the coast twice this month. Come with me next time if you like.
   A: I need to get back in shape first, I think. I've joined the gym and I've **only** lost a few kilos.
3 A: Sorry, have you **been waiting** long? My bus was late.
   B: No, don't worry. I've only **just** got here.
   A: OK, have you ever decided which film you want to see?
4 A: Where have you been? I've been trying to call you ~~for~~ all morning.
   B: Sorry, I've been at the dentist's **for** hours.
   A: Oh, are you OK?
   B: Yes, but my tooth has **been hurting** since last night.

VOCABULARY Lucky escapes

2 passed out, could've drowned
3 had a hairline fracture, could've broken it/might've broken it
4 was paralysed from the waist down, could've been killed
5 banged her head, might've knocked herself out
6 twisted my ankle, might've broken it/could've broken it

LISTENING

A

1 mixed	2 around the world
3 Australia	4 warm-up
5 space to play	6 opposition
7 stuff	8 fitness
9 stamina	10 hand-eye
11 ages	12 level
13 shape	14 her husband

PRONUNCIATION Not pronouncing sounds

A

1 You can play in men's, women's and mix**ed** teams.
2 It's similar to rugby but withou**t** the tackling.
3 We ge**t** people of all shapes, sizes, and ages.
4 It's so simple that after two to three games you ge**t** the basic skills.
5 It's up to you to kee**p** playing and develop your game.
6 I use**d** to travel a lot for work.
7 I couldn'**t** find the time to exercise.
8 I wanted something my husband and I coul**d** do together

VOCABULARY BUILDER QUIZ 5

A

1 post, others to do with sewing
2 dive, others to do with tennis
3 tackle, others are people
4 comic, others are to do with football
5 disallowed, others are physical problems

B

1 breath	2 fitness
3 shape	4 fool

C

1 self-employed	2 self-catering
3 self-taught	4 self-esteem
5 self-conscious	6 self defence

D

1 off	2 out
3 into	4 up

E

1 fai**r**	2 w**a**ndering
3 clos**e**	4 fi**x**ed
5 **s**ack	6 **d**rowning

UNIT 6

VOCABULARY Where you stayed

A

1 facilities, incredible, weather, unbearably hot
2 middle, nowhere, a bit of a dump
3 overlooked, muddy, filthy
4 stunning views, beaches, deserted
5 incredibly welcoming, whole, spotless

B

5 a   1 b   2 c   3 e   4 f

GRAMMAR Modifiers

A

1 The room was **quite** spacious, considering the price we paid.
2 I've never met him but people say he's **a bit of** a joker.
3 The main square was **absolutely** packed with tourists all weekend.
4 The tenants left **rather** a mess everywhere.
5 The food was **a bit too** spicy for my liking.
6 Rents in this area are **very** high just now.
7 The trip was a **complete** disaster from start to finish.
8 I thought the area around the flat was **quite** nice.

B

1 What's the matter? You're in a bit of **a** bad mood today.
2 There was hardly **anything** to do at the resort. The kids were really bored.
3 The place was deserted. There was **hardly** anyone staying at the hotel.
4 I'm going to be a **bit** late, but only about five minutes.
5 I'm going to send this steak back. It's **not** very nice.
6 There are hardly **any** vacancies during the summer.
7 Turn the TV down. It's a bit too **loud**.

C

2 The hotel was a bit too expensive.
3 The campsite was a bit of a nightmare.
4 The hotel room was not particularly big.
5 The food was absolutely delicious.
6 The weather was completely awful.
7 The campsite was a right dump / mess!
8 The view was really interesting.

DEVELOPING CONVERSATIONS Negative questions

1 g   2 a   3 c   4 f   5 b   6 d

LISTENING

A

1 in a field, tent
2 their own home, a TV presenter
3 a chambermaid and a manager, posh hotel

B

1 t   2 f   3 t   4 t   5 f   6 f   7 f
8 t   9 f

PRONUNCIATION Diphthongs

B

1 /aɪ/   2 /ɔɪ/
3 /eə/   4 /ɪə/

C

1 n**ow**adays   2 f**i**xed
3 l**i**ar   4 l**ea**der

GRAMMAR have / get something done

1 She's going to have to get her shoe repaired.
2 She wants get her ears pierced.
3 They're going to get a tattoo done of each other's names.
4 He needs to have central heating installed.
5 They should have had the roof checked before they bought it.
6 He's just had his motorbike stolen.

VOCABULARY Understanding idioms

1 having a whale of a time
2 in small doses
3 make ends meet
4 through rose-coloured glasses
5 costs an arm and a leg
6 finding my feet
7 taking the mickey
8 out of pocket

DEVELOPING WRITING An email – giving news

A

1 b   2 e   3 a   4 d   5 c

B

work
the journey
getting to know people
accommodation

C

1 we get on
2 feel homesick
3 hectic
4 missing
5 locals
6 broke the ice
7 it was a relief
8 find our feet

D

1 g   2 f   3 a   4 b   5 d   6 e   7 c

D

Student's own answers.

READING

A

c

B

1 f
2 t
3 t
4 f
5 doesn't say
6 f
7 t
8 doesn't say
9 t

C

where = East London
which piece = which piece of art
They = the researchers
Her = Dr Kanwal Mand
those = images
there = Bangladesh
them = the children
its = Bangladesh's
those = the people
that = Bangladesh

D

1 with   2 up
3 in   4 into
5 out

Vocabulary builder Quiz 6

A

1 N 2 P 3 P 4 N 5 N 6 P

B

1 blast   2 over
3 hook   4 itself
5 put   6 away

C

1 less   2 ed
3 over   4 y
5 un   6 trans

D

1 staggered   2 spot
3 glared   4 limped
5 strolling   6 glanced
7 rushing

UNIT 7

Vocabulary Weather and natural disasters

A

1 tsunami   b
2 forest fire a
3 tornado   b
4 famine   b
5 floods   b
6 earthquake   a
7 volcanoes   b
8 drought   b

B

1 storm, loud, lightning, soaked, out
2 froze, melt
3 mist, thick, lift
4 heat, humid, blowing, strong
5 pouring, eased, spitting, slight

Grammar Narrative tenses

A

1 watched   2 I'd never seen
3 was filmed   4 showed
5 had formed   6 hadn't realised
7 was coming   8 had worked
9 couldn't believe 10 were speeding
11 was moving   12 was
13 managed   14 died

B

1 d   2 a   3 f   4 b   5 c   6 e

Developing conversations Exaggerating

1 c   2 b   3 e   4 a   5 d   6 f

Listening

A

c

B

1 E   2 J   3 E   4 J   5 J   6 E

Grammar Participle clauses

A

1 cutting down   2 recycling
3 reached   4 becoming
5 invested   6 polluted
7 affected   8 living

B

1 going   2 built
3 created   4 living
5 invested   6 visiting

Student's own answers.

Reading

A

b

B

1 C   2 A   4 D   5 B

C

1 D   2 A   3 B   4 C   5 D   6 A
7 C   8 B

D

1 look   2 boasts
3 take   4 surrounded
5 catch   6 provide

Vocabulary Plants and trees

1 roots   2 stem
3 leaves   4 herbs
5 palm tree   6 weeds
7 seeds   8 flower
9 bushes   10 oak

Developing writing A story – using the first line

A

1 when   2 before
3 On this particular night   4 While
5 later   6 Within seconds
7 suddenly   8 just

B

1 fright   2 scared
3 death   4 panic
5 fear

C

1 f   2 d   3 c   4 e   5 b   6 a

D

1 was, appeared, started
2 had walked, realised, had remembered
3 had just settled, heard, didn't dare
4 turned, seemed, had never needed
5 fall, dawned, hadn't told
6 was strolling, heard, had ever seen
7 became, could, was going to be
8 had explored, had never experienced, would never

E

Student's own answers.

VOCABULARY BUILDER QUIZ 7

A
1 shade, others are disasters
2 melt, others are weather conditions
3 subsidy, others to do with inheriting things
4 breed, others are to do with plants
5 invasive, others are to do with plants

B
1 thunder
2 foggy
3 lightning
4 flooded
5 breeze

C
1 over
2 with
3 was deemed
4 member
5 dare
6 invaluable
7 off
8 rightful

D
1 exaggeration
2 aging/ageing
3 harassment
4 intimidation
5 resumption
6 subsidised
7 violation

UNIT 8

VOCABULARY Crimes

A
1 robberies
2 kidnapping
3 fraud
4 speeding, murder
5 bombings, riots
6 bribery

B
1
1 had set fire
2 had just gone off
3 was killed
2
1 got caught
2 've gone
3 was only doing
3
1 was held captive
2 vanished
3 'd been seized
4
1 'd never been broken into
2 'd smashed
3 hadn't stolen
5
1 never comes back
2 's found dead
3 'd been stabbed
6
1 came up to
2 'd grabbed
3 'd got hold

DEVELOPING CONVERSATIONS
Comments and questions

A
1 A: We had our car stolen last weekend.
  B: What **a** shame!
2 A: My dad has been a victim of identity theft.
  B: Oh, you**'re joking**!
3 A: We had to come back off holiday early because there were riots in the capital.
  B: You must **have** been a bit scared.
4 A: They closed the airport due to a bomb scare.
  B: That's ~~very~~ dreadful!

5 A: The band's singer was caught speeding on the motorway.
  B: That**'s** awful!
6 A: Some kids broke into the local sports centre.
  B: Oh, no~~t~~!

B
a 3   c 5   d 2   e 6   f 1   h 4

GRAMMAR Modals + present and past infinitives

A
1 can't
2 should've
3 must
4 be feeling
5 can't
6 been investigating
7 might
8 doing

B
2 You must have been shocked by the robbery.
3 He might've been at the scene of the crime.
4 You should've protected all your personal information.
5 She can't be guilty of fraud.
6 She might not be living in this area anymore.
7 There could have been a nasty accident.
8 The burglar couldn't have been more than 15 years old.

LISTENING

A
a

B
1 f   2 f   3 t   4 t   5 t   6 f   7 f

PRONUNCIATION Diphthongs

B
1 /ʊə/
2 /əʊ/
3 /aʊ/
4 /eə/

C
1 kn**ow**
2 c**ou**rt
3 s**ou**r
4 dr**ea**dful

VOCABULARY Agreeing and disagreeing

A
2 A: People who speed should lose their licence.
  B: I couldn't agree ~~with~~ more.
3 A: The council should install more cameras in public places.
  B: That's not a ~~very~~ bad idea.
4 A: He was bound to fall into a life of crime.
  B: I don't really see it like that ~~for~~ myself.
5 A: People think the crime rate is worse than it really is.
  B: I know what you ~~do~~ mean.
6 A: Demonstrators should pay towards the cost of policing their march.
  B: Well, that's ~~a~~ one way of looking at things.
7 A: I think burglary is one of the worst crimes.
  B: That's ~~a~~ complete rubbish!
8 A: Putting people in prison just doesn't work.
  B: I ~~am~~ agree with you up to a point.

GRAMMAR Nouns and prepositional phrases

A
2 focus on
3 need for
4 excuse for
5 return to
6 quality of
7 damage to
8 involvement in

B

1 a with   b for
2 a on   b in
3 a for   b of
4 a on   b of
5 a for   b with

DEVELOPING WRITING
An online forum – giving opinions

A
b

B

1 to
2 being watched.
3 about
4 would
5 truth
6 to
7 to
8 chance
9 freedom
10 done

C

1 nothing
2 research
3 far
4 lack
5 role
6 go on
7 case
8 drop

D

1 pro
2 anti
3 anti
4 anti
5 pro
6 anti
7 pro
8 pro

E
Student's own answers.

READING

A
c

B

1 Shaun Greenhalgh
2 Shaun Greenhalgh's father, George
3 expert from the British Museum
4 Shaun Greenhalgh's father, George and his mother, Olive
5 Shaun Greenhalgh
6 Shaun Greenhalgh
7 experts from the British Museum and auction house Christie's
8 Shaun Greenhalgh

C

1 conspiracy
2 defraud
3 accomplished
4 unassuming
5 forgeries
6 imprisonment
7 enquiries

VOCABULARY BUILDER QUIZ 8

A

1 burglary
2 blackmailing
3 fraudulent
4 kidnappers
5 robbery
6 suspiciously
7 appalling
8 rehabilitation

B
-**or** dictator, projector, inspector
-**er** defender, labourer, container

C

1 d   2 f   3 c   4 a   5 b   6 e

D

1 The house has been broken **into** three times in a year.
2 How long have they **been** held captive?
3 I couldn't believe I'd **gone** overdrawn by £500.
4 I've always **been** opposed to the death penalty.
5 He vowed **to** never commit a crime again.

UNIT 9
VOCABULARY Working life

A

1 got made redundant
2 've got the hang of everything
3 don't get a raise
4 're getting on-the-job training
5 haven't been promoted

B

1 g   2 e   3 f   4 b   5 c   6 a   7 d

GRAMMAR Conditionals with present tenses

A

1 If you haven't taken all your holiday by the end of the year, you **can't** carry it over.
2 Staff get promotion if they have **achieved** all the goals outlined by their line manager.
3 If employees are feeling demotivated, we **give** them on-the-job training.
4 The reps get a bonus if they ~~will~~ reach their sales targets.
5 If you ~~don't~~ miss a deadline, you lose ten per cent of your marks.
6 Students get better results if they **have** control over their work.

B

1 are you going, don't pass
2 goes, 'll be starting
3 don't get, 'll hand
4 fails, 'll have to
5 give, have
6 might look, don't get
7 comes, 'll be made
8 should report, 's been bullying

DEVELOPING CONVERSATIONS Feelings about the future

A

1 Probably not.
2 Definitely.
3 I doubt it.
4 Definitely.
5 I'm bound to

B
Student's own answers.

LISTENING

A

1 c   2 b   3 a

B

1 b   2 b   3 a   4 a   5 b   6 a

PRONUNCIATION Stress on abbreviations

A
1 I think **PE** and **RE**.
2 I'm **not** with **Greg** on **ICT**.
3 I would **do away** with **PSHE**.

B
BBC British Broadcasting Company
UCLA (The) University of California, Los Angeles
ATM Automated Teller Machine
VAT Value Added Tax
UN United Nations
FBI Federal Bureau of Investigation
IMF International Monetary Fund
PC Political Correctness/Personal Computer
SMS Short Message Service
ISP Internet Service Provider

GRAMMAR Conditionals with past tenses

A
1 give up / didn't have to
2 was made / wouldn't bother
3 'd get / pushed herself
4 didn't work / might sign up
5 had / lent
6 would make / were
7 wasn't / 'd get
8 could drop / 'd choose

B
2 If I'd been good at Music, I wouldn't have dropped it when I was 14.
3 If I'd worked for them for more than one year, I'd have got some redundancy pay.
4 If my parents had had the opportunity, they would have gone to university.
5 If I had been able to get a job in my field, I wouldn't be working in a factory.
6 If the boss had helped her, she would've got the hang of the job quickly.
7 I wouldn't have got ill if I hadn't been working really long hours.
8 I would've taken up Spanish if my school had taught modern languages.

READING

A
b

B
1 a   2 f   3 g   4 h   5 d   6 c   7 e

C
1 applicants for the job
2 contract for the job
3 cost in Australian dollars of marketing campaign
4 finalists
5 countries the finalists are from
6 species of fish that live around the island

D
adventurous   fit
articulate   bright
outgoing

E
1 e   2 f   3 c   4 d   5 a   6 b

VOCABULARY Starting presentations

A
1 tell, overview, make
2 talk to, outlining, consider
3 summarise, reviewing, highlight
4 take, commenting, focus

B
a 3   b 1   c 4   d 2

C
1 What I'm going to try and do today is tell ~~to~~ you about the best ways to look after your collection. I**'d** like to begin by showing you a short video and then after that I**'ll** move on to the main do's and don'ts.
2 What I'm going to try and do today is summarise ~~about~~ the changes in sales patterns in our new markets. I'd like to begin by reviewing ~~of~~ the main trends and then after that I'll move on to make ~~up~~ some recommendations for future growth.
3 What I'm going to try and do today is take a look~~ing~~ at the history of the car industry in the area. I'd like to begin by comment**ing** on why this area has always been synonymous with cars and then after that I'll move on to highlight ~~on~~ some of the most successful models.

DEVELOPING WRITING
A personal statement – varying sentence structure

A
c

B
a 7   b 4   c 1   d 6   e 3   f 5   g 2

C
1 c, f   2 d, i
3 e, j   4 b, h
5 a, g

D
Student's own answers.

VOCABULARY BUILDER QUIZ 9

A
1 c   2 a   3 b   4 e   5 d

B
1 drain**ing**   2 redundan**cy**
3 **mis**understood.   4 afford**ability**
5 **de**centralise   6 **re**structured

C
1 undervalue   2 underage
3 Underdeveloped   4 understaffed
5 underestimate

D
1 mind   2 role
3 influence

E
1 hand   2 merge**r**
3 **a**round   4 ran**k**
5 **st**ock   6 **t**ray

UNIT 10

VOCABULARY Birthdays

1 get-together 2 bunch
3 cosy 4 spree
5 fancy-dress 6 pretending
7 theme

GRAMMAR The future perfect

A

1 'll have made 2 'll have become
3 'll have got 4 'll have found
5 will've got 6 'll have met
7 won't have set 8 should've been

B

Student's own answers.

DEVELOPING CONVERSATIONS Arranging to meet

1 Can we make it after lunch? I'm in a meeting until midday.
2 Could we make it somewhere nearer the office? I haven't got the car with me today.
3 Any chance we can make it the following week? We won't have got back from holiday.
4 Can we make it somewhere a bit cheaper? I'm a bit short of cash just now.
5 Could we make it something a bit less strenuous? My wrist is still hurting after that accident.

DEVELOPING WRITING A web page – do and dont's

A

c

B

1 shake 2 Making
3 uncomfortable 4 unless
5 space 6 initiate
7 awkward 8 turns
9 code 10 norms
11 round 12 be
13 assume 14 mind

C

1 'Out and about'
2 'The home front'
3 'The art of conversation'
4 'Out and about'
5 'Meet and greet'
6 'Out and about'

D

1 smoke
2 that you will chat during the meal
3 taking a gift
4 using your chopsticks correctly
5 to take off your shoes
6 don't drink too much

E

Student's own answers.

VOCABULARY Making mistakes

A

1
1 organising a surprise party
2 sending a private email
3 copying in everyone
2
1 burst out crying
2 hadn't realised
3 put your foot in it
3
1 top politician
2 turned up
3 dressed casually
4
1 is due
2 isn't actually pregnant
3 made a stupid joke
5
1 live on air
2 didn't have a clue
3 meant to be a joke
4 didn't see the funny side

READING

A

a

B

1 t 2 f 3 f 4 t 5 f 6 f
7 t 8 t

C

1 Maddie's father and mother
2 police
3 Maddie's father and mother
4 Maddie
5 gatecrashers
6 neighbours
7 Maddie
8 police

GRAMMAR Question tags

A

1 haven't I 2 shouldn't I
3 aren't I 4 aren't you
5 didn't they 6 doesn't he
7 isn't she 8 have you

B

2 The new CD wasn't worth it, was it?
3 We'll meet at 12.30, shall we?
4 Your team haven't been playing very well, have they?
5 The food isn't very tasty, is it?
6 You couldn't close the window, could you?
7 They didn't play well, did they?
8 Turn the light on, will you?

C

1 hasn't she? 2 can't you?
3 aren't you? 4 has she?
5 hasn't it? 6 were they?

VOCABULARY Taking about parties

A
1 dragged, left 2 up, host
3 chat, lost 4 each other, off

B
1 throwing a surprise party
2 spent a fortune
3 setting up a marquee
4 went to waste
5 got a bit out of hand
6 break it up
7 burst into tears

C
1 g 2 b 3 e 4 a 5 h 6 d
7 f 8 c

LISTENING

A
hen do children's party
graduation party retirement party
wedding

B
3 There's no point throwing a party for a shy person.
6 I'd like to have a less busy social life.
4 Graduation celebrations used to be quite simple.
1 I spent more than I wanted to.
2 Children's parties have become much more elaborate.
5 People buy gifts for no special reason.

PRONUNCIATION Linking vowel to vowel

B
1 She‿is, and I don't mean to sound horrible. (/j/)
2 Modern mums like to‿organise an event or a (/w/)
  function.
3 It means the parents have to go‿along too. (/w/)
4 Tell me‿about it! (/j/)
5 She's insisting on a fancy dress do‿and the whole (/w/)
  family has to be there.
6 Now you're just winding me‿up. (/j/)

VOCABULARY BUILDER QUIZ 10

A
1 cosy 2 casual
3 light-hearted 4 gorgeous
5 stuffy

B
1 handed in his resignation
2 put me at ease
3 on air
4 making ... remarks
5 in top form
6 got out of hand

C
1 publicity 2 security
3 responsibility 4 speciality
5 humidity 6 activity

D
1 dress 2 get
3 safe 4 public
5 burst 6 split
7 out 8 waste

UNIT 11

VOCABULARY Problems with vehicles

2 spare 3 flat
4 bald 5 engine
6 overheat 7 front
8 windscreens 9 wing mirrors
10 fill 11 tank
12 brakes 13 scratches
14 dents 15 battery
16 flat

DEVELOPING CONVERSATIONS Expressing shock

2 At 2.30 in the morning? Isn't there an earlier flight?
3 Six weeks? Isn't there another room available sooner?
4 An extra €150? What mistake have they made?
5 160kph? Why was he going so fast?
6 An hour and a half? Can't he get here any quicker?

DEVELOPING WRITING A story – using the last line

A
Five
1 I'd got a flat tyre.
2 Fitting the spare took over an hour.
3 I also got filthy but had no time to stop and change.
4 the engine just stopped. I had put petrol in a diesel car.
5 got to the wedding in dirty jeans and a T-shirt
Putting petrol into a diesel car

B
When I <u>set off</u> I <u>had</u> no idea how difficult a simple trip <u>would become</u>. My best friend <u>had asked</u> me to be the best man and of course I'<u>d said</u> yes. I <u>decided</u> to hire a car to get to the wedding, as I <u>wanted</u> to be there nice and early.
After checking I <u>had</u> my suit, the rings and my speech, I <u>picked up</u> the car. The journey through town <u>was</u> fine, but <u>no sooner had I reached</u> the motorway than things <u>started</u> to go wrong. Suddenly the car <u>felt</u> very bumpy. I <u>pulled off</u> the motorway and <u>realised I'd got</u> a flat tyre. <u>Fitting the spare was a nightmare</u> and <u>took</u> over an hour. I also <u>got</u> filthy but <u>had</u> no time to stop and change.
While I <u>was trying</u> to make up time, I suddenly <u>realised</u> I <u>needed</u> fuel. I <u>stopped</u>, <u>filled up</u> the tank, <u>set off</u> again but a few metres up the road the engine just <u>stopped</u>. I <u>had put</u> petrol in a diesel car. I <u>couldn't believe</u> how stupid I'<u>d been</u>.
I finally <u>hitched</u> a lift with a lorry driver and <u>got</u> to the wedding in dirty jeans and a T-shirt. I can safely say it <u>was</u> the worst journey I've ever had.

C
2 Not only did we catch the wrong train but we also left our bags on the platform.
3 At no time did they explain that we had to return the car by midday.
4 Hardly had we set off than we ran out of petrol.
5 Little did we know how rough the crossing would be.
6 No sooner had I got to the check-in than I realised I'd left my passport at home.

D
1 get 2 lose
3 damage 4 miss
5 cancel 6 turn up

E
Student's own answers.

GRAMMAR Uncountable nouns

A
1 less furniture
2 more information
3 great deal of experience
4 hardly any traffic
5 enough money
6 plenty of work

B
1 You've got hardly any luggage.
2 There won't be much cheap accommodation left by now.
3 Have you had any information on the flight delays?
4 The agent gave us loads of advice before we left.
5 There hasn't been much progress up to now.
6 We had a bit of trouble finding our way here.

READING

A
technology

B
1 c   2 b   3 a   4 c

C
1 Nico	2 Zoltan
3 Richie	4 Val
5 Val	6 Val

D
1 commute	2 keeping
3 across	4 grumpy
5 feedback	6 bearable

VOCABULARY Driving

A
1 overtake the car in front
2 doing a hundred and fifty
3 slam on your brakes
4 drive in the middle lane
5 look in your mirror and indicate

B
1 d   2 a   3 e   4 c   5 b

GRAMMAR Emphatic structures

A
1 What's good is **the** fact that people are using the trains more.
2 **What** really makes me annoyed is people speeding in residential areas.
3 The thing that irritate**s** me is the lack~~ing~~ of staff on the stations.
4 It's harmful to the environment fly**ing** everywhere.
5 What gets me is the amount **of** empty buses you see on the roads.
6 The thing **that** bothers me about flying is the amount of hanging around.
7 It's dangerous when people **don't** follow the rules of the road.
8 What I hate is ~~that~~ people not moving their stuff off the seat on a train.

B
1 It really irritates me when people use their horn for no reason.
2 It's much more tiring driving at night.
3 What I love about travelling around by train is the freedom.
4 What's encouraging is the number of people changing to public transport.
5 What was totally unexpected was the fact that the airline gave us a refund.
6 The thing that really annoyed me was they didn't explain the delay.

LISTENING

Speaker 1 d   Speaker 2 a
Speaker 3 f   Speaker 4 e
Speaker 5 b

PRONUNCIATION

A
1 D   2 S   3 D   4 D   5 S   6 D

VOCABULARY BUILDER QUIZ 11

A
1 fare, others are parts of car
2 fuel, others are parts of road
3 crossing, others are adjectives
4 appeal, others are thing you do when driving

B
1 c   2 a   3 e   4 b   5 d

C
1 dented	2 remote
3 covers	4 worn
5 flash	6 spillage
7 in	

D
1 word	2 peak
3 row	

E
1 infuriating	2 spiritual
3 breathtaking	4 disrepair
5 remarkably	6 worthwhile

UNIT 12

VOCABULARY Health problems

A
1 have	2 suffer from
3 remove	4 be
5 use	

B
1 faint	2 bump
3 pin	4 high blood pressure
5 bruises	6 scratches

DEVELOPING CONVERSATIONS Passing on messages

A
1 Give, regards
2 Give, tell
3 apologies, say
4 Send, love
5 Give, congratulations
6 Tell her, take
7 Say, we're thinking

B
a 5   b 2   c 3   d 6   e 4   f 7   g 1

GRAMMAR *supposed to be –ing* and *should*

A
1 I'**m** supposed to be having a check-up tomorrow but I've got too much work.
2 My knee hurts a bit now but it should~~n't~~ be OK in a few days.
3 I shouldn't ~~to~~ need to be in hospital for very long.
4 She's supposed to **be** walking with crutches but she just refuses.
5 I'm afraid the side effects of the drugs **will** last a few days.
6 They'**re** supposed to be launching a new flu treatment but it's been delayed.

B
1 am supposed to be visiting; shouldn't take
2 should feel; am supposed to be playing
3 should clear up; are supposed to be going
4 is supposed to be giving; shouldn't be

LISTENING

A
Kate: stressed, cautious, a control freak
Sam: easy-going, confident, good fun

B
1 Sam   2 Kate
3 Kate   4 Kate
5 Sam   6 Sam
7 Kate   8 Kate
9 Sam

PRONUNCIATION Intonation on question tags

A
1 falling   2 falling
3 rising   4 rising
5 falling   6 rising
7 rising   8 falling

VOCABULARY Parts of the body and illnesses

A
1 lung   skin
2 skull   hip
3 brain   liver
4 ribs   wrists
5 big toes   fingers
6 elbow   knee
7 kidneys   ankles

B
1 arthritis   2 diabetes
3 Alzheimer's   4 stroke
5 tuberculosis

READING

A
1 c   2 d   3 a   4 b

B
2 t   3 t   6 t   8 t

C
1 nap   2 snore
3 night's sleep   4 insomnia
5 lying   6 like a baby
7 awake   8 amount of sleep

GRAMMAR Determiners

A
1 another   2 Half
3 This   4 All
5 many   6 a

B
1 some, is   2 that, None of
3 other, some   4 another, none
5 any, both

DEVELOPING WRITING A letter – showing sympathy

A
b

B
1 expresses sympathy
2 asks how Erik is now
3 makes a joke
4 asks about future treatment
5 offers help
6 makes a promise
7 tells Erik about a gift
8 passes on a message

C
1 e j   2 a i   3 d h   4 c f   5 b g

D
Student's own answers.

VOCABULARY BUILDER QUIZ 12

A
1 bruise   2 deposit
3 gamble   4 transplant
5 boast

B
1 inconvenience   2 silence
3 independence   4 negligence
5 violence

C
1 replace   2 regulate
3 refer   4 recuperate
5 relieve

C
1 They had to postpone ~~out~~ her operation.
2 Don't let this problem detract ~~out~~ from your success.
6 There's a nasty bug going round ~~out~~ at my kids' school.

E
1 inhaler   2 bandage
3 crutches   4 stitches

UNIT 13

VOCABULARY Life events

A

moving house family life
giving birth family life
a couple getting together/splitting up family life
changing careers education and work
dropping out of college education and work
being sacked education and work
getting a degree / Masters/PhD education and work
being sent to jail results of bad decisions
being kicked out of somewhere results of bad decisions
getting killed the end of life
passing away the end of life

B

1 a couple getting together
2 changing careers
3 moving house
4 passing away
5 being sacked
6 being sent to jail
7 getting a degree / Masters/PhD
8 dropping out of college

C

1 spread   2 rough, retrained
3 bribes, get   4 labour
5 been, knocked   6 out
7 call

GRAMMAR Past perfect simple and continuous

A

2 He gave up the course after he had been studying for only two years.
3 Before he started working in catering, he had been unemployed for six months.
4 By the time he set up his business, he had been working in catering for five years.
5 By the time he married Lucy, they had already known each other for eight years.
6 He set up his own business ten years after he had left school.

B

1 hadn't seen
2 had been
3 hadn't been getting on
4 had spent
5 had nearly given up
6 had been living
7 hadn't been
8 had come down with

DEVELOPING CONVERSATIONS Showing uncertainty

1 far   2 to
3 Apparently   4 As
5 what   6 told

LISTENING

A

a

B

was a teacher of French 4
ran an environmental campaign 6
organised a strike 2
did voluntary work in Africa 3
retired 5
set up a writing group 7

PRONUNCIATION strong and weak forms

A

1 /ə/   /æ/
2 /ɒ/   /ə/
3 /uː/   /ə/
4 /ɜː/   /ə/
5 /ɒ/   /ə/

GRAMMAR be always -ing / wish and would

A

1 wish / would buy a round
2 always leaving
3 is constantly getting
4 wish / wouldn't be
5 always organising
6 wish / wouldn't have
7 are constantly borrowing
8 wish / was

B

a 3   b 6   c 5   d 1   e 8   f 7
g 2   h 4

READING

A

a

B

Facts – 1, 2   Opinions – 3, 4, 5

C

1 b   2 c   3 a   4 c   5 a

D

1 faded   2 constant
3 of   4 earth
5 went   6 fit

VOCABULARY Birth, marriage and death

A

1 expecting   2 due
3 had   4 straightforward
5 went   6 rushed
7 in   8 leave

B

1 bride and groom   2 town hall
3 reception   4 best man
5 honeymoon   6 cemetery
7 mourners   8 condolences
9 coffin   10 grave
11 ashes

DEVELOPING WRITING
A description – using vivid language

A

b

B

1 incredibly	2 demanded
3 chattered	4 gulped
5 weary	6 endless
7 hurrying	8 beamed
9 deafening	10 identical to
11 enormous	12 burst into tears

C

1 pride	2 embarrassment
3 nerves	4 disappointment
5 pleasure	6 confusion
7 sadness	8 laughing

D

Student's own answers.

VOCABULARY BUILDER QUIZ 13

A

1 b   2 e   3 d   4 c   5 a

B

1 It's time to call **it** a day and go home.
2 Don't let the children get **their** own way all the time.
3 She'll be going on maternity **leave** quite soon.
4 He's so serious. I wish he would lighten **up** a bit.
5 Why was he kicked **out** of university after only one term?

C

1 reach	2 losing
3 on	4 for
5 has	6 buried
7 condolences	8 toast

D

1 disrupting	2 upbringing
3 overreact	4 falling-out
5 counsellor	6 underlying
7 commuter	

UNIT 14

VOCABULARY Banks and money

A

1 I'm	2 cash point
3 withdraw	4 account.
5 of	6 limit
7 good	8 got
9 credit	10 rating
11 facility	12 cash
13 loan	14 borrowing

B

1 pay in an	2 be in a
3 be good with	4 be in
5 run up	

C

1 make good money
2 withdraw some money
3 get into debt
4 apply for a loan
5 strengthen the economy
6 pay off my student loan
7 buy/on credit
8 run out of money

DEVELOPING CONVERSATIONS
Apologising and offering explanations

1 A: I've been waiting ages.
  B: I do apologise ~~for~~. There must have been some kind of mix-up.
2 A: I only need a short-term loan.
  B: I'm very sorry. I'm afraid there's absolutely ~~not~~ nothing we can do.
3 A: I've been trying to get cash for 20 minutes.
  B: I'm ~~have~~ really sorry. I'm afraid the system is down at the moment.
4 A: I was told I could withdraw all the money today.
  B: I do apologise. I'll have a word with my manager ~~about~~ and see what I can do.
5 A: I'd like to extend my overdraft.
  B: I'm awfully sorry. I'm afraid I'm not authorised ~~for~~ to make that decision.
6 A: Why is each customer taking so long?
  B: I'm terribly sorry ~~about~~. The computers are being very slow today.
7 A: A thousand pounds has gone missing from my account.
  B: I do apologise. I'll ~~take~~ look into the matter at once.

GRAMMAR Passives

A

1 I was given a bad credit rating but the debts were run up **by** my girlfriend.
2 When I looked at my bank statement I couldn't believe what **had** happened.
3 Money from organised crime is currently launder**ed** through online businesses.
4 I'll never forget **being** refused credit in a shop. It was so embarrassing.
5 I don't know why my loan application **was** turned down.
6 correct
7 All customer signatures have to **be** check**ed** before any cash is handed over.
8 correct

B

1 is, made	b
2 are, stored	a
3 be spent	c
4 were, first seen	b
5 were used	a, c
6 was, recently introduced	b
7 were, launched	c
8 is destroyed	b

LISTENING

1 c   2 b   3 a   4 c   5 a

PRONUNCIATION Silent letters

A

1 I've been trying to pay for over ha<u>l</u>f an <u>h</u>our.
2 Did Eric tell you he'd applied for a mor<u>t</u>gage?
3 He's already up to his eyes in de<u>b</u>t.
4 They paid the <u>wh</u>ole lot off.
5 Come on, support our campai<u>g</u>n.
6 I was about to go out and buy some champa<u>g</u>ne.
7 I was looking at the <u>w</u>rong ticket.
8 I went strai<u>gh</u>t to the bank to sort it out.

GRAMMAR wish

A
1 c 2 g 3 a 4 f 5 b 6 h 7 d
8 e

B
2 I wish I'd never taken it out.
3 I wish I had better job.
4 I wish I didn't have to go to see my bank manager about my overdraft.
5 I wish we could have sold it two months earlier.
6 I wish we could afford something bigger.
7 I wish my parents would be a bit more understanding about my spending.
8 I wish my flatmate wouldn't chat for so long.

READING

A
1 f 2 d 3 a 4 c 5 g 6 b

B
1 t 2 f 3 t 4 f 5 f 6 t

C
1 currency   2 voucher
3 bank notes   4 counterfeiting
5 worth   6 economic
7 stable

VOCABULARY Metaphor

1 gambles **M**, gambling **L**
2 stake **L**, stake **M**
3 lottery **M**, lottery **L**
4 earned **M**, earn **L**
5 waste **L**, waste **M**
6 odds **M**, odds **L**
7 jackpot **L**, jackpot **M**
8 bets **L**, bet **M**

DEVELOPING WRITING
An online guide – giving information and advice

A
1 a 2 e 3 d 4 b 5 c 6 f

B
1 e 2 a 3 f 4 c 5 b 6 d

C
1 is often included
2 included
3 fare
4 to
5 to haggle
6 give
7 less
8 lower

D
Student's own answers.

VOCABULARY BUILDER QUIZ 14

A
1 rope, others to do with large houses
2 launder – the only crime
3 proof, others to do with money
4 mortgage, others to do with gambling

B
1 lengthen   2 weaken
3 strengthen   4 widen
5 tighten

C
1 remote   2 compulsive
3 penniless   4 frugal
5 stern   6 reluctant

D
1 **b**ranches.   2 fa**st**
3 **g**listening   4 **g**amble
5 odd**s**

E
1 flow   2 -social
3 down   4 cheque
5 arguments

UNIT 15

VOCABULARY Food and cooking

A
1 fennel   2 pumpkin
3 basil   4 radish
5 raisins   6 eel

B
(Sample answers given in brackets)
1 chickpeas (lentils, kidney beans)
2 almonds, peaches, coconut, grapefruit (plums, cherries)
3 trout (cod, eel)
4 courgette, parsley (celery, red pepper)
5 chocolate (cake, biscuits)

C
1 steam   2 blend
3 Sprinkle   4 peel
5 crush   6 Soak
7 Chop

DEVELOPING CONVERSATIONS Vague language

1 A: What's that smell? It's **kind of** sweet and spicy at the same time.
  B: It's mulled wine. It should be ready in 10 minutes **or so**.
2 A: I'm not that hungry so just a small**ish** portion for me, please.
  B: Sure. It's a **sort of** light stew anyway so it shouldn't be that filling.
3 A: I love Thai cooking. All those hot and citrus**y** flavours.
  B: Mm. It's OK if it's mild**ish** but I can't stand too much chilli.
4 A: What's 'mizuna'? Is it **sort of** like spinach?
  B: Not really. It's a Japanese vegetable with a mild mustard**y** flavour.
5 A: I saw this big**gish** fruit in the market just now. I think it was called a 'pomelo'.
  B: Oh, I know. It's **like** a grapefruit but with much thicker skin.
6 A: How much sugar do I need to add?
  B: The fruit is sharp so I'd say **roughly** double the amount of berries.
7 A: How's your salad?
  B: Very soggy. They must have used **about** a litre of dressing on it.

GRAMMAR Linking words

A

1 Despite
2 until
3 Once
4 in case
5 Otherwise
6 Provided

B

1 once
2 so
3 if
4 then
5 for
6 However
7 unless
8 as
9 during
10 although

LISTENING

A

salads **food heaven**
tofu **food hell**
fish **food hell**
burger and fries **food heaven**
tea **food hell**
garlic **food hell**
curry and rice **food heaven**
meatballs and spaghetti **food heaven**

B

1, 2, 4, 6, 7

PRONUNCIATION Connected speech

A

2 So_I'd have to say the good_old_American burger_and fries.
3 My children just think_I'm_old-fashioned, but_it's_not for me.
4 I got the taste for spicy food when_I was_in the_army.
5 My favourite thing_is_meatballs_and spaghetti_in tomato sauce.
6 That's_it from me_and the people here_in Brighton.

VOCABULARY Prefixes

A

1 ex
2 super
3 re
4 pre
5 multi
6 out
7 pro
8 over
9 dis
10 mis
11 semi
12 non

B

1 over
2 re
3 non
4 mis
5 super
6 multi

READING

A

1 the least appetizing
2 the most dangerous
3 the hottest
4 the least accessible
5 the most valuable

B

1 C
2 D
3 E
4 B
5 C
6 A
7 C
8 A

C

1 poisonous
2 appetising
3 valuable
4 spiciness
5 scarcity
6 specialist

VOCABULARY Food in the news

A

1 fast food advertising
2 food shortages
3 food poisoning
4 food waste
5 food production

B

1 d
2 e
3 a
4 c
5 b

GRAMMAR Reporting verbs

A

1 to give
2 all our friends
3 to get
4 our booking
5 on adding
6 trying
7 on.
8 to divide

B

1 Jane blamed me for burning the burgers.
2 Mum advised me to send the food back.
3 Ellie suggested we order the set menu to be delivered.
4 Dad promised not to forget to take it out of the oven.
5 The managing director denied using any product that had been genetically altered.
6 Mark reminded me to ask Meena about her secret ingredient.
7 Lili apologised for not making it on Saturday.
8 The health minister declared all the affected premises closed.

C

1 e
2 b
3 c
4 h
5 f
6 d
7 g
8 a

DEVELOPING WRITING An anecdote – a food experience

A

1 trying
2 prepare
3 put
4 hit
5 brought
6 chew
7 cough
8 spitting
9 took
10 fade

B

1 sinking **positive**
2 undercooked **negative**
3 smothered **positive**
4 smeared **negative**
5 mouthful **negative**
6 succulent **positive**
7 crave **positive**
8 wrong **negative**

C

Student's own answers.

VOCABULARY BUILDER QUIZ 15

A

1 d
2 c
3 a
4 e
5 b

B

1 publicise
2 summarise
3 authorise
4 specialise
5 emphasise

C

1 lid
2 roughly
3 stock
4 fake
5 muttering
6 tide

D

1 squeeze
2 fuss
3 bid
4 heavily

E

1 up
2 alleged
3 outbreak
4 originated
5 hygiene

UNIT 16

VOCABULARY Reasons for phoning

1 arrange / time
2 check / stock levels
3 pass on / thanks
4 remind / appointment
5 chase up / payment
6 let / make
7 see / taking
8 confirm / booking
9 apologies / losing
10 enquire / options

DEVELOPING CONVERSATIONS Using *would* to be polite

1 If you wouldn't mind, I'd rather give it a miss.
2 Would you mind spelling your surname?
3 Would 3.30 tomorrow be at all possible?
4 Would you happen to have the figures with you?
5 I was wondering if you'd like to come to dinner?
6 Any time would suit me.
7 Would it be possible to email me directions to your office?

GRAMMAR The future continuous

A

1 won't make / 'll be working
2 'll be travelling / won't be
3 'll be finishing / 'll deal
4 going to be taking / 'll send
5 won't manage / 'll be finalising

B

1 Will you be seeing the new recruits later?   d
2 If you'll be popping down to the canteen later   e
3 As you won't be coming to the dinner,   b
4 When will you be leaving for the conference?   f
5 If you won't be using the pool car today,   c
6 Will you be doing any photocopying later?   a

DEVELOPING WRITING An email – chasing an order

A

1 placed
2 in
3 in order to
4 due
5 me
6 despatched
7 Despite
8 over
9 debited
10 in
11 would
12 receipt

B

1 I am writing to enquire about an order
2 the operator assured me that the package had been despatched and would be with me within 48 hours.
3 Despite repeated calls
4 my current account and can confirm that it has been debited to the sum of £81.99
5 I would be grateful if you could look into the delay and make sure the watch is delivered to me within 48 hours.
6 Please acknowledge receipt of this message. I can be contacted at the above email address.

C

State the date of your order and any reference numbers.
an order I placed online on 14/9/09Order number: D61290X

Include your full name.
Marcus Linnemann

Say where you can be contacted.
I can be contacted at the above email address.

State what you ordered and the price.
the item in question is a watch priced £69.99

Say clearly when the order was meant to be delivered.
I paid £12.00 for special delivery in order to receive the watch the following day.

Confirm that you have paid for the order.
debited to the sum of £81.99

State what action you want to be taken.
you could look into the delay and make sure the watch is delivered to me within 48 hours.

D

Student's own answers.

VOCABULARY Building up a business

A

1 floated / stock
2 subject / takeover
3 set up / company
4 raise / capital
5 run / loss
6 break / even
7 having / turnover
8 making / profit
9 plough / business
10 face / competition

READING

A

b

B

| 1 f | 2 t | 3 t | 4 f | 5 t | 6 f |
| 7 t | 8 f |

C

1 Levi's grandmother
2 Levi's family
3 one of the Dragon's
4 Levi
5 Sainsbury's or another outlet
6 a fan

D

1 pitch	2 brand
3 entrepreneur	4 inspiration
5 budding	6 struck
7 passion	8 marketing

GRAMMAR Ways of expressing necessity and ability

A

1 I can't talk now so I'll ~~must~~ call you back later.
2 It will be great not **to** have to commute to work every day.
3 When do you think you'll **be** able to finish the report?
4 This new software will **enable** us to protect the system from viruses.
5 It's unfair to force people **to** take reduced hours at short notice.
6 Why won't my password let **me** access the file?
7 What do you need to enable you **to** finish the project on time?
8 Sadly we've been force**d** to make some redundancies.

B

1 had to buy in
2 won't be able to offer
3 are not allowing, to bring
4 not being able to park
5 will be forced to look for
6 has made me wonder
7 Don't let, get
8 will be able to keep

VOCABULARY Collocations in business

A

1 up
2 up
3 to
4 out of
5 up
6 in
7 with
8 up
9 up
10 over
11 out of
12 into
13 out into

B

| 1 e | 2 f | 3 c | 4 b | 5 d | 6 a |

C

1 do a lot of market research
2 exploit a gap in the market
3 launch a product line
4 develop and then 5 market the products
6 fulfil orders
7 improve sales and marketing
8 boost sales
9 expand the business
10 have a controlling stake in the company

LISTENING

Speaker 1 b
Speaker 2 f
Speaker 3 a
Speaker 4 d
Speaker 5 e

PRONUNCIATION Sounds that aren't pronounced

A

1 two
2 four
3 two
4 two
5 two
6 two
7 four
8 two
9 two

VOCABULARY BUILDER QUIZ 16

A

1 up
2 on
3 out
4 over
5 even

B

1 delivery
2 enquiry
3 recovery
4 discovery
5 mastery

C

1 flag
2 ware
3 out
4 turn
5 collar

D

1 float
2 deal
3 network
4 stake
5 at

E

1 entrepreneurial
2 strategic
3 negotiating
4 instability
5 expansion

CD1 TRACK	ITEM	
1	titles	–
2		1
3		2
4	1.1	3
5		4
6		5
7		6
8	1.2	
9	2.1	
10	2.2	
11		Speaker 1
12		Speaker 2
13	3.1	Speaker 3
14		Speaker 4
15		Speaker 5
16	3.2	
17	4.1	
18	4.2	
19	5.1	
20	5.2	
21		1
22	6.1	2
23		3
24	6.2	
25	6.3	
26	7.1	
27	7.2	
28	8.1	Part 1
29		Part 2
30	8.2	
31	8.3	
32	9.1	
33	9.2	
34	9.3	
35	10.1	
36	10.2	
37	10.3	
38		Speaker 1
39		Speaker 2
40	11.1	Speaker 3
41		Speaker 4
42		Speaker 5
43	11.2	
44	12.1	
45	12.2	
46	13.1	
47	13.2	
48		1
49		2
50	14.1	3
51		4
52		5

CD1 TRACK	ITEM	
53	14.2	
54	15.1	
55	15.2	
56		Speaker 1
57		Speaker 2
58	16.1	Speaker 3
59		Speaker 4
60		Speaker 5
61	16.2	